THE EURO AT TEN:
The Next Global Currency?

THE EURO AT TEN:
The Next Global Currency?

JEAN PISANI-FERRY & ADAM S. POSEN, editors

PETERSON INSTITUTE FOR INTERNATIONAL ECONOMICS
BRUEGEL
Washington, DC
June 2009

Jean Pisani-Ferry is director of Bruegel, the Brussels-based think tank, and professor at Université Paris-Dauphine. He is also a member of the European Commission's Group of Economic Policy Analysis and of the French prime minister's Council of Economic Analysis. He was executive president of the French prime minister's Council of Economic Analysis; senior adviser to the French minister of finance; director of CEPII, the French institute for international economics; and economic adviser with the European Commission. He has held teaching positions with various universities including the Ecole polytechnique in Paris and the Université libre de Bruxelles. Recent books he coauthored or coedited include *Coming of Age: Report on the Euro Area* (2008), *An Agenda for a Growing Europe* (2004), and *Exchange Rate Policies in Emerging Asian Countries* (1999).

Adam S. Posen is deputy director of the Peterson Institute for International Economics (PIIE), where he has been a senior fellow since 1997. He has been a visiting scholar and consultant at central banks worldwide, including on multiple occasions at the Federal Reserve Board, the European Central Bank, and the Deutsche Bundesbank. In 2006 he was on sabbatical leave from PIIE as a Houblon-Norman Senior Fellow at the Bank of England. He is the author of *Restoring Japan's Economic Growth* (1998), coauthor with Ben Bernanke et al. of *Inflation Targeting: Lessons from the International Experience* (1999), and editor and part-author of *The Euro at Five: Ready for a Global Role?* (2005) and *The Japanese Financial Crisis and its Parallels with U.S. Experience* (2000).

PETER G. PETERSON INSTITUTE FOR INTERNATIONAL ECONOMICS
1750 Massachusetts Avenue, NW
Washington, DC 20036-1903
(202) 328-9000   FAX: (202) 659-3225
www.piie.com

C. Fred Bergsten, *Director*
Edward A. Tureen, *Director of Publications, Marketing, and Web Development*

BRUEGEL
33 Rue de la Charité/Liefdadigheidsstraat 33
B-1210 Brussels, Belgium
Phone: +32 2 227 4210
Fax: +32 2 227 4219
www.bruegel.org

Jean Pisani-Ferry, *Director*
Andrew Fielding, *Editor*

Copyediting: Madona Devasahayam
Tables and figures: Xcel Graphic Services
Typesetting: Susann Luetjen
Printing: Edwards Brothers, Incorporated
Cover design: Susann Luetjen
Cover photo: © Stasys Eidiejus—Fotolia.com

Printed in the United States of America

11 10 09   5 4 3 2 1

Library of Congress Cataloging-in-Publication Data

The euro at ten : the next global currency? / [edited by] Adam S. Posen, Jean Pisani-Ferry.
    p. cm.
  Includes index.
  ISBN 978-0-88132-430-3 (pbk.)
  1. Euro. 2. Currency question. 3. Financial crises. 4. Money--European Union countries. I. Posen, Adam Simon. II. Pisani-Ferry, Jean.
  HG925.E867843 2009
  332.4'94--dc22
                              2009010655

Contents

Preface

The euro has now celebrated the tenth anniversary of its successful launch on January 1, 1999. In the midst of the greatest financial crisis of the last 70 years, the world's only transnational major currency has delivered price stability to the people of the euro area, retained its value in international markets, and proven capable of weathering the storm—which at present came from both internal as well as external asset price busts and imbalances. While a few increasingly shrill and lonely naysayers remain, the euro has amply demonstrated its sustainability. Also euro-denominated assets, particularly corporate bond issues, and euro-invoiced trade have come to make up an increasingly large share of the global total in real and financial commerce.

The global role of the euro, however, remains much more uncertain. Many would argue that the current crisis is the euro's moment: With the US economy at least perceived in many quarters to have brought on the crisis, and with that crisis attributed in part to global imbalances associated with excess consumption by the United States, it would seem time for markets in general and governments holding reserves to look anew at the euro as the one viable dollar alternative. Prospects for sustained budget deficits and inflation in the United States when the crisis abates, as well as recently and sharply expressed concerns about dollar stability by such major US debt holders as the Chinese government, would seem to add momentum to this possibility for the euro to emerge as codominant with the dollar on the global scene. Historical echoes of the British pound's loss of world role to the dollar before the Second World War, and of the dollar seemingly saving in its role in the 1970s and 1980s only through the absence of an alternative currency, are ringing loudly. Many eastern European members hit hard by the crisis have expressed a wish to accelerate their euro entry.

Yet the current crisis has produced to date a flight to the dollar as a safe haven and an extended appreciation of the dollar against the euro. In addition, even those governments voicing concerns about the dollar's medium-term value are not advocating a shift into the euro as a new reserve; those market participants who vote with their feet are not shifting portfolios into euro assets either. The monetary stability of the euro has neither solved the problems of coordination on financial stability within the euro area nor increased the willingness of euro area members to extend that monetary stability to other EU members. If anything, the response of the euro area governments to the crisis has been to move in a defensive direction regarding the euro's global role by complaining of competitive depreciations by near neighbors, refusing to adjust the euro area entry criteria or accelerate consideration of new members, making no effort to extend euro swap lines on the scale that the Federal Reserve has offered in dollars, and asking the IMF to administer conditional loans to crisis-hit Eastern European economies.

In October 2008 the Institute and our European sister Bruegel held a joint high-level conference to examine the euro's potential to move beyond its success as a currency for a large region into a broader global role. This book, edited by Bruegel Director Jean Pisani-Ferry and PIIE Deputy Director Adam S. Posen, comprises the papers and panel discussion presented at that conference. European officials representing the Commission, the European Central Bank, and a major euro area central bank assess the current use of the euro as a global currency, and the willingness and requirements to have the euro's role expand. In more specific studies, contributing authors from around the world assess the progress of the euro project after ten years, the fundamental drivers of global currency usage and how the euro performs on these criteria, and the perspective of other major regions on usage of the euro. A panel of current and former senior policymakers examines the implications for the global monetary system and for transatlantic relations of the euro's potential to rise in importance at a time of dollar vulnerability.

One important objective of the book is to identify areas of common interest and of common vulnerability between American and European policymakers, as the euro evolves and as the crisis continues. A second objective is to better inform policymakers and the American public about the euro and thereby dispel unrealistic concerns on the US side of the Atlantic about whether the euro "can survive." The authors make clear that this question has long since been settled in the affirmative. The questions at hand are: What is required for the euro to attain codominance with the dollar globally? Does the financial crisis make this more likely or reveal relative weaknesses in the euro's position as well? What might occur if the euro does not take on a leading monetary role at this time?

The development of the euro and its implications for the international financial system have been of major interest to the Institute since the first pre-Maastricht proposals were made. Adam S. Posen edited a conference volume on *The Euro at Five: Ready for a Global Role?* (2005) that took an earlier look at this issue, and provides a benchmark for comparison with this volume's assessment of the euro's progress since then. C. Randall Henning's *Cooperating with Europe's Monetary Union* (1997) and the Institute's earlier conference volume on *Reviving the European Union* (1994) foreshadowed these questions of a bipolar monetary world. My own article "The Dollar and the Euro" in *Foreign Affairs* in 1997 was one of the first by a US economist to suggest that not only would the euro succeed but also that it would challenge the dollar. This research was part of the Institute's continuing agenda on the leadership of the global economic system and on international monetary regimes.

The Peter G. Peterson Institute for International Economics is a private, nonprofit institution for the study and discussion of international economic policy. Its purpose is to analyze important issues in that area and to develop and communicate practical new approaches for dealing with them. The Institute is completely nonpartisan.

The Institute is funded by a highly diversified group of philanthropic foundations, private corporations, and interested individuals. About 22 percent of the Institute's resources in our latest fiscal year were provided by contributors outside the United States. We gratefully acknowledge funding from the European Commission's Economic and Financial Affairs Directorate and External Relations Directorate for the October 2008 conference and this volume, as well as its support for our ongoing work with Bruegel researching transatlantic approaches and cooperation in macroeconomic policy (Grant No C1/2008/TD under grant agreement n°SI2.507359). The views expressed in this publication are the sole responsibility of the authors and do not necessarily reflect the views of the European Commission, of the Institute, or of Bruegel, or any of their respective officers.

The Institute's Board of Directors bears overall responsibilities for the Institute and gives general guidance and approval to its research program, including the identification of topics that are likely to become important over the medium run (one to three years) and that should be addressed by the Institute. The director, working closely with the staff and outside Advisory Committee, is responsible for the development of particular projects and makes the final decision to publish an individual study.

The Institute hopes that its studies and other activities will contribute to building a stronger foundation for international economic policy around the world. We invite readers of these publications to let us know how they think we can best accomplish this objective.

C. FRED BERGSTEN
Director
April 2009

Introduction

The Euro at Ten—Successful, but Regional

JEAN PISANI-FERRY AND ADAM S. POSEN

The euro is now in its tenth year of usage, successfully performing all the functions of a currency for European citizens using it and providing price stability to the euro area.[1] The monetary union and its central bank are in the process of passing the test of a major financial crisis and have held up well so far. In spite of market commentaries and spreads contemplating the euro area's breakup, one result of the crisis has been that more countries want to join the euro area than before, not fewer.

Given its success to date, however, the euro could be more than an anchor for some participating countries and an aspiration for others. At a time when voices in China and other emerging countries advocate a multipolar monetary regime, the euro could become a currency for all of Europe or even a global currency. At a time when investors wonder about fiscal sustainability in the United States and ponder the risks of monetization, it could represent a partial alternative to the US dollar as a store of value. The papers in this volume address this issue of the euro's impact on the international monetary system so far and its potential role beyond the euro area over the next decade.

All authors started from two questions. The first was: Is the euro en

Jean Pisani-Ferry is the director of Bruegel. Adam S. Posen is deputy director and senior fellow at the Peterson Institute for International Economics. The papers in this volume are based on a conference at the Peterson Institute on October 10, 2008, jointly organized by Bruegel and the Peterson Institute with the support of the European Commission.

1. A general assessment of the impact of the euro on the euro area's and the European Union's own economic performance is given in Pisani-Ferry et al. (2008), DG ECFIN (2008), and ECB (2008). An earlier assessment predicting that the euro would be successful on its own terms, but without an important global role, is in Posen (2005).

route to becoming a global currency and thus to either challenging or equalling the dollar in its reserve and leadership role? Their largely common answer is that it has already become a dominant regional currency, whose role extends to areas bordering the euro area or the European Union, but it is very far from rivalling the US dollar on a number of fundamental criteria. One can consider this a success or a failure but, more importantly, it is a fact: By all standards the euro is an overwhelming success in the European Union and its neighborhood, and by all standards it is junior to the US dollar in international monetary affairs.

The second question for all authors was: What has the global financial crisis, and the euro area policy response to it, revealed about the resilience of the euro and its international prospects? Again the largely common answer is that the existence of the euro contributed to macroeconomic stability within the euro area, and thus to stability globally, but that the crisis revealed weaknesses in the governance and crisis management capabilities of the euro area. Doubts about the euro area's ability to respond to cross-border banking problems also persist. Furthermore, the euro did little to improve the crisis response of neighboring countries in Central and Eastern Europe.

Responses to these two questions together highlight the gap between the euro's current reality and its potential. But they also highlight the regional role and responsibilities of the euro area. The euro, as a successful regional currency but not a global currency, provides stability to its current members and helps some of them ward off the effects of the crisis—and this should be a primary policy objective for euro area decision-makers. At the same time, the Eastern and Southeastern European countries tied to the euro area include some of the emerging markets worst hit by the crisis (some of which belong to the European Union and are among its major trading partners). Even if the formal mandates of the European Central Bank (ECB) and the Eurogroup (where the ministers of finance of the area meet) do not formally include it, broader stability in the region should be a major economic and political objective as well. Inability to provide it (beyond the provision of balance-of-payments assistance within the framework of the International Monetary Fund [IMF] programs) must accordingly be seen as a failure of euro area policymaking and needs to be rectified. In essence, while the crisis promoted the attractiveness of euro area membership for those within it, the euro area's limited crisis response demonstrated the defensive crouch in which European policymakers continue to treat shocks to the euro area—and thus undercut its regional importance, not to mention its positive influence.

As with many other aspects widely discussed—such as the Stability and Growth Pact on fiscal policy, the criteria for enlargement, or the insistence on ERM2[2] membership prior to euro area entry—the European

---

2. ERM2 is the exchange rate mechanism that links the euro and EU countries in a formal

Union's approach to monetary arrangements appears to be bound by a narrow and exceedingly formal definition of its objectives, be it monetary stability within its borders or equal treatment across candidates whatever the circumstances. This is at the potential expense of both broader stability, political and economic, over the long term and Europe's ability to address strategic challenges. The analogous focus on national responses to banking crises, when there are major two-way spillovers between the euro area and Eastern European financial systems, reinforces this tradeoff—and the air of defensiveness as though the euro's viability indeed were deemed fragile by its very guardians.

Similar concerns arise as regards the euro area's role in global monetary arrangements and their likely evolution. The facts that flight to safety by investors during the current crisis has been primarily to dollar-denominated assets and that calls by Chinese and other governments for post-dollar-dominated reserve currency arrangements have primarily focused on non-euro alternatives underscore the limitations on the global role of the euro to date. But as one of us quotes sage Rav Hillel in the opening of his paper regarding the euro's geopolitical limitations (Adam Posen in chapter 2), "If I am not for myself, who will be for me? Yet, if I am for myself only, what am I? And if not now, when?" In other words, if the euro is neither eagerly promoted nor widely adopted as the alternative to the dollar at a time when US policymakers have made arguably the greatest postwar errors and when dollar-denominated asset values and credibility have suffered the greatest losses, will it ever become a global currency? The authors in this volume expect that there will be steady increases in the euro's share in foreign exchange reserves, in financial and trade transactions, and even in exchange rate pegs and baskets in the coming years, where trade and financial linkages with the euro area grow for real-side market-driven reasons. They do not, however, expect any sudden shift to the euro as a global currency, as a result of either the crisis or fundamentals. And they are pessimistic for the long term as the weight of Europe in the world economy is set to diminish.

Does the euro's lack of global role really matter? Empirically, it is an interesting question both on its own terms of forecasting significant capital flows and as a means of testing various fundamentals as explanations of the euro's (and dollar's) relative performance. Normatively for policy, the importance of the issue is less self-evident. As Lawrence Summers puts it in the closing discussion in chapter 4, "My view is that the United States is best served by not conceptualizing itself as in competition with the euro.... To have two currencies trying to be in complete equipoise risks substantial instability, as things rush from one direction to the other. None of this is

peg to it. It succeeded the exchange rate mechanism of the European Monetary System when the euro was introduced in 1999. Membership in the ERM2 is a precondition for joining the euro area.

to say that the United States should seek to thwart the euro." Similarly, Erkki Liikanen states, "I think we, as European central bankers, should not promote the euro [into a bipolar role with the dollar], and that the euro's international role should rather reflect the economic development of the euro area." We, the editors, acknowledge this responsible view of senior policymakers and admire its freedom from nationalist cant on both sides of the Atlantic. It is no doubt correct to consider the euro primarily in terms of the economic performance of the euro area and in those terms to view it as a success.

Yet, we believe this focus is too narrow in three senses and that under the present circumstances the lack of serious discussion about the potential global currency status of the euro is reason for some concern:

- First, the fundamental factors limiting the euro's international role and usage do reveal weaknesses in the European Union's economic integration and performance, which need to be addressed (we summarize our authors' evidence from chapter 2 on this score in the next section).

- Second, the erosion of US monetary and financial leadership may well be secular and even accelerated by the current crisis, in which case, absent a globally ready euro, a vacuum in the international economic system may arise and potentially cause instability.[3] We recap below the likely developments in regional ties to the euro and in regionalization of monetary arrangements (particularly but not only in Asia) as set out by our authors in chapter 3.

- Third, as already noted, we view the insufficient response of the euro area to the crisis impact in Eastern Europe, particularly among the European Union's newer member states, as harmful to solidarity and performance within the union, if not to the European project itself.[4] It is ironic that at the very same time that euro area membership becomes all the more appealing, even for traditionally reluctant states like Denmark and Poland, the entry criteria are losing relevance: (1) the inflation criterion is becoming too easy to fulfill, and (2) the budgetary criterion is becoming virtually impossible to reach. Lack of consideration for regional spillover effects of national choices and lack of flexibility turn euro area enlargement into a mechanical exercise at a time when Europe is confronted with a strategic choice.

Drawing on the work of our authors and our own additional research, we outline some practical steps to reduce these harms.

---

3. The classic statement of the dangers from such an absence of monetary leadership at a time of economic contraction is given in Kindleberger (1986).

4. See also Darvas and Pisani-Ferry (2008).

Why Has International Success Been Limited?

Several reasons account for the euro's limited international success so far. The most obvious one is the dollar's incumbent status. Scholars of international monetary history have often warned that inertia resulting from network externalities makes the status of dominant international currency hardly contestable (Matsuyama, Kiyotaki, and Matsui 1993). Some have also argued that shifts in dominant currency, when they occur, take place abruptly rather than gradually, and that policy errors in the home country can provide the opportunity for a switch, if an alternative currency is available (Bergsten in chapter 4). More recent historical interpretations of the lengthy decline of the pound's role in the 20th century, among other cases, suggest however that reserve or leading currencies can coexist (Eichengreen 2005, Eichengreen and Flandreau 2008). So the incumbent role of the dollar is a less compelling argument than is sometimes suggested.

However much weight one chooses to put on the network effects and persistence of incumbent currency status, the gap between the euro and dollar in reserve portfolio holdings, in number and breadth of countries pegging (soft or hard) to them, in commodities priced in them, in share of trade invoiced in them, and in share of investment portfolios is far larger than one would expect based on the euro area's economic size and price stability relative to the US economy (Chinn and Frankel 2007; Portes, Papaioannou, and Siourounis 2006). Furthermore, all but one of the countries pegged to the euro are major trading partners of Europe whereas a large number of countries whose currency is pegged to the dollar trade with Europe as much as with the United States—if not much more as in the case of Ukraine. This is evidence of strong asymmetry.

On one measure—that of private-sector financial depth in some assets, particularly regarding international bond issuance—the euro area has roughly caught up with the United States (see Kristin Forbes' paper in chapter 2).[5] This if anything emphasizes the difficulty in explaining the gap between the euro's and dollar's global role by network externalities: If market preferences have been revealed and changes have happened on international bond markets, why not for other markets? Similarly, if bipolar monetary systems have been known to exist in the recent past, and the US relative economic performance, or at least relative policy credibility, has been damaged by the current financial crisis, then it is all the more difficult to understand why there has not been a greater shift to the euro in various channels than has been seen over the past two years.

Thus, both the euro's relatively limited global role versus what some

---

5. The usual Bank for International Settlements data on the relative role of the dollar and the euro in international bond markets give a distorted image of reality as they count intra-euro area cross-border holdings as international. Corrected data put euro bond outstanding second to dollar outstanding, but by a narrow margin.

simple economic factors would indicate and its limited take-up as a result of the US-initiated financial crisis (and arguably US global imbalances, at least as widely perceived) instead argue that we need a better understanding of the sources of global currency adoption. The papers in this volume provide specific reasons why the euro has not yet achieved world currency status:

- *Limited economic base.* The euro area is somewhat smaller in economic weight than the US economy (16.1 percent of world GDP at purchasing power parity exchange rates compared with 21.4 percent in 2007, according to the IMF) but more importantly, it does not have a strong growth potential. Medium-term projections indicate that absent significant enlargement or revolutionary increase in productivity trend, its weight in the world economy will shrink continuously (Posen 2004; Forbes and Pisani-Ferry and Sapir in chapter 2).

- *Financial fragmentation.* It was initially assumed that monetary integration would trigger financial integration within the euro area. In the event, Europe's financial center is London, not Frankfurt or Paris, there are several euro-denominated government bond markets instead of one, and cross-border securities trading has developed to a much lesser extent than anticipated.[6] In other words, monetary union has not driven full financial integration. This has proved workable in normal times, but the sustainability of this combination of offshore markets, national bank oversight, and euro area–wide monetary operations is questionable in the long run. During the recent crisis, governments have further realized that whatever comparative advantage some countries could have in the banking industry, an industrial specialization model might not be viable because it implied too large a banking sector for national budgets in case of the need to bail out distressed banks. This threat to the existing model of cross-border integration may lead to a return to fragmentation.

- *Uncertain governance.* Although monetary policy is centralized within the euro area, and product and capital market regulations are to some extent harmonized throughout the European Union, countries within the euro area still have different fiscal, tax, and labor-market policies. There are no prospects of centralization, so how to combine monetary centralization and fiscal/structural/financial decentralization should be a matter for consensus, but there is enduring disagreement as regards the desirable degree of coordination of national policies in these areas. Furthermore, the crisis has exposed the degree to which ac-

---

6. In contrast, cross-border banking and bond issuance have blossomed but are not sufficient to constitute full financial integration. Forbes, Martin, Mayer, and Liikanen in this volume all make balanced assessments of the data supporting this characterization.

countability to domestic taxpayers can trigger competing or contrasting reactions. Although somewhat fashionable in the United States or the United Kingdom, talk of a euro area breakup is mistaken, based at best on shallow comprehension of the functioning of the Economic and Monetary Union (EMU). Nevertheless, as long as the rest of the world sees the future of the euro area and its membership as partially uncertain, this will remain a limiting factor. Thomas Mayer's market view in chapter 3 of this volume depicts this perception in a very reasoned manner, emphasizing the market impact from likely intra–euro area strains of adjustment, rather than an infeasible breakup—but these market discounts are real.

- *Noneconomic limitations.* The euro area is certainly not a hard power. It includes countries with differing stances on international affairs, and there is no common foreign and security policy as yet. So long as the United Kingdom keeps its national currency, the euro area does not include the country with the largest military projection capacity in the European Union. As one of us (Posen 2008) has argued, the few non-neighboring countries that have pegged to the euro tend to be those with security ties to euro area members (notably France, the one hard power within the euro area), while a number of countries pegged to the dollar have geopolitical ties with the United States that outweigh their trade and financial linkages. In chapter 2 of this volume, Posen further contends that this noneconomic factor is a significant brake on the international development of the euro and that strictly economic rules–based treatment of crisis-hit Eastern European countries may actually weaken the euro's global role by demonstrating the limits of political commitment.

- *A discouraging stance toward a global role.* The ECB and the European Union are officially neutral as regards the international role of the euro, as Lorenzo Bini Smaghi (chapter 1) and Liikanen (chapter 4) state in this volume. However, while professing that it neither discourages nor encourages its development, as with the position taken by the Bundesbank and the Bank of Japan in the 1980s (Eichengreen 2005), the European Union has come out clearly against the de jure adoption of the euro by third countries.[7] During the 2008–09 crisis the ECB adopted a cautious approach toward the provision of euro liquidity to neighboring, de facto partially euroized countries, unlike the US Federal Reserve, which early on extended dollar swap lines to several central banks throughout the world. Clearly, the euro area does not fully see itself as a monetary hub and does not take action to become one.

---

7. Prior to the crisis, unilateral euroization by EU members with euro currency boards in place was prevented. The ECOFIN Council had already formally adopted in November 2000 the position that unilateral euroization is not compatible with the treaty and cannot be a way to bypass the convergence process required for euro membership.

It is not easy to delineate the role of each of these factors in the limited development of the international role of the euro. Our conclusion from the studies in this volume is that they jointly represent a significant force beyond the dollar's incumbency offsetting the euro area's economic size and stability.

What Are the Consequences?

Is the euro area consciously or unconsciously squandering part of the potential benefits—either to its members or to the world economy—that could be realized if the euro became a global currency? The advantages of issuing an international currency are often overestimated by observers and politicians, and an economist's first reaction is always to emphasize that the benefits of monetary unification are first and foremost domestic. It should also be recognized that being a global currency has potential costs as well[8]: As illustrated by the "conundrum" of low long-term interest rates prior to the crisis and the role of global imbalances in the crisis, the issuance of an international currency implies that the demand for securities denominated in this currency partially depends on external rather than solely domestic developments. This can affect both the exchange rate and market interest rates as has been the case in the United States. Europe's fragmented markets and uncertain governance in some way partially protect it from instability coming from abroad. As long as it is not equipped with strong enough policy institutions to respond to such shocks, this might be a blessing in disguise.

However, these considerations should not lead policymakers to overlook the potential but not always realized international benefits of issuing a world currency. Seigniorage is a second-order issue here (and the euro area actually already benefits from it since the euro is widely used in the region, including for illegal or semilegal purposes). A much more significant gain to the issuer of a global currency is that the international role of the currency contributes to increasing transactions of securities denominated in it, and thereby to the depth and liquidity of the markets for its government bonds and ultimately the demand for them. In spite of mone-

8. Bergsten and Henning in contributions to this volume question whether the United States has actually benefited on net from the global role of the dollar, with Bergsten claiming less certain dollar dominance might have led to greater discipline. We and most of our authors agree with Summers' characterization of that threat as likely to do more harm than good and believe that having a global currency does little harm so long as it is consistent with the economic fundamentals. The United Kingdom trying to maintain a global role for sterling long after the UK economy declined was indeed harmful. The euro area presents the opposite situation, however, where the global currency status is far short of its economic weight and thus of its potential stabilizing influence on the international financial architecture and on its neighbors.

tary union, government bond markets in the euro area remain fragmented and the largest one, that of the German Bund, is about one-fourth the size of the US federal bond market. For non-European residents this reduces the attractiveness of euro government assets and thereby the liquidity and depth of corresponding markets, as indicated in Kristin Forbes' paper (chapter 2). The widening sovereign risk spreads of some euro area debt issuers over Bunds during the crisis, while far smaller than they would have been absent the euro, are in part also indicative of these costs.[9] Other potential benefits to issuing a global currency include low exchange rate risk and transaction costs. As indicated by Linda Goldberg (chapter 2), trade invoicing in euros is still limited. Even France and Germany invoice about a third of their exports in US dollars, and the Asian countries almost never use the euro. Finally, the dollar remains the dominant currency for the quotation of commodities.

In the absence of the euro's exerting itself globally, countries around the world are finding monetary stability harder to come by as the dollar suffers through a relative decline (whether temporary or lasting). Contributors to this volume systematically examine the role of the euro in various regions of the world. Unsurprisingly, C. Randall Henning (chapter 3) finds that it remains modest in East Asia in spite of the roughly equal weights of the United States and the European Union in the region's foreign trade and in spite of stated intentions to move to a more balanced international system. Instead of baskets involving the euro, except perhaps the special drawing rights (SDR), Asian monetary integration has received a boost— which, though unlikely to culminate soon, adds to global fragmentation. Similarly, Maria Celina Arraes (chapter 3) finds that despite the increase in trade and investment linkages between Latin America and the euro area— and, it should be added, the emergence of Brazil as a G-20 member and world economic player—the strongest monetary relationship in the region remains with the US dollar, even beyond Mexico. Mohsin Khan (chapter 3) makes the assessment that Middle East and North Africa (MENA) and the Gulf Cooperation Council area are dollar zones and likely to remain so, in spite of trading more with Europe than with the United States. This reinforces and is reinforced by the pricing of oil and gas, as well as most commodities, in dollar terms, which may be optimizing but also increases the impact of dollar swings on the world economy.

György Szapary (chapter 3) shows that only in Central and Eastern European countries has the euro taken a dominant role, including in the non-EU member countries of Southeastern Europe. Even Russia has included the euro in its reference currency basket. Real integration in trade as well as cross-border investment—including in the banking sector— have driven this process. It would have been a shock not to see the euro

---

9. Part of the spreads reflects solvency concern and part liquidity premia. There is no established methodology to separate the first effect from the second.

emerge as dominant here. So the picture is one of clear regional success and global limitations. Yet that brings us back to the concern that the euro area's inward orientation if not defensive insecurity is exacerbating the divisions within Eastern Europe in ways that will ultimately be harmful to the euro area economies as well, when more assumption of at least regional responsibility would pay off. One of us (Posen) contends in chapter 2 that economic disregard may turn into politically driven monetary diversification or self-insurance.

Impact of the Crisis

Most of the preceding paragraphs could have been written before the crisis. The global financial crisis, however, has made some of the euro's strengths and weaknesses more apparent and has pointed to the need for immediate responses to the latter.

On the positive side, in 2007 and 2008 the ECB reacted to episodes of acute liquidity shortage more decisively and forcefully than generally expected. The ECB's hands-on stance was made very clear in Lorenzo Bini Smaghi's presentation at the conference, which took place at the height of the liquidity crisis (see chapter 1) and is also pointed out in the paper by Pisani-Ferry and Sapir in chapter 2. Both the Federal Reserve and the Bank of England played catch-up with and learned from the ECB's actions in this regard, and if anything the ECB benefited from being a newer central bank with a repo system better suited to today's markets.

On the less positive side, the crisis has exposed how difficult it can be for an institutional construct like the euro area to depart from fixed routes and explore new avenues in response to unforeseen problems. This was most evident in the cases of bank bailouts and the response to the widening of government bond spreads within the euro area. In chapter 2 Pisani-Ferry and Sapir contrast a "fair weather" governance regime that is based on rules and aims at predictability with the requirements of "stormy weather" governance: initiative, flexibility, and even when needed centralization (in chapter 3 Mayer uses parallel imagery of a happy childhood giving way to a troubled adolescence for the euro). At the height of the crisis in October 2008 a coordinated response to the banking crisis was found outside the normal institutional framework, but with meltdown breathing down the policymakers' necks and only through ad hoc means—including pressure from UK actions outside the euro area. The one institution intended to act flexibly because it was not bound by rules and procedures, the Eurogroup, failed to seize the initiative. This indicates the limits of existing institutional arrangements, despite decent crisis management in the worst of the crisis so far.

In addition, the euro area's response to the widening of bond spreads within it is still unclear. Country risk differentiation is natural in a union where governments remain solely responsible for their own debt. However, levels reached by the spreads in winter 2009 indicate that the possibility of a funding crisis for some euro area member states must be considered seriously. Apart from saying that they would not call the IMF, policymakers in the euro area have not clearly indicated so far how they would respond in the event of such a crisis. As Mayer points out in chapter 3, what would happen, for example, if banks of a fiscally troubled member country presented bonds dedicated to bail out these very banks to the ECB's discount window? Euro area policymakers have tried to calm markets but without being specific about the modalities and limits of potential assistance to a member government. The assumption of the Maastricht Treaty and the euro area's design was that there was no need for crisis management because, by being part of a single currency, members would eliminate the risk of national financial crisis. This may not be sufficient in situations that could arise in the context of deteriorating public finances and persistent market nervousness.

In short, the euro area has an incomplete governance problem. Among other things, for example, this leads to the bizarre result that EU members that are not euro area members are eligible for financial assistance, but euro area members are not because of the no-bailout restrictions. No European instrument could completely substitute for the IMF, especially given the reluctance of EU political institutions to impose conditionality on fellow members. But there are some alternatives short of that and these alternatives would be better than assuming that crises cannot occur within the euro area.

A Pragmatic Agenda

Our first conclusion from the analyses presented in this volume is that for the euro's international role to develop, participants in the single currency need first and foremost to act on the domestic front. Their priority should be to address the weaknesses exposed by the crisis. This requires strong action on financial integration and clarification of cross-border bank supervision, beyond that already called for in the Lisbon Agenda or in the May 2009 Commission communication on European banking supervision (European Commission 2009), neither of which will be enough to remove the limitations and thus the risks identified here. This also requires a rethinking of multilateral surveillance on the basis of lessons learned from the failure to spot vulnerabilities ahead of the crisis and the adoption of principles and procedures for crisis management—including for possible crises within the euro area.

Such improvements in euro area internal governance are a prerequisite to the necessary consolidation of external governance. The fragmented external representation of euro area membership at the IMF and other international financial institutions reveals the constraints on the euro area's ability to respond to global—and thus external—shocks. While some incumbent member states' reluctance to give up their exaggerated roles is part of the reason why consolidation of external representation has not yet occurred, we believe that there is more to it. Internal decision-making is unclear, making citizens and their member states reluctant to centralize external representation. We fear in fact that there may now be even less appetite for consolidated external representation than before the crisis. Awareness of fault lines in euro area governance, the natural, if unfortunate, political pressures to look after one's parochial interests in times of hardship, and the perception of larger member states that direct participation in the G-20 serves their interests better than lengthy negotiation to define a common position among the EU-27 all contribute to reluctance. As Commissioner Joaquín Almunia says in his contribution to chapter 1, "Current events provide a strong case for deepening coordination with the euro area...and to present a united front in international fora to better influence the global decision making process." This is indeed correct but also indicates that in the absence of progress toward the former objective, attainment of the latter may be jeopardized.

If other factors limiting the euro's global role, like the persistence of trade invoicing in dollars or the absence of hard power projection by the European Union (let alone the euro area), are beyond domestic influence, so be it. The euro area will have enough to do and sufficient benefits for itself, for the full EU membership, and arguably for the world by being the best regional currency it can be.

This brings us to our second conclusion, which is that the regional dimension has to be taken very seriously, so the euro area can do much beyond the domestic agenda. If a currency is not a successful regional currency, it does not become a global currency and an effective influence for stability, let alone one of the international financial architects. We have argued that a successful regional currency role comes with responsibilities toward countries in the region that have adopted the euro as an anchor or whose financial systems are partially euroized. That requires playing beyond the script as envisaged by the treaty, considering the situation not just of full club members but also of shadow members, honorary members, and future members. The euro area has to confront this reality. So far the euro area has taken some initiative to stabilize specific countries—mostly in support to IMF programs—but it has not recognized the full extent of its regional responsibilities.

In the near term, the Eurosystem needs to provide more aggressive support to the euroized and near-euro EU member states. This would start with extending swap lines in euros to a number of emerging markets, as the Federal Reserve has done, and, as discussed by Henning, has even been strengthened in East Asia. The euro area is now in a position of sufficient stability and size to no longer fear being disrupted or left hanging by such measures. The Eurosystem could also begin to accept non-euro assets for repos, with appropriate discounts, for countries that are integrated with the euro area financial system but have been prevented from euroizing. There remains too great a risk of financial crisis responses in euro area countries with financial headquarters disadvantaging banking systems in Eastern Europe, although to date it has not been a major problem (both the Commission and the European Bank for Reconstruction and Development have played constructive ad hoc roles in forestalling such issues). The euro area should coordinate with Eastern European governments on crisis responses concerning such things as deposit guarantees and lending limits that have potentially major spillovers.

An immediate agenda is for the euro area to provide a clearer and more sensible path to euro membership for EU members in Eastern Europe. Note that we said more sensible, not easier, path. At a minimum the Commission and Eurogroup should offset the ways in which the crisis has made euro accession more distant even for countries with good policies. While the Maastricht criterion on inflation is now interpreted to exclude calling for deflation,[10] when that is the average of the three lowest inflation rate economies (as it would be today), surely setting a floor for the inflation criterion at no lower than the ECB's long-term goal of near 2 percent harmonized index of consumer price inflation would be sensible. While some measure of exchange rate stability vis-à-vis the euro must be a prerequisite to euro area entry, surely it would make sense to disregard the sudden huge depreciation of all Eastern European currencies in fall 2008—irrespective of their economic fundamentals—rather than resetting the ERM2 clock to zero (or even keeping the waiting period so long).[11] An analogous case can be made with regard to the debt and deficit criteria, given (as Pisani-Ferry and Sapir point out in chapter 2) that even paragons of fiscal virtue like Ireland and Spain have seen their positions completely erode following their busts. In chapter 3 Szapary notes that many new member states will now have challenges meeting the fiscal deficit and long-term interest rate criteria for reasons beyond their control.

---

10. When calculating the average inflation of the three best performers among the EU-27 as called for by the treaty, countries whose inflation is negative are counted as having zero inflation. In a deflationary environment this implies that the reference inflation rate is zero instead of being negative (we are grateful to Marco Buti of DG ECFIN for clarifying this point). The fact of this decision, which is not explicit in the treaty, shows that there is more room for sensible reinterpretation and evolution than commonly acknowledged, as was seen with the 2005 reform of the Stability and Growth Pact.

11. Goldberg reminds us in her contribution to this volume that "If the periphery countries use the center country's currency on their bilateral international trade transactions, they are more sensitive to the center country's monetary policy, and their own national monetary policies are less effective at influencing prices in local markets." In other words, euro area monetary policy is responsible for a meaningful share of outcomes in EU member economies that are "only" trade integrated, absent formal monetary arrangements.

Behind our specific policy suggestions, the euro area has a broader principle and approach to adopt regarding its Eastern European neighbors. We believe that it is harmful to European solidarity, not just to the euro's global role, and eventually to European economic and political stability over the medium term to set member state against member state in trying to distinguish themselves. The Czechs insist they are not the Hungarians, the Estonians that they are not the Latvians, the Bulgarians that they are not the Romanians, and that each must be treated accordingly—and the euro area's present approach encourages this behavior. In a narrow rules-based mindset, such a separating equilibrium seems to make sense, for all that matters are the membership criteria. And indeed competition for performance has more than once been a powerful recipe for virtuous convergence. As we have argued, however, in a crisis such inflexibility will lead to bad outcomes.

In the run-up to the euro's creation 10 years ago, southern EU member states undertook many short-term measures to get through the hoops, strictly speaking, for euro area entry. The result has been that those same countries have continued to suffer from justified doubts about their ability to undertake real adjustment and control their fiscal situations, despite euro area membership. So the premise that enforcing rules, even under the guise of IMF conditionality, will force Hungary or Romania to see the error of their ways is empirically suspect and at best highlights the hypocrisy of enforcement within euro core versus periphery. At worst, the euro area would be pushing a number of Eastern European member states down a very dangerous path economically and politically, which would hurt the competitiveness and stability of their neighbors as well. The euro area needs to step up to its regional responsibilities and can do so only by taking a long-term view of what the region needs, rather than going into a defensive crouch of sticking to the fair weather rules.

References

Chinn, Menzie, and Jeffrey Frankel. 2007. Will the Euro Eventually Surpass the Dollar? In *G7 Current Account Imbalances: Sustainability and Adjustment*, ed. Richard H. Clarida. Chicago, IL: University of Chicago Press.

Darvas, Zsolt, and Jean Pisani-Ferry. 2008. *Avoiding a New European Divide*. Bruegel Policy Brief no. 2008/10. Brussels: Bruegel. Available at www.bruegel.org.

DG ECFIN (Directorate General Economics and Finance). 2008. *EMU@10—Successes and Challenges after Ten Years of Economic and Monetary Union*. Brussels: European Commission. Available at http://ec.europa.eu.

Eichengreen, Barry. 2005. Sterling's Past, Dollar's Future: Historical Perspectives on Reserve Currency Competition. Tawney Lecture delivered to the Economic History Society, Leicester, UK, April 10. Available at www.econ.berkeley.edu.

Eichengreen, Barry, and Marc Flandreau. 2008. *The Rise and Fall of the Dollar, or when Did the Dollar Replace Sterling as the Leading International Currency?* NBER Working Paper 14154 (July). Cambridge, MA: National Bureau of Economic Research.

ECB (European Central Bank). 2008. *Monthly Bulletin: 10th Anniversary of the ECB*. Frankfurt. Available at www.ecb.int.

European Commission. 2009. European Financial Supervision. Commission Communication 2009 (252), May.

Kindleberger, Charles P. 1986. *The World in Depression, 1929–1939*, 2d. ed. Berkeley, CA: University of California Press.

Matsuyama, K., N. Kiyotaki, and A. Matsui. 1993. Toward a Theory of International Currency. *Review of Economic Studies* 60: 283–307.

Pisani-Ferry, Jean, et al. 2008. *Coming of Age: Report on the Euro Area*. Brussels: Bruegel. Available at www.bruegel.org.

Portes, Richard, E. Papaioannou, and G. Siourounis. 2006. Optimal Currency Shares in International Reserves: The Impact of the Euro and the Prospects for the Dollar. *Journal of the Japanese and International Economies* 20, no. 4: 508–47.

Posen, Adam S. 2008. Why the Euro Will Not Rival the Dollar. *International Finance* 11, no. 1: 75–100.

Posen, Adam S., ed. 2005. *The Euro at Five: Ready for a Global Role?* Washington: Institute for International Economics.

Posen, Adam. 2004. Fleeting Equality: The Relative Size of the US and EU Economies to 2020. *US-Europe Analysis Series* (September). Washington: Brookings Institution.

A Challenging Anniversary

The Euro at Ten and the Financial Crisis

JOAQUÍN ALMUNIA

I had planned to focus on the role of the euro in the world economy, but I cannot ignore the exceptional events we have witnessed recently. Nevertheless, even in these testing times, there are still good grounds to celebrate the euro. Despite our imperfect institutional framework, the Economic and Monetary Union (EMU) has sheltered European economies from turbulence over the last decade, and we can be assured that the current crisis would be having an even more severe impact were we without the single currency today. I would also argue that the euro has allowed Europe to play its part in setting out policy actions that will strengthen the global financial system in the future—something that will no doubt be a central concern in the months ahead.

The current events—far from pushing the euro to the background—have highlighted the advantages of a single currency and shown the value of deepening euro area coordination. The European Commission has prepared a major report, *EMU@10*, on the first 10 years of the EMU. When we analyzed the advantages and difficulties of the bold decision to create the euro, our assessment was, and is, very optimistic and positive. Over the 10 years of its existence, the euro has been an undisputed success. It has anchored macroeconomic stability in the euro area and brought historically low inflation and interest rates for much of the last decade. Despite the euro area's lower-than-expected growth rate—due largely to too few structural reforms—the macroeconomic stability combined with the boost to trade and investment brought by the euro has helped to create 16 million new jobs, more than in the United States in the same period. The

Joaquín Almunia is the European commissioner for economic and monetary affairs.

euro's rapid rise to the status of a global currency in less than a decade is a reflection of its success.

Today the EMU is limiting the impact of the crisis in Europe and in the rest of the world as well. The single currency has provided stability in several ways. First, it has prevented the exchange rate and interest rate tensions among its members that used to be common during financial stress. Second, as we argue in our *EMU@10* report, our stability-oriented macroeconomic policy framework has reduced the level and volatility of inflation and interest rates, as well as output fluctuations, in the euro area. Third, since the start of the financial turmoil in 2007, the European Central Bank (ECB) has adopted a prudent monetary stance and has skillfully managed liquidity. This has helped to anchor inflation expectations and to ease conditions in the interbank market.

In short, the EMU has created a pole of relative stability in Europe that world economies have also benefited from, especially those that have strong trade and monetary links with the euro area. Its balanced current account position has also helped reduce the risks for the world economy associated with large global imbalances.

A Deepening Financial Crisis

Financial markets around the world have been going through an extraordinarily difficult period. The upheaval that began here in the United States has engulfed Europe and is now spreading rapidly across the international system.

The crisis intensified sharply as confidence in financial markets collapsed. As the flow of credit ground to a halt, central banks around the world stepped in to provide massive injections of liquidity.

The ECB was among the first to provide liquidity in euros and US dollars in coordination with the Federal Reserve and the Bank of England. This high level of coordination was evident again on October 8, 2008, when the ECB together with the Federal Reserve and five other central banks made an emergency interest rate cut of half a percentage point.

But the actions of central banks are not enough to restore confidence to markets. Risk aversion has now reached extreme levels. Deleveraging has accelerated as market participants are forced to sell off assets that are rapidly losing value.

Market sentiment has plummeted, brought down by deterioration in the banking sector. It is difficult to predict how far the crisis will go and when it will end. Following the spate of bank failures here in the United States, problems started spilling over to European banks.

Urgent Measures to Contain the Crisis

In the first year of the financial crisis, Europe saw the failure of a few national banks, mostly in the United Kingdom and Germany. Governments' swift actions were consistent with the need to rescue their own national banks, such as Northern Rock, IKB, and WestLB.

In September 2008, we saw for the first time the need to support financial institutions with cross-border presence. While providing such support was expected to be impossible, action by governments was fast and effective, as in the cases of Fortis and Dexia.

Confronted with the depth of the crisis and the acceleration of national responses, the European Union then quickly moved to establish close cooperation at the European level. Leaders of the four EU economies that are members of the G-8—Germany, the United Kingdom, France, and Italy—together with the three institutions of the euro area (the Eurogroup, the ECB, and the European Commission) met in Paris in early October 2008 and agreed on a series of measures to stabilize the EU financial system. Leaders pledged to protect individual savings and to take all necessary actions to guarantee the solvency and stability of the EU financial system.

Subsequently, the 27 finance ministers agreed to support the recapitalization of systemically important financial institutions. They agreed that in view of the different national situations there can be no uniform solution in the European Union but that national actions should follow eight commonly agreed principles. Countries now have the flexibility to act at a national level, while not compromising the common European interest and avoiding negative spillovers and a beggar-thy-neighbor race.

The Ecofin ministers also agreed on a series of measures concerning accounting standards and retail deposit protection. The Commission will now urgently bring forward a proposal to promote convergence of deposit guarantee schemes.

The European parliament has also pledged its support and readiness to act quickly and support necessary legislation. The heads of state and government of the European Union, who gathered on November 7, 2008, in Brussels, further supported these measures and stressed the need for coordination. These decisions are unique and consistent with our EU framework.

More recently, as our banking sector faced systemic crisis, several EU national governments announced broad measures. The United Kingdom announced in October 2008 partial nationalization of its banking sector, and actions have been taken by Ireland, Denmark, Germany, Spain, and Italy. Others may follow. Such actions are broadly in line with the principles agreed by the Ecofin ministers, and all countries have pledged to comply with state aid and competition rules.

But the events in the financial markets point to the fact that systemic problems are a global phenomenon and that the solvency of the global financial system is at stake. At the October 2008 meeting in Paris, EU leaders called for a summit with international partners to devise a coordinated approach to the crisis and to lay the foundations for the reform of the global financial system. I sincerely hope that further progress on coordination can be achieved here in Washington.

Reforms for a More Resilient EU Financial Sector

The crisis has raised deeper questions about the financial system and how it should be regulated. In this respect, the October 2007 Ecofin roadmap, which is in line with initiatives at the global level and in particular with the Financial Stability Forum recommendations, remains the basis for the EU policy response in the medium term.

EU leaders agreed in early October 2008 to further accelerate this roadmap. The Commission has already put forward changes to the capital requirement directive to limit risk exposure and to improve supervision of banks operating in more than one country by creating a college of supervisors. The Commission adopted a new legislative proposal for credit rating agencies in November 2008, providing for tighter rules. We are developing additional proposals covering market transparency, valuation standard of accounting of assets, prudential risk management and supervision, and further improvement of coordination.

Effects on the Real Economy

Restoring confidence and normal functioning to financial markets is especially urgent given the mounting evidence that the crisis is beginning to take its toll on the real economy. The risk that this will result in a vicious circle, with events in the financial markets and in the economy feeding off one another, is now a very real and worrying possibility.

Declining confidence, reduced availability of credit and its increased costs to households and businesses, together with oil and commodity price hikes earlier in 2008, are all affecting growth.

Recent indicators point to further weakening of the EU economy in 2008, with the revised growth forecast down to 1.4 percent and with growth weak and well below potential in 2009.

To support economic activity through additional financing, EU leaders have asked that the European Investment Bank increase its loan program to small and medium-sized businesses by 30 billion euros. And we shall ensure that our Lisbon Agenda of reforms is vigorously pursued to help accelerate the adjustments and increase growth and employment.

The crisis will clearly impact public finances, and public deficits will increase. The Stability and Growth Pact, when correctly applied, has sufficient flexibility and allows the implementation of expansionary fiscal policies in the short term, while remaining prudent in the medium term. However, we must prevent deficits from spiralling out of control, and governments should strive to respect the 3 percent limit for budget deficits and 60 percent ceiling for government debts.

Stronger International Coordination

Current events provide a strong case for deepening coordination within the euro area, both to develop solid and decisive policy action in the face of crisis and to present a united front in international fora to better influence the global decision making process.

The euro area's recent actions have demonstrated that when it manages to swiftly agree on a coordinated position, it can be instrumental in finding agreement in the European Union as a whole and even internationally. It is vital we now build on this success, not least because beyond European coordination, there is now a serious need for global coordination.

The financial crisis has revealed how interlinked the world's economies and financial markets are. In addition, there are signs of major shifts in the geopolitical balance. Apart from the current turmoil in the banking sectors in Europe and the United States, let me point out the weakness of the dollar and the fact that advanced economies are slowing down while emerging markets are picking up the slack.

When this crisis is over, other challenges for the global economy will remain. Our future international system will have to absorb ongoing financial innovation, rapid shifts in capital flows, and the further unwinding of global imbalances. This is the main reason why we have no alternative; we need to pursue multilateral solutions.

I believe the European Union and the United States will lead this global movement together. We have long enjoyed a steady and cooperative relationship across the Atlantic. The situation in the 21st century demands that we build on our relationship and together reach out to our new partners.

We need to establish a global dialogue and a new framework that takes in the rising powers of the emerging world. International cooperation needs to rise to the new challenges as it seems that our multilateral institutions are finding it increasingly difficult to provide the answers we need. Our international institutions need to be made more inclusive and more effective.

Within a reformed governance system, there is scope for the International Monetary Fund (IMF) to play a more active role to steer international financial cooperation. The IMF may need to carry on its reforms if it is to exploit its full potential. Overall, I see value in continuing the IMF-led multilateral consultations and extending their scope to global financial stability. And I call on the euro area to continue to be a committed and active partner in this process.

Conclusion

It is clear that the international financial system is in crisis and the stability of the world economy is at risk. What is less clear is how to overcome these challenges.

I believe that if we work together—at both European and global levels—we will find effective solutions. We need to strive for common answers that will safeguard the stability of our economies and financial markets for years to come.

I am convinced that a new global governance framework will emerge from this crisis. Within this new framework, Europe should speak with one voice and win a stronger political role for itself. I have already called for a consolidated representation for the European Union and the euro area in international bodies—which, incidentally, will free up room for emerging economies.

The EMU has made a positive contribution to world stability—and will continue to do so—and this implies new global responsibilities. Because the euro is now a global currency, the euro area should play an active role in international coordination.

The unravelling financial crisis only reinforces the need for Europe to move and speak as one on the world scene. We must rise to the challenge and promote a multilateral resolution of the global financial crisis.

The Internationalization of Currencies—A Central Banking Perspective

LORENZO BINI SMAGHI

It is an honor to be here to celebrate the tenth anniversary of the euro. It is a privilege to represent the institution—the European Central Bank (ECB)—that over the past 10 years has watched over the first steps of the euro and brought it up to be the second most important international currency in the world. The euro is now leaving behind its childhood and entering adolescence. As with many adolescents, it faces a common question: "What would you like to do when you grow up?"

The ECB, like any parent, might tend to be overoptimistic about its child's future. This is why we have adopted a policy of neither encouraging nor discouraging the international use of the euro. It should be an entirely demand-driven process. Like modern parents, we recognize that the euro does not belong to us but should develop according to its own ambitions. We are here to ensure that it has a few key virtues, the first being stability.

Several people—including in the United States, where the euro's birth was considered improbable a decade ago—predict a bright future for the euro, anticipating that it will surge to become the dominant international currency in the coming decades (Chinn and Frankel 2008). Others, however, think that the euro is unlikely to overtake the US dollar (Eichengreen and Flandreau 2008a).

I will not try to review what the euro has already achieved over the last decade. The ECB regularly publishes a report that can be easily consulted (ECB 2008a). I will instead assess the implications, in particular from a central banking point of view, of becoming an international cur-

Lorenzo Bini Smaghi is a member of the Executive Board of the European Central Bank. He thanks Maurizio Habib for his input in the preparation of these remarks.

rency. I will analyze both the advantages and the challenges. I will then try to assess whether the euro has the potential to further increase its role and examine the main obstacles to achieving such a status.

Implications of an International Currency

Even though the euro is currently not the dominant international currency, it has become an alternative to the US dollar as a reserve currency. Euro banknotes are a popular means of payment and store of value in the European Union's neighboring countries. What are the implications for the ECB and the euro area as a whole? I shall try to answer this question, drawing on the economic literature.

Countries can obtain two well-identified advantages from having an international currency. First, microeconomic gains stemming from lower transaction costs. Whether the currency is used for international trade, borrowing in the international markets, or simply tourism, the costs of conversion to a foreign currency and the exchange rate risk attached to these operations are eliminated. Second, the monetary authority issuing an international currency has larger seigniorage revenues to the extent that foreigners hold that currency in the form of non-interest-bearing liabilities, in particular as coins and banknotes. These gains are, however, relatively small and are estimated at less than 0.05 percent of GDP for the euro area, as only a small fraction of the total cash in circulation—10 to 15 percent—is held by non–euro area residents. International seigniorage gains are only slightly larger for the United States, at about 0.1 percent of GDP, as more than half of its stock of currency is estimated to circulate abroad (European Commission 2008, ECB 2007).

Other, broader implications of issuing an international currency are less well documented and not as easily quantifiable. Both the United Kingdom in the period before the First World War—from 1870 to 1913—and the United States in the period after the Second World War enjoyed a so-called exorbitant privilege from being at the center of the international monetary system (Meissner and Taylor 2006).

The privilege stemmed from the possibility to issue low-interest domestic currency–denominated liabilities to finance higher-yield investments abroad. Both the United Kingdom before 1913 and the United States until the end of the 1980s were net creditors toward the rest of the world, and this exorbitant privilege may be seen as their remuneration for being the "bankers of the world." Over the past 20 years, the United States has shifted to a relatively large debtor position vis-à-vis the rest of the world, but its income balance has stayed positive thanks to a positive return differential between its external assets and its liabilities. For some economists, this is the result of the transformation of the United States from world banker to "venture capitalist" with a "leveraged" position, where fixed-income domestic-currency liabilities finance riskier foreign assets taking the form of equity and direct investment (Gourinchas and Rey 2005).

The greater ability to issue domestic-currency liabilities has another important implication from a macrofinancial stability perspective. To the extent that external liabilities are mainly in domestic currency, whereas external assets are denominated in foreign currency—as in the case of equity and foreign direct investment and often also debt securities—issuers of international currencies tend to have a "long" position in foreign currency. As a result, fluctuations in exchange rates tend to produce countercyclical valuation effects on net external assets. When the exchange rate appreciates, foreign-currency assets shrink in domestic-currency terms and as a share of GDP. Conversely, following sharp devaluations—often associated with economic and financial stress—the foreign currency–denominated assets grow in domestic-currency terms and liabilities are unaffected, improving the overall investment position when it is more needed (Lane and Milesi-Ferretti 2005). As an example, after the currency crises in both 1949 and 1967, the pound sterling's status as an international currency—with most of the large overseas liabilities still denominated in pounds—allowed the United Kingdom to cushion somewhat the impact of the devaluations (Cairncross and Eichengreen 2003).

The issuance of an international currency could potentially also have significant implications for the implementation of monetary policy. Let's consider the experience of the euro over the past 10 years in that regard.

On the one hand, it has been essential for the euro area to have its own monetary policy in order to face idiosyncratic shocks and focus on the maintenance of domestic price stability. This result would not have been possible without the introduction of the euro and the creation of a large internal economic and trade area free of exchange rate risk. On the other hand, the external demand for euro-denominated assets may affect domestic monetary aggregates, complicating their relationship with inflation over the long run. Recent ECB staff research shows that it is necessary to place money demand in the context of portfolio flows and international asset prices in order to explain euro area money supply dynamics and measure excess liquidity, which can pose risks to price stability (ECB 2008b).

In addition, successful international currencies are used as external anchors by a number of countries that prefer to fix the exchange rate and relinquish their monetary independence.

Such currency pegs eliminate one channel of adjustment of external imbalances for the anchor currency. As long as the pegging countries are smaller than the issuing country, this might not be a major problem. However, when the aggregate economic weight of all pegging countries becomes large, the margin for adjustment of the nominal effective exchange rate of the anchor currency becomes constrained. As a consequence, the adjustment of the nominal effective exchange rate might require a more than proportional adjustment of the bilateral rates of the remaining floating currencies.

Moreover, fluctuations in the demand and supply of the euro among international investors, from both the private and public sectors, may have implications for the exchange rate. The increasing attractiveness of euro-denominated assets as a potential alternative to US dollar securities may generate sudden shifts in portfolio flows and unwelcome volatility in foreign exchange markets. Another potential indirect channel of disturbance in the dollar-euro exchange rate is the role of the US dollar in the invoicing of oil and other major commodities. Over the past few years, the surge in oil prices and other commodities—in US dollar terms—has been associated with a negative relationship with the exchange rate of the US dollar against the euro. In the case of oil prices, this could be the result of policies by oil-exporting countries to try to defend the purchasing power of a barrel of oil in terms of a basket of international currencies, including, in particular, the euro. It must be acknowledged that it is difficult to detect and isolate the direction of causality between the oil price and the US dollar.

Overall, for the ECB and the euro area, the international role of the euro offers positive opportunities and serious challenges. This explains the ECB's neutral stance aimed at neither directly promoting nor hindering the international use of the euro.

Determinants of the International Use of Currencies

What conditions cause currencies to dominate international markets? Do these conditions favor a growing role for the euro?

There is a large body of literature on the determinants of the international use of currencies. Most studies focus either on the store of value function of currencies and their role in foreign exchange reserves (see Chinn and Frankel 2008 for a recent review) or on the unit of account and means of payment functions, including the invoicing of international trade (see Kannan 2007). In the first case, users of an international currency are mainly concerned with its ability to maintain a stable purchasing power over time. In the second, users care about transaction costs and the economies of scale that are obtained from tapping into a large network.

In both cases, a number of economic, financial, political, and institutional factors contribute to increasing the popularity of an international currency. I will review these factors with particular reference to the euro.

Economic and Financial Conditions

Let me start with the economic and financial conditions supporting the international role of currencies. The size of the economy and its foreign trade flows are crucial to promoting the international status of a currency. This is because there are scale economies and network externalities in using the currency that is also used by other agents in international transactions. The larger the economy and its trade flows, the more likely it is that smaller economies will adopt the currency of the larger trading partner. In this respect, the critical mass of the euro area, in economic terms, is large enough to exert gravitational attraction on the rest of the world. In 2007 the euro area accounted for about 16 percent of world GDP, measured at purchasing power parity, and its external trade was equal to more than 18 percent of world trade, at current exchange rates.

In the invoicing of international trade, however, network externalities tend to generate only one "winner." For several decades, the US dollar has served as a medium of exchange and unit of account for homogeneous goods traded in organized exchanges, such as commodities and oil. In this case, inertia is very important, and it is very difficult to dislodge the incumbent currency, whose use is associated with low information and transaction costs. Yet even in this case, it would be possible to switch to a parallel invoicing system, including the euro, if agents expected others to start using the new currency and technological progress diminished transaction and information costs (Mileva and Siegfried 2007).

Transaction costs are important not only in international trade but also in the use of currencies as financing or investment instruments. For this reason, truly international currencies must be backed by large, deep, liquid, and efficient financial markets. In terms of size, credit quality, and liquidity, US dollar financial markets still have an edge over the euro markets, although this gap seems to have narrowed since the launch of the euro in 1999 (Galati and Wooldridge 2006). The US Treasury bond market remains the most liquid segment of the global bond market, whereas sovereign issuances are inevitably fragmented in the euro area. However, this structural problem has been mitigated by the removal of exchange rate risk since the introduction of the euro. Government bond yields have converged across euro area countries and are increasingly driven by common factors, although local factors continue to play a role (ECB 2008c). Indeed, the bid-ask spreads of sovereign bonds denominated in euros are not much higher than the spreads of those denominated in US dollars (Dunne et al. 2006). Interestingly, the euro area bond market for "corporate" issuance is quite well integrated (ECB 2008c), and effective bid-ask spreads are possibly even lower than in the United States (Biais et al. 2006).

I have argued so far that investors take into account liquidity and transaction costs when dealing with international currencies. Once these structural and cost differentials converge across currencies, traders and investors can discriminate among various alternatives on the basis of the return on their investment. In brief, international currencies must be able to preserve their external value, avoiding inflation and sharp nominal devaluations. It is well known that the erosion of the status of the pound sterling as leading international currency was caused by a series of large shocks accelerating a declining trend. The First and Second World Wars accelerated the fading of the United Kingdom as a major political and imperial power. The economic decline was highlighted by at least three devaluations in 1931, 1949, and 1967, which progressively undermined the confidence of international investors in the ability of the pound sterling to preserve its external value. Recent evidence suggests that the pound sterling lost its dominance already in the mid-1920s but then regained the lead in the second half of the 1930s (Eichengreen and Flandreau 2008b). The jury is still out on this case, but it is evident that inertia in the international use of currencies is much stronger in the case of the invoicing of trade, where network effects favor the use of only one currency. Inertia is somewhat less powerful when investors decide how to allocate their portfolio, leaving greater room for currency competition.

Obviously, inflation and devaluations accompanying the demise of world currencies are not natural accidents but the result of wrong macroeconomic policies and structural weaknesses. These often take a long time to emerge in the form of an erosion of external competitiveness and a rise in external imbalances, fiscal profligacy and internal imbalances, low productivity, and, eventually, sluggish growth and high unemployment. Conversely, strong and balanced economic performances foster the international status of currencies.

Where does the euro stand in terms of policies and performance? The euro area fares relatively well compared with major economic partners, although a greater effort has to be made to raise productivity and lift the potential growth rate of the economy. The external position is fairly balanced. The Stability and Growth Pact guards against the emergence of public deficits and debt. Over the past 10 years, inflation has been kept relatively low in spite of large supply-side shocks. The institutional setting of the ECB, with its independence from political pressure and its mandate to preserve price stability, helped to rein in inflationary pressures and indirectly fostered the confidence of domestic and foreign residents in the capacity of the euro to preserve its value.

Political and Institutional Conditions

Let me turn to the political and institutional conditions for currencies to steadily take on an international role. This is clearly a more complicated issue.

Historically, countries with stable political systems and the capacity to enforce the rule of law, both inside and outside their borders, had currencies that were widely traded and accepted internationally. Certainty with regard to property rights, which may be undermined by political instability, and the ability of the issuer of the international currency to rule and to raise revenues to repay its financial obligations are crucial in this case.

The existence of "hard power" certainly contributes to the ability to enforce property rights, domestically and internationally, and thus helps in developing an international role for the currency. From this point of view, Europe cannot compete at present with other providers of hard power. On the other hand, the success of the Economic and Monetary Union provides Europe with a form of "soft power." This power is translated in different ways, such as the anchoring of several currencies to the euro, the adoption of the independent central bank model in the Maastricht Treaty, technical assistance on issues related to monetary policy, payment systems, supervision, banknote issuance, and the like.

Good economic governance is also a fundamental ingredient of successful international currencies. The Dutch guilder in the 17th and 18th centuries, the pound sterling in the 19th and early 20th centuries, the US dollar in the late 20th century, all were (or are) international currencies backed by strong empires and states but also supported by the economic power and success of their issuers.

Some academics regard political and economic governance as the "Achilles' heel" of the euro (e.g., Cohen 2007). They claim that the delegation of monetary and economic responsibilities across member states and EU institutions is unclear, and they lament the lack of a single unitary governance structure, the so-called commander in chief, behind the euro. Over the past year, the financial turbulence has posed a serious test for monetary authorities throughout the world. The reaction of the ECB has shown that the central bank can act rapidly and effectively to address liquidity issues.

As the crisis has evolved from a liquidity to a solvency problem, the challenge has moved increasingly to supervisory authorities and finance ministers. The ability to provide a coordinated European response is being tested. On specific occasions, such as the bailout of the banks Fortis and Dexia, the framework has functioned properly.

On the more general response to the crisis of confidence in the financial system, it is paradoxical that the relatively healthier European banking system might have to suffer more because of the uncoordinated and piecemeal reaction of national authorities. There is also a risk of a renationalization of the single market for financial services, as a result of different solutions being implemented in different countries.

The fear of many academics and observers has long been that, without a specific framework for crisis resolution, the European banking system would be unable to address major shocks. The problem might turn out to be a different one. The absence of a crisis resolution framework does not prevent effective solutions from being found and implemented. But since these solutions are different from country to country, they may lead to problems of discrimination and difference of treatment, undermining the functioning of the single market. This certainly would not contribute to the international role of the euro. And this is confirmed by the recent weakening of the exchange rate.

Another important institutional condition for the international success of currencies—closely linked to good economic governance—is trade and financial liberalization. By definition, only currencies that can be freely converted for trade or investment purposes have the potential to achieve the status of international currencies. According to Barry Eichengreen, the US dollar owes part of its success in maintaining its position as main reserve currency to the absence of truly convertible competitors since the Second World War. In his view, the international use of potential reserve currencies—such as the French franc, the Japanese yen, or the Deutsche mark—was directly or indirectly discouraged by the respective governments (Eichengreen 2005).

Convertibility is not an issue in Europe, but protectionism, especially against foreign capital, might be. We are currently observing attempts in different countries to limit the inflow of capital from foreign countries, in particular in so-called strategic sectors. However, the definition of "strategic" remains vague and can give rise to quite imaginative interpretations.

Concluding Remarks

To sum up, currencies emerge as international players thanks to a combination of a number of conditions. These include geopolitical influence, political stability, and the enforcement of the rule of law, as well as good political and economic governance. Only large economies generating meaningful network externalities possess international currencies. They must also be economies with deep, efficient, and open financial markets where it is possible to invest without the risk of incurring large transaction costs or capital losses. Eventually, once all these factors have been accounted for, the quality of economic governance and economic institutions and the ability to devise policies that support confidence in the external value of the currency can make the difference. Obviously, inertia in the international use of currencies is strong, and sudden changes in their relative position are unlikely, barring very large shocks.

Since its introduction 10 years ago, the euro has emerged as the second most important currency in the world. The euro area offers the opportunity of a large, deep, and increasingly integrated financial market for foreign operators willing to hold euro-denominated assets. The monetary policy conducted by the ECB has certainly contributed to supporting confidence in the euro. We now face a different type of challenge, related to the integrity and sustainability of the single market in the face of a major financial crisis.

Given the dimension of the current turmoil, it is not surprising that market participants view the ongoing developments with some concern. After all, the birth of the euro was followed by a substantial depreciation of the euro against all other currencies. The young currency and the young central bank needed to be tested in good and in bad times. The premature death of the euro was preannounced several times. But the skeptics had to concede.

In light of Europe's past experience, one element has to be taken into account in analyzing the current situation. Either a strong response is provided to the challenges posed by the current turmoil to the single financial market within the existing institutional framework or the framework itself is changed in favor of a more centralized system of supervision and crisis resolution. After all, this is how the euro was born, as it became clear, in particular after the 1992–93 foreign exchange crisis, that it was not sustainable to run different monetary policies within a single market. The same logic could apply in the case of financial regulation and supervision. And national authorities know it.

References

Biais, B., F. Declerck, J. Dow, R. Portes, and E-L. von Thadden. 2006. *European Corporate Bonds Markets: Transparency, Liquidity, Efficiency.* London: Centre for Economic Policy Research.

Cairncross, A., and B. Eichengreen. 2003. *Sterling in Decline: The Devaluations of 1931, 1949 and 1967,* 2d ed. Basingstoke and New York: Palgrave Macmillan.

Chinn, M., and J. A. Frankel. 2008. *The Euro May Over the Next 15 Years Surpass the Dollar as Leading International Currency.* NBER Working Paper 13909 (April). Cambridge, MA: National Bureau of Economic Research.

Cohen, B. J. 2007. Enlargement and the International Role of the Euro. *Review of International Political Economy* 14, no. 5 (December): 746–73.

Dunne, P., M. Moore, and R. Portes. 2006. *European Government Bonds Markets: Transparency, Liquidity, Efficiency.* London: Centre for Economic Policy Research.

ECB (European Central Bank). 2003. *Review of the International Role of the Euro.* Frankfurt.

ECB (European Central Bank). 2007. *Review of the International Role of the Euro.* Frankfurt.

ECB (European Central Bank). 2008a. *The International Role of the Euro.* Frankfurt.

ECB (European Central Bank). 2008b. The External Dimension of Monetary Analysis. *ECB Monthly Bulletin* (August). Frankfurt.

ECB (European Central Bank). 2008c. *Financial Integration in Europe.* Frankfurt.

Eichengreen, Barry. 2005. *Sterling's Past, Dollar's Future: Historical Perspectives on Reserve Currency Competition.* NBER Working Paper 11336 (May). Cambridge, MA: National Bureau of Economic Research.

Eichengreen, Barry, and M. Flandreau. 2008a. Why the Euro Is Unlikely to Eclipse the Dollar. *Financial Times,* April 3.

Eichengreen, Barry, and M. Flandreau. 2008b. *The Rise and Fall of the Dollar, or When Did the Dollar Replace Sterling as the Leading International Currency?* NBER Working Paper 14154 (July). Cambridge, MA: National Bureau of Economic Research.

European Commission. 2008. *EMU@10: Successes and Challenges after 10 Years of Economic and Monetary Union.* Brussels: Directorate-General for Economic and Financial Affairs.

Galati, G., and P. Wooldridge. 2006. *The Euro as a Reserve Currency: A Challenge to the Pre-eminence of the US Dollar?* BIS Working Paper no. 218 (October). Basel: Bank for International Settlements.

Gourinchas, P., and H. Rey. 2005. *From World Banker to World Venture Capitalist: US External Adjustment and the Exorbitant Privilege.* NBER Working Paper 11563 (August). Cambridge, MA: National Bureau of Economic Research.

Kannan, P. 2007. *On the Welfare Benefits of an International Currency.* IMF Working Paper 07/49 (March). Washington: International Monetary Fund.

Lane, P. R., and G. M. Milesi-Ferretti. 2005. *Financial Globalization and Exchange Rates*. IMF Working Paper 05/03 (January). Washington: International Monetary Fund.

Meissner, C. M., and A. M. Taylor. 2006. *Losing Our Marbles in the New Century? The Great Rebalancing in Historical Perspective*. NBER Working Paper 12580 (October). Cambridge, MA: National Bureau of Economic Research.

Mileva, E., and N. Siegfried. 2007. *Oil Market Structure, Network Effects and the Choice of Currency for Oil Invoicing*. ECB Occasional Paper no. 77 (December). Frankfurt: European Central Bank.

The Euro and the International Monetary System

DOMINIQUE STRAUSS-KAHN

We are facing a very serious situation in the financial markets and the global economy. We have to make some hard choices, and we must start making them very soon. I will therefore spend most of my time today on what needs to be done to contain the crisis and on its implications for the global economy.

I apologize in advance if it seems like I have spoiled a birthday party for the euro by talking too much of the storm outside. But I want to take advantage of this gathering, as well as the broader gathering of the fall 2008 World Bank/International Monetary Fund (IMF) meetings, to discuss what we need to do. We can solve the problems in the financial markets and the global economy so long as we act quickly, forcefully, and cooperatively.

In October 2008, the IMF gave its assessments of what is happening in the financial markets and the global economy. Let me talk first about the outlook for financial markets and the actions we must take there because, as we all know, the heart of the problem is in financial markets.

An Action Plan for the Financial Markets

First, the numbers. In the IMF's October 2008 *Global Financial Stability Report*, we estimated that financial-sector losses could be about $1.4 trillion, almost 50 percent higher than our estimates in the spring, which others thought to be pessimistic. About half of these losses have been realized, but there are still significant losses in the system.

Dominique Strauss-Kahn is the managing director of the International Monetary Fund.

But the problems in the financial markets now go beyond the cash losses. We are facing a crisis of confidence. The private sector cannot restore confidence on its own. Macroeconomic policy measures by governments will not restore confidence on their own. Piecemeal measures on financial markets will not restore confidence on their own. What will restore confidence is government intervention that is clear, comprehensive, and cooperative between countries. A few simple principles should govern action:

- **Principle 1:** Government action needs to have a clear objective so that effective oversight of how public money is used is possible.
- **Principle 2:** National plans need to be comprehensive. They must contain guarantees to depositors and assurances to creditors that are sufficient to ensure that markets function. They must deal with distressed assets and provide liquidity, and, most importantly, they must include bank recapitalization.
- **Principle 3:** Action should be coordinated, at the global level and at the regional level when appropriate, for example, in the European Union.
- **Principle 4:** Action should be fair, in that taxpayers, who are taking on the downside risks, should be able to share upside gains once the crisis passes.

How might this be applied in practice? I would highlight four sets of actions. First, as many governments have now concluded, the fragility of public confidence has reached a point where some explicit public guarantee of financial-system liabilities is unavoidable. This means not only retail bank deposits but probably also interbank and money market deposits, so that activity may restart in these key markets. Of course, such a step should be temporary and include safeguards such as heightened supervision and limits on deposit rates offered.

Second, the government needs to take out troubled assets and force the recognition of losses. Asset purchases should be done at fair value. Why fair value? Because transparent bank recapitalization and restructuring of balance sheets is essential to the process. If capital is to be attracted to banks, it is better to pay a lower price now, recognize losses, and give banks an upside if the implied loss turns out to be smaller than expected.

Third, private money is scarce in today's environment. Therefore, support from the government is needed. One strategy that has worked in past crises is to match new private capital subscriptions with government capital, which imposes a market test for the use of public funds.

Fourth, a high degree of international cooperation has become urgent. The collapse in confidence in the markets has been almost matched by a collapse in confidence between countries. We saw a very bad trend toward unilateral measures taken with national interests in mind, with unintended beggar-thy-neighbor consequences for others.

We are beginning to see a turnaround in this. At the Ecofin meeting in early October 2008 some principles were agreed to, and on October 8 we saw coordinated moves by major central banks. We need more coordination. Financial institutions now span many countries, and credible rescue plans must be consistent across many jurisdictions. I urge European countries especially to work together.

There is no domestic solution to a crisis like this one. I know, having myself served as a minister of finance of my country, how difficult it is in the European Union to reach consensus and make decisions. I do not underestimate the problems. Nevertheless, cooperation and coordination in actions is the price of success at both the European and global levels. The weekend's meetings will be an opportunity for finance ministers to talk about how to bring about the needed cooperation. All kinds of cooperation have to be commended. All unilateral actions have to be avoided, if not condemned.

How Is the Financial-Sector Turmoil Affecting the Global Economy?

One of the reasons action is so important is that the turmoil in the financial markets is having serious effects on the global economy. Even if strong and coordinated action along the lines I have been talking about is taken, we think the world is going to experience a serious slowdown.

We foresaw this in spring 2008. At that time, we were criticized for being too pessimistic. Now I am afraid that it seems we were too optimistic. Our best forecast now is that world growth will be around 3 percent in 2009, which may not sound so bad. But the projection for advanced countries is worse: very close to zero until at least mid-2009, with a slow recovery during the rest of that year. World growth will be driven increasingly by growth in emerging and developing countries. And they will grow at a lower rate than they have in the recent past: 7 percent in 2008 and 6 percent in 2009. The financial-market crisis is also going to have longer-term effects.

The United States

In the United States, a new generation of households, businesses, and banks will now have fresh and vivid memories of a financial crisis. They will be more cautious and take fewer risks. This is not a bad thing. In fact it is part of a long-term correction that is due. Before the crisis, people—and especially banks—took too many risks. Now changed attitudes to risk will reshape patterns of consumption and investment. We are already beginning to see this.

How should macroeconomic policymakers in the United States respond to this? My answer is that they should not try to fight the long-term change but that if both private investment and private consumption fall sharply in the short term—as private saving rises—then there may be a need for the government to support the economy. The options for fiscal policy will be constrained by the large addition to the federal debt caused by the recently passed rescue package. But fiscal stimulus measures may still be justified in the near term so long as they are balanced by longer-term measures that promise to contain deficits and debt, especially reform of entitlement programs.

Europe

In terms of economic impact, Western Europe was hit at least as hard as the United States in 2008, partly because of the appreciation of the euro.

But let me make one point, which is very relevant to the subject of this conference. We have not yet seen a foreign exchange crisis. Sure, we have seen a couple of days when the euro-dollar rate has moved by a couple of percent, and we have seen some equally sharp movements of the pound sterling and other currencies. But none of this approaches a crisis, and we have certainly not seen the kind of abrupt and disruptive movements of exchange rates that characterized the Asian crisis.

Why is this? One reason is obviously the success of the euro. For example, consider what 2007 might have been like if Europe had not had the euro. If the past is any guide, the appreciation pressure on the euro would have gone disproportionately into the Deutsche mark, which may have appreciated much more than the euro now has. In other countries, political and business forces would have lined up in favor of decoupling or devaluing against the mark.

Anticipating the possibility of exchange rate realignments, market participants would have withdrawn capital from countries at risk of realignment, driving up interest rates and risk spreads and potentially causing current account financing problems. Higher interest rates would have undermined housing markets and choked growth.

As in the past, exchange rate realignments would likely have been needed to restore order, and these exchange rate realignments in turn would have caused inflationary pressures in countries that devalued. So there is no question that the euro has contributed to the stability of its member countries during this crisis. And for its members it has become an essential element of the global monetary system.

However, European countries still face major challenges in dealing with the current crisis, and policy options are constrained. Many European countries have limited scope for fiscal stimulus because of already high debt and aging populations. There is more leeway in monetary policy. Indeed, the European Central Bank took appropriate action in early October 2008.

Emerging Economies

In 2009 almost all global growth will come from the emerging economies. But the effects of the turbulence are also beginning to mount in their financial markets and economies.

Emerging economies are generally in a much better position than in the past. They have large reserve buffers, solid current account positions, and healthier banks. However, there is still a large group of countries that are very exposed to global financial conditions due to high external financing needs and in some cases banking system fragilities.

Policy responses will need to be tailored to the circumstances of individual countries. For those with high reserve levels, there could be room to draw them down to finance a temporary and sudden shortfall in capital flows—not to defend a particular exchange rate but to mitigate adverse effects on banks or corporations associated with depreciation. Other countries, though, will need to raise policy interest rates in line with rising risk premia to stem outflows and bolster confidence in their currencies.

Finally, some emerging economies may need help and possibly substantial help. For our part, the Fund is supporting member countries with advice, and if needed we are ready to support them with financing. We have activated emergency procedures to respond quickly to urgent requests, with high-access financial programs based on streamlined conditionality that focuses on crisis response priorities. We have plenty of liquidity to support our members if they need financing.

Before concluding, let me talk about two other issues.

Food and Fuel Crisis

The first issue is the other crisis in the world economy, which is affecting many developing countries. High food and fuel prices continue to put enormous pressure on developing countries. Prices have eased in recent months but remain well above their levels at the onset of the recent price surges.

About 50 countries are really hurting, with uncomfortably weak reserve positions. National budgets are also under pressure, and inflation is on the rise. In low-income countries the average inflation rate is expected to exceed 13 percent by the end of 2008. Inflation hurts the poor most because they are least able to protect themselves, and it leads to greater inequality and sometimes to unrest.

Developing countries can help themselves, for example, by shifting budget support toward subsidies for goods particularly consumed by the poor, or, when feasible, better-targeted social safety net programs that protect the poor in a cost-effective manner.

But developing countries also need help from others. The Fund is doing its part—together with the World Bank—with advice and technical assistance. The Fund has also increased financial support to 15 countries, and we have changed our Exogenous Shocks Facility so that we can provide assistance more quickly, in larger amounts, more flexibly, and with more focused conditionality. Donors must also help. One complication is that the budgets of advanced countries will be under more strain because of the financial crisis. It is very important that they not respond to the crisis by cutting aid, which goes to the poorest and most vulnerable people in the world.

Looking Beyond the Crisis

The second issue is that even though we are still in the midst of the financial crisis, we need to draw some lessons from it.

Lessons in Regulation and Supervision of the Financial Sector

For the financial sector we have a good start in the recommendations and technical work of the Financial Stability Forum (FSF), much of which was done in collaboration with the IMF. But of course, strong as they were, the FSF recommendations have not been adopted in time to prevent the crisis from unfolding. In fact, the crisis is the result of three failures: regulatory and supervisory failure in advanced economies, failure in risk management in the private financial institutions, and failure in market discipline mechanisms. Now we need to go further. Let me emphasize a few points.

We need to have more flexibility and less procyclicality of some of the Basel II norms, including on the question of "fair value." The rating agencies have to adapt to the new complexity of the financial sector, limit conflicts of interest, and accept supervision. We need to close loopholes and fill information gaps in financial regulation and supervision. This includes looking again at regulation for covering securitization, private equity companies, and mechanisms that increase leverage. We also need to give more thought to regulating hedge funds, either directly or indirectly, by regulating their counterparties.

How should we tackle this work? Let me be blunt. I think the IMF can help in coordinating this effort, drawing on the expertise of others. Why? Two reasons: First, the Fund—with its universal membership and demonstrated financial diplomacy (for example, its work on sovereign wealth funds)—can bring together the different actors in a global forum that discusses risks to global stability and policy responses, and second, the Fund has the machinery for follow-up through bilateral surveillance and Financial Sector Assessment Programs (FSAPs).

Improving the Financial Architecture

Like a forest fire that leads to renewal of the soil, every crisis gives birth to new ideas, and especially new ideas to improve the international financial architecture. Earlier in October 2008, Robert Zoellick made an inspiring call for a "new multilateralism."

Let me add a few ideas to the debate. One can trace most of the problems in the architecture to either lack of legitimacy or lack of effectiveness. Legitimacy must be conferred by reliance on broader groups. One very simple change that could be made is to extend the G-8 to at least China, India, and Brazil, and perhaps others.

But this needs to be accompanied by greater reliance on multilateral institutions with near universal membership, so that no country that wants to participate in the international system is left out. Of course, the institutions themselves have to be representative as well as universal, and especially we need to see an increasing role for and responsiveness to emerging markets. Both the reform of Fund quotas and the broader governance reform that we are undertaking are very important for this.

As to effectiveness, I would like to see greater simplicity and more follow-up. To achieve more simplicity we need better coordination between international organizations. It sometimes seems that you need a scorecard to keep track of the players in development: development banks, the UN Development Program, the World Food Program, and national administrations. The roles of the different multilateral institutions need to be better defined so that there are fewer overlaps between them.

We also need better follow-up of agreements and communiqués. There is a certain poignancy in reading past communiqués. They remind me of a discarded children's board game. They once inspired great passion but are quickly forgotten. (This has not changed since I was finance minister in the 1990s.) One way to better follow up the work for the "Gs" would be to have a kind of secretariat.

The current crisis is, if nothing else, a wake-up call. Put simply, we have to manage the system better than we have so far. And I believe that we can do better. This is a time of serious challenges, but it is also a time when we can think imaginatively and act boldly.

2

Underlying Determinants of Global Currency Status

Financial Network Effects and Deepening

KRISTIN J. FORBES

Many factors determine global currency usage. This paper focuses on one of them: demand for a country's financial liabilities due to financial deepening and liquidity. This focus does not imply that financial-market development is the only factor determining global currency usage, but, as I argue in this paper, it has been one of the most important determinants of demand for the dollar and will play an important role in determining the future of the euro. This topic is closely related to the financial crisis currently unwinding around the globe. What happens to European financial markets, and especially how European policymakers support and regulate their markets in response to the financial crisis, will be critical in determining the long-term demand for European investments and the euro.

I first describe the insatiable demand for US liabilities over the past few years. Second, I talk about the determinants of foreign investment in the United States, drawing from theoretical and empirical studies. Finally, I draw lessons from demand for European liabilities and the euro and link it to the current financial crisis.

Insatiable Foreign Demand for US Liabilities

It is well known that there has been an insatiable demand for US liabilities over the last few years. The statistics are so astounding that they merit a quick review. In 2007, as the US financial crisis was in its early stages,

Kristin J. Forbes is a nonresident visiting fellow at the Peterson Institute for International Economics and associate professor at the Massachusetts Institute of Technology's Sloan School of Management.

the United States attracted $2.1 trillion of new capital flows from abroad.[1] This $2.1 trillion does not include any new sales; that is $2.1 trillion of new money coming into the United States. These capital inflows funded the US current account deficit plus US capital outflows. Moreover, this was not a one-year event. From 2003 through 2007, $7.8 trillion of new foreign investment flowed into the United States. This is over $5 billion a day of foreign capital purchasing US liabilities—including equities, government bonds, corporate bonds, foreign direct investment (FDI), and bank loans. Even after the subprime crisis started to unfold, the money kept "rolling in" to the United States, albeit at a slower pace. For example, in the first quarter of 2008, the United States attracted $411 billion of new capital flows, compared with $693 billion in the first quarter of 2007. Unfortunately, data for the last few months of 2008, as the financial crisis deepened, are not yet available, but the recent strengthening of the dollar suggests that foreign demand for US financial liabilities has remained strong. This large and sustained demand for US financial liabilities has been a key support for the US dollar.

Where is this $2.1 trillion of foreign capital flows into the United States going? Figure 2.1 illustrates the use of foreign capital inflows from 2003 to 2007. Some commentators incorrectly imply that most of these capital inflows are used to purchase US treasuries. In fact, only 16 percent of total capital inflows (including private- and official-sector flows) are used to purchase US treasuries. More important is the 22 percent of capital inflows used to purchase corporate bonds and 17 percent for FDI and equities. Therefore, foreign capital flows into the United States represent a diverse range of investments—not primarily US treasuries.

Not surprisingly, these massive capital inflows of over $5 billion a day into the United States have given foreigners a substantial ownership share of major US financial classes. As shown in table 2.1, foreigners now own 11 percent of US equities, 24 percent of US corporate bonds, and 57 percent of marketable US treasuries. These ownership shares have increased rapidly over the past few years and further reflect the importance of foreign demand for US liabilities in supporting the dollar.

Determinants of Foreign Demand for US Liabilities: The Evidence

Why are foreigners willing to invest over $5 billion a day in the United States? There are several possible explanations, and this section briefly explores them one at a time.[2]

One potential reason is that foreigners earn high returns on their US

---

1. All statistics in this paragraph are from the Bureau of Economic Analysis website, www.bea.gov (accessed in October 2008).

2. See Forbes (2007 or 2008) for more details on these explanations.

Figure 2.1 Composition of gross foreign capital inflows, 2003–07
(percent)

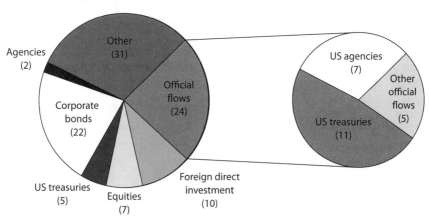

Source: Bureau of Economic Analysis, *Survey of Current Business,* July 2008, US international transactions table.

Table 2.1 Share of foreign holdings of US liabilities, as of June 2007

Class	Total outstanding US liabilities (billions of dollars)	Percent foreign-owned
Equity	27,768	11.3
US treasuries	3,454	56.9
Agencies	6,105	21.4
Corporate debt	11,391	24.0
Total	48,718	18.8

Note: US treasuries are marketable treasuries and exclude central bank holdings.

Source: US Treasury Department, June 2008.

investments. This is one of the standard talking points of US Treasury secretaries. For example, Secretary Henry Paulson Jr. argued: "We have deep and liquid capital markets and a growing economy that provides opportunities for foreign investors to earn an attractive return on their capital."[3] His predecessor, Secretary John Snow, stated: "Today we are in a situation where sound, growth-enhancing policies in the United States have made it an extremely attractive place to invest."[4] These arguments are important

3. Prepared remarks before the Economic Club of Washington, March 1, 2007, available at www.treas.gov.

4. Prepared remarks at Chatham House, the Royal Institute of International Affairs, London, November 17, 2004, available at www.treas.gov.

Figure 2.2   Average annual returns on private-sector investment, 2002–06

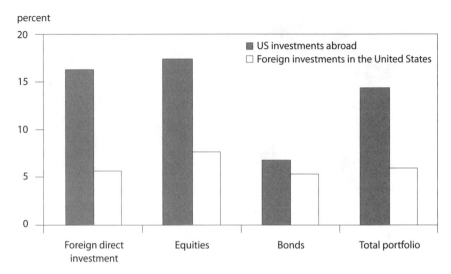

percent

Source: Bureau of Economic Analysis, *Survey of Current Business,* July 2008, US international transactions table.

because the academic literature provides evidence that investors chase re-turns (see Bohn and Tesar 1996, Sirri and Tufano 1998). If foreigners were investing in the United States and earning high returns, then combined with the evidence that investors chase returns, this would suggest that foreigners would continue to invest in the United States.

Is this the case?[5] The returns on foreign investment in the United States can be calculated in a number of ways, but no matter which statistics you calculate, the findings are similar to those in figure 2.2. The figure focuses only on private-sector investment—excluding "official-sector" investment (i.e., governments) as governments may place less emphasis on returns than the private sector when making investment decisions. For each asset class, the white bars are the returns that Americans earned when investing abroad from 2002 to 2006 (the last five years for which data are available) and the shaded bars are the returns that foreigners earned in the United States. The pattern is striking. For each asset class—FDI, equities, bonds, and portfolio investment (equities and bonds)—foreigners have earned less investing in the United States than Americans have earned abroad over the last five years. This pattern continues to hold if one adjusts for cur-rency movements and makes rough adjustments for risk. No matter how

---

5. For discussions of problems in measuring return differentials across countries and evidence for longer periods, see Curcuru, Dvorak, and Warnock (2008) and Lane and Milesi-Ferretti (2007).

Table 2.2   Country exposure to the United States (percent)

Exposure	Equities	Debt
Global market share	35.8	38.2
Mean	4.3	14.8
Median	1.3	9.1
Minimum	0	0.1
Maximum	27.8	67.1
Number of countries	82	54

Notes: Debt includes corporate, government, and agency debt. Foreign holdings include foreign official holdings.

Source: Based on analysis in Forbes (2008) using data from the US government.

one cuts the data, foreigners investing in the United States have earned substantially lower returns versus what they would have earned if they kept their money abroad—even within the same asset classes. Therefore, foreigners are clearly not investing in the United States because they have earned high returns year after year and are chasing returns.

A second reason why foreigners might be willing to invest over $5 billion a day in the United States is that this is a natural reduction of home bias that has been occurring around the world over the past decade. Individuals tend to be "overweight" in domestic holdings, and as they seek to diversify their portfolios internationally, it is not surprising that they would increase their investments in the largest market in the world.

Again, is this the case? To test the validity of this theory, it is useful to look at whether countries are over- or underinvested in the United States versus what a simple portfolio allocation model would predict. More specifically, a simple portfolio allocation model predicts that countries hold US liabilities so that the share of US holdings in their portfolio equals the share of the US market in the global portfolio.[6] Table 2.2 makes these comparisons.[7] The top row shows that the US share of the global equity market is about 36 percent, and the US share of the global debt market (which includes corporate, agency, and government debt) is about 38 percent. For investors with a well-diversified portfolio, about 36 percent of their equity exposure should be to the US equity market and about 38 percent of their debt exposure to the US debt market. The second row of the table, however, shows that the mean exposure to US equity and debt markets for countries around the world is far lower. On average, foreigners

---

6. This simple framework assumes that investors care only about the mean and variance of the real return of their invested wealth, markets are efficient, and cross-border barriers to investment are small.

7. See Forbes (2008) for additional details on this calculation and specific country statistics.

hold only 4 percent of their equity investments and only 14 percent of their debt investments in the United States. The median exposures to the US markets are even lower, suggesting that most countries do not have nearly as much exposure to US markets as standard portfolio diversification models would predict.[8] Most countries are underexposed to US equity and debt, and achieving more diversification in their portfolios could be an important factor driving investment in the United States. In other words, countries seeking to reduce their home bias and diversify their portfolios may generate a natural capital flow into the United States and support a continued strong demand for US liabilities (at least for a limited time).[9]

In addition to return chasing and portfolio diversification, a third factor that could drive US capital inflows is differences in financial-market development and the quest for more liquid and efficient financial markets. This explanation has recently received a substantial amount of attention in the academic literature (such as Caballero, Farhi, and Gourinchas 2008; Ju and Wei 2006; Mendoza, Quadrini, and Ríos-Rull 2006). Although the models and explanations in each of these papers are slightly different, the main idea is that countries around the world that are generating huge surplus earnings and savings (such as China and the Middle East) need to invest these earnings somewhere. Since financial markets in these countries are less developed—as measured by liquidity, efficiency, range of instruments, and the like—investors or governments choose to invest this money in another country that has more developed financial markets. Since the United States has the world's largest, most developed, and most liquid financial market, it has been the recipient of the bulk of this surplus earnings and savings. (Granted, many of these perceived advantages of the US market before 2007 may now be perceived as liabilities after the financial crisis, but these weaknesses were not widely appreciated before 2007.)

A fourth reason foreigners might invest in the United States is their trade links or other forms of "closeness." There is some evidence that when a country trades more with another country, it also tends to hold more of its financial liabilities (see Obstfeld and Rogoff 2001, Antràs and Caballero 2007). There is also evidence that countries that are "closer" tend to buy more of the other country's financial assets, with "closeness" measured not only by distance but also by ties through measures such as a common language, a colonial heritage, or a cheaper cost of communications (see

---

8. It is worth noting that China is one of the few countries that is "overexposed" to the United States versus the predictions of these simple portfolio allocation models (with about 50 percent of its debt exposure in the United States).

9. If foreign countries reduced their home bias against the United States, however, this would not necessarily generate an increase in net US capital inflows because US investors could simultaneously reduce their home bias and increase gross capital outflows (which could be even greater than the increase in gross capital inflows).

Portes, Rey, and Oh 2001; Daude and Fratzscher 2006). Any countries that trade more with the United States or are "closer" based on this broad definition would have a stronger demand for US financial liabilities.

A fifth and final factor that could drive foreign investment into the United States is perceived strong US corporate governance. I realize that statement may seem rather contradictory given the recent problems in US financial markets—such as in the markets for subprime housing and credit default swaps, to name a few. Prior to this crisis, however, there was a widespread belief that the United States had the gold standard of corporate governance in its financial markets, and if anything many analysts worried that the Sarbanes-Oxley Act of 2002 and recent reforms to US corporate governance may have been too stringent, rather than too loose. This perceived strong corporate governance may have been one factor attracting investment to the United States. Investors may have been willing to purchase US liabilities, even with the expectation of a lower return relative to other investment opportunities, due to the country's strong institutions, perceived good accounting standards, and belief that their investments would not be confiscated by the government.

Which of these five factors is actually important in driving foreign capital flows into the United States? In Forbes (2008), I perform a detailed empirical analysis to attempt to sort out the relative importance of factors such as return differentials, diversification, financial-market development, trade and closeness, and corporate governance in driving foreign investment into the United States.[10] The models, econometric issues, and lengthy series of results are beyond the scope of this paper, but the key findings can be briefly summarized. The main result of this analysis (which I confess was not my expectation) is that the relative development of US financial markets has been the key driver of foreign capital into the United States. Countries with less developed financial markets sought to take advantage of the more liquid and more efficient financial markets in the United States.

To get a sense of the magnitude of this effect, consider the case of China. China held $894 billion in US bonds at the end of 2007. Then assume that China developed its own financial markets, such as by increasing its private bond market capitalization to GDP to a size comparable to that in South Korea in 2006 (before the financial turmoil hit). This development of China's domestic bond market would make domestic investment more attractive and reduce China's need to invest its surplus savings abroad in US financial markets. Using the central estimates from Forbes (2008), the magnitude of this effect would be substantial; China would reduce its holdings of US bonds by $250 billion. Although this amount is small

---

10. For other analyses of the determinants of cross-border investments and capital flows, see Bertaut and Kole (2004), Chan, Covrig, and Ng (2005), Lane and Milesi-Ferretti (2008), and Faruqee, Li, and Yan (2004).

relative to the size of total US bond markets, it would undoubtedly have some effect on US financial markets—especially if sales of US bonds by the Chinese were accompanied by sales in other countries.

Although this empirical analysis found that relative levels of financial-market development appear to be the most important factor driving foreign investment into the United States, it also found that other factors were important. More specifically, the analysis found a moderate role for trading and closeness in driving capital flows: Countries that trade more with the United States and are closer through cultural ties, a common language, distance, or the cost of communications also tend to invest significantly more in the United States. Finally, the analysis found a small role of return chasing in explaining investment in US equity markets (although not bond markets). Surprisingly, there is no evidence that diversification motives are an important factor driving foreign investment in the United States.

Implications for the Euro

What are the implications for the euro? The role of financial-market development is the key lesson from this analysis of foreign investment in the United States and the corresponding demand for the dollar. How do European bond and equity markets compare with those in the United States? Euro bond markets have been growing in size and liquidity and are closing the gap with dollar bond markets. This increase in size will correspondingly make the euro bond markets more attractive and increase foreign investment. Equity market capitalization in the euro area, however, is still only about half of the equity market capitalization in the United States. As a result, in the near future European equity markets will not be as attractive an alternative for foreign investment that places a substantial importance on size and liquidity.

The key factor affecting the future of European equity and bond markets, however, will undoubtedly be how they perform during the current financial crisis and what new structure emerges. The responses by European regulators and policymakers will be critical. At the time of this writing, the immediate response to the crisis is sending a strong signal that there is no "European market" and instead Europe is a collection of individual markets with differentiated rules and governance. Each regulator and each government has been responding in the interests of its own country. If this approach continues, it may significantly detract from the attractiveness of European capital markets. Since a key factor driving foreign investment is the quest for large and liquid markets, the realization that European markets are not one large, combined, liquid, efficient, and deep market will deter foreign capital inflows.

In addition to financial-market depth, the empirical analysis discussed earlier suggested several other factors that can affect the demand for a country's financial liabilities. One factor is trade flows and "closeness." It is hard to see significant changes in these variables over the next few years that will affect demand for European financial liabilities, but I will leave this topic to the other papers in this volume, which focus more on trade. Another factor driving demand for foreign investment in equity markets is return chasing. Over the three years from 2006 to 2008, European equity markets outperformed US equity markets. For example, the total return on the Eurofirst 300 over this period was 26 percent, while the return on the S&P 500 was 22 percent. The stronger return in European equity markets may have attracted more foreign investment over this period. Since the start of 2008, however, this pattern has reversed. From January 1, 2008 to October 6, 2008, the return on the Eurofirst 300 was –31 percent while the return on the S&P 500 was –28 percent. This weaker performance of the European equity markets may reduce demand for European equities in the immediate future, but given the unprecedented turmoil in all financial markets, it is likely that any such effect would be overwhelmed by other factors and it is impossible to make any prediction about relative returns going forward.

One result from the analysis of the drivers of foreign demand for US liabilities was the relatively unimportant role of diversification and a reduction in home bias. Even if this was an important factor, however, it is unlikely to be a major factor driving future demand for European financial liabilities as foreigners' portfolios are already more exposed to Europe than to the United States. As shown in table 2.3 (part of which replicates statistics in table 2.2), US equity markets are 35.8 percent of global equity markets, and the average holdings of US equities by foreigners are only 4.8 percent of their total equity portfolios. This indicates that foreigners hold only 13.5 percent of the optimal share of US investments in their equity portfolio.[11] Making a similar calculation, foreigners hold only 24.9 percent of the optimal share of US investments in their debt portfolio. The same calculations for the major European markets suggest that foreigners are still underweight in European equity and debt versus the optimal portfolio shares but substantially less underweight than they are for the United States. For example, foreigners hold 28.3 and 33.6 percent of the optimal shares of French and German equities, respectively, and 41.5 and 71.7 percent of French and German debt, respectively. This suggests that most countries around the world already have more exposure to European equity and debt markets than they do to US markets. As a result, any increase in diversification and reduction in home bias by foreign investors would actually drive a greater increase in demand for US liabilities than European liabilities.

---

11. The 13.5 percent is calculated as 35.8 percent divided by 4.8 percent. Note that these numbers are substantially smaller if the numerator is median foreign holdings instead of mean foreign holdings.

Table 2.3 Country exposure to the United States and Europe (percent)

Country	Global market weight	Mean	Percent of global market weight
France			
Equity	4.5	1.3	28.3
Debt	4.9	2.0	41.5
Germany			
Equity	3.0	1.0	33.6
Debt	5.9	4.2	71.7
United States			
Equity	35.8	4.8	13.5
Debt	38.2	9.5	24.9

Notes: Debt includes corporate, government, and agency debt. Foreign holdings include foreign official holdings.

Source: Based on analysis in Forbes (2008) using data from the International Monetary Fund's Coordinated Portfolio Investment Survey.

Conclusion

Key factors driving foreign demand for US equity and debt over the past few years are unlikely to be replicated in a surge in demand for European equity and debt and the corresponding demand for the euro. A key factor determining future demand for the euro will be how European financial markets emerge from the current crisis. If regulators and policymakers treat European equity and debt markets as one coherent, large, and liquid market, this will attract additional foreign investment in the future.

On the other hand, if they continue to treat Europe as a collection of individual markets with different regulations and different backstops, this will make European financial markets less attractive to foreigners in the future. Since foreigners place such a large premium on the size, liquidity, and depth of financial markets when allocating their investment, how European markets evolve in these terms will be a key factor driving future demand for the euro.

References

Antràs, Pol, and Ricardo Caballero. 2007. *Trade and Capital Flows: A Financial Frictions Perspective*. NBER Working Paper 13241. Cambridge, MA: National Bureau of Economic Research.

Bertaut, Carol, and Linda Kole. 2004. *What Makes Investors Over or Underweight?: Explaining International Appetites for Foreign Equities*. International Financial Discussion Paper 819. Washington: Board of Governors of the Federal Reserve System.

Bohn, Henning, and Linda Tesar. 1996. US Equity Investment in Foreign Markets: Portfolio Rebalancing or Return Chasing? *American Economic Review: Papers & Proceedings* 86, no. 2 (May): 77–81.

Caballero, Ricardo, Emmanuel Farhi, and Pierre-Olivier Gourinchas. 2008. An Equilibrium Model of 'Global Imbalances' and Low Interest Rates. *American Economic Review* 98, no. 1 (March): 358–93.

Chan, Kalok, Vicentiu Covrig, and Lilian Ng. 2005. What Determines Domestic Bias and Foreign Bias? Evidence from Mutual Fund Equity Allocations Worldwide. *Journal of Finance* 60, no. 3 (May): 1495–534.

Curcuru, Stephanie, Tomas Dvorak, and Francis Warnock. 2008. The Stability of Large External Imbalances: The Role of Returns Differentials. *Quarterly Journal of Economics* 123, no. 4 (November): 1495–530.

Daude, Christian, and Marcel Fratzscher. 2006. *The Pecking Order of Cross-Border Investment.* European Central Bank Working Paper 590. Frankfurt: European Central Bank.

Faruqee, Hamid, Shujing Li, and Isabel Yan. 2004. *The Determinants of International Portfolio Holdings and Home Bias.* IMF Working Paper WP/04/34. Washington: International Monetary Fund.

Forbes, Kristin. 2007. Global Imbalances: A Source of Strength or Weakness? *Cato Journal* 27, no. 2 (Spring/Summer): 193–202.

Forbes, Kristin. 2008. *Why Do Foreigners Invest in the United States?* NBER Working Paper 13908. Cambridge, MA: National Bureau of Economic Research.

Ju, Jiandong, and Shang-Jin Wei. 2006. *A Solution to Two Paradoxes of International Capital Flows.* NBER Working Paper 12668. Cambridge, MA: National Bureau of Economic Research.

Lane, Philip, and Gian Maria Milesi-Ferretti. 2007. Where Did All the Borrowing Go? A Forensic Analysis of the US External Position. Unpublished working paper. Photocopy.

Lane, Philip, and Gian Maria Milesi-Ferretti. 2008. International Investment Patterns. *Review of Economics and Statistics* 90, no. 3 (August): 518–37.

Mendoza, Enrique, Vincenzo Quadrini, and José-Víctor Ríos-Rull. 2006. *Financial Integration, Financial Deepness and Global Imbalances.* NBER Working Paper 12909. Cambridge, MA: National Bureau of Economic Research.

Obstfeld, Maurice, and Kenneth Rogoff. 2001. The Six Major Puzzles in International Macroeconomics: Is There a Common Cause? *NBER Macroeconomics Annual* 15: 339–90.

Portes, Richard, Hélène Rey, and Yonghyup Oh. 2001. Information and Capital Flows: The Determinants of Transactions in Financial Assets. *European Economic Review* 45, no. 4-6 (May): 783–96.

Sirri, Erik, and Peter Tufano. 1998. Costly Search and Mutual Fund Flows. *Journal of Finance* 53, no. 5 (October): 1589–622.

International Trade in Financial Assets

PHILIPPE MARTIN

A few years ago, Andrew K. Rose of the University of California, Berkeley started a whole literature on the effects of common currencies on trade. His message was that the effect was very large, suggesting that the euro would also have a large effect on trade (Rose 2001). The estimated size of the euro's trade effect has since been reduced from very large to modest.

Richard E. Baldwin's bottom line is that the "euro probably did boost intra-Eurozone trade by something like five to ten percent" (Baldwin 2006). There are good reasons to focus on the euro's effect on trade in goods since as economists we believe that increasing trade has large welfare gains. Also, the datasets on trade flows on which these effects can be estimated are rich and of good quality. But this is not the case for financial flows. Still, it is surprising that there has been little research on the effect of the euro on trade in financial assets.

The euro's impact on trade in financial assets should be of particular interest because the euro may more directly affect transaction costs on financial markets than on goods markets as it can be considered a driver of financial integration.

A second reason to study the impact of the euro on financial integration is that, following the orthodox view, financial integration brings welfare gains. The role of financial markets to smooth transitory asymmetric shocks may be all the more important in the euro area, where asymmetric shocks cannot be stabilized by different monetary policies.

Before I report on the large and visible effect of the euro on financial

Philippe Martin is a professor at Sciences Po (Paris) and research fellow at the Centre for Economic Policy Research (London).

markets, it is important to question whether the orthodox view is sound. This view on the welfare gains of deeper, more integrated, and larger financial markets is (or was) certainly shared among many policymakers for whom bigger financial markets, more financial assets are better. There is an implicit or explicit assumption in this conference (and even in its title) that countries or groups of countries (in the case of the euro area) should strive to have larger financial markets, more financial instruments, and, therefore, compete with each other to attract financial activities. Many interpreted the creation of the euro as part of this competition, and indeed one of the coveted prizes of being a "global currency" is that it supposedly comes with financial-market (or supermarket) dominance. The present financial crisis should, however, oblige us to question these assumptions.

We know the arguments that make sense theoretically: Bigger, more liquid financial markets (1) should allow more investment projects to be financed and, therefore, foster long-term growth and (2) should also allow risk diversification. Both arguments are linked because risk diversification is the mechanism that allows publicly traded firms to specialize in their core business and provide higher returns. However, when one compares the empirical literature on the gains brought by trade integration and the literature on the gains brought by financial integration and financial-market development, it is clear that the case for the latter is weaker or even absent.

The present crisis is obviously raising more doubts about the assumption of efficiency of financial markets and the assumption that they can diversify rather than aggravate aggregate risk in the economy. Bigger financial markets may indeed enable financing of more investment projects, but this is welfare enhancing only when financial markets are efficient. It is not yet clear that financial markets enable financing of the most efficient investment projects when they themselves are not efficient. In the presence of bubbles, the fact that more projects can be financed is not necessarily a good thing. Going even further, the competition among different countries to attract financial activities may have played a role in causing the present crisis by pushing toward excessive laxity in the rules and regulations of financial institutions.

In the present context, interpreting the creation of the euro as part of the global competition game to attract financial activities may lead to the conclusion that the euro has not been an element of global financial stability. The creation of the euro may have fostered more risk sharing and financial stability through other more standard mechanisms, but using the euro to foster competition between financial markets may be a dangerous game. Hence, I would not derive any strong unambiguous welfare implication from the empirical results suggesting that the euro has had a more visible and impressive effect on trade in financial assets than on trade in goods.

There is a small, recent literature on the euro-asset-trade link. For example, Philip Lane (2006) looks at the impact of the Economic and Monetary Union (EMU) on bond portfolios. R. De Santis and B. Gerard (2006) analyze the impact of EMU on portfolio weights rebalancing. Another line of research follows the lead of Andrew Rose by analyzing the financial gravity equation (see Portes and Rey 2005 or Aviat and Coeurdacier 2007).

The first decade of the euro has demonstrated the powerful effect of a single currency on financial integration. The euro has led to a fall in transaction costs in cross-border trade in financial assets and weakened, but not eliminated, the financial home bias. The increase in intra–euro area holdings during 1999–2006 fully explains the increase in the share of advanced countries in cross-border world financial trade (Lane and Milesi-Ferretti 2008). From this point of view, the euro's effect seems to be much more visible and impressive on trade in financial assets than on trade in goods. An open question is how the current crisis will affect this integration process. Given the national nature of supervision and guarantees, there is a risk that the integration brought by the euro may be partially reversed.

Nicolas Coeurdacier and I recently studied the euro's impact on trade in financial assets using a theoretically derived financial gravity equation (Coeurdacier and Martin 2007). The theory is derived from a simple model (Martin and Rey 2004, 2006) of risk diversification in which the demand for assets (domestic and foreign) depends on income, relative returns, and various transaction costs that can be influenced by the creation of the euro. The advantage is that the model generates simple testable implications. Coeurdacier and I use two datasets—a cross-country one on bilateral asset holdings (bonds, equity, and banking assets) and a Swedish one on both holdings of foreign assets and outflows. Sweden is interesting to study because it is very open for both trade and financial flows; it is a member of the largest and most integrated regional trade agreement, the European Union, but is outside the euro area.

In this paper I first disentangle the different effects of the euro on asset holdings for countries both within and outside the euro area. In theory, the euro may have several effects on the cost of transacting assets: on transactions inside the euro area, on purchases of euro assets by countries outside the euro area, and on purchases of non-euro assets by euro area countries. For example, the elimination of currency risk had several effects. It decreased transaction costs of trading across different financial markets in the euro area. It led to more integration of national equity markets. In particular, due to local-currency mandates on many institutional investors, the replacement of national currencies by the euro meant that the feasible universe for such investors was greatly enlarged (Lane 2008).

As in trade theory, these relative changes in transaction costs may also result in diversion if, for euro-based investors, transaction costs to buy euro assets decrease more than to buy non-euro assets. From this point of view, the EMU is one of the drivers of financial integration, but it is different from the other drivers (financial deregulation, financial innovation, and liberalization of international capital flows) because it is asymmetric.

In addition, and as noted by Lane (2006), the single currency and single monetary policy may increase the correlation between returns of euro assets and make them closer substitutes. This may actually have a negative effect on the holdings of euro assets by countries in the euro area. The reason is that the increased elasticity of substitution between euro assets magnifies the impact of any remaining transaction cost on cross-border holdings within the euro area.

Coeurdacier and I (2007) find evidence that the euro affects both transaction costs and the elasticity of substitution, but the effect is different for different classes of assets and also depends on whether countries are in or outside the euro area. Our estimates (which depend on our estimated elasticity of substitution between assets) suggest that the transaction costs to buy assets from the euro area are lower by around 17 percent for equity and 14 percent for bonds. This unilateral financial liberalization effect of the euro benefits countries both in and outside the euro area.

In addition to this effect that benefits all countries, countries inside the euro area benefit from a decrease in transaction costs for equities and bonds of around 10 and 17 percent, respectively. This is the preferential financial liberalization aspect of the euro. Hence, for a country inside the euro area, the transaction cost of cross-border purchase of a stock or a eurobond is lower by around 27 and 31 percent, respectively. Overall, this translates into large effects on cross-border asset holdings. The euro increases bilateral bond holdings between two euro area countries by 150 percent while equity holdings rise by around 45 percent.

However, the impact on bank assets is not significant. The numbers for equities and bonds are very large, and one may think that, as for the early effects of the single currency on trade, they are too large to be true. But these numbers are not driven by the fact that euro area countries are more financially developed, have better institutions, and are closer to the other main financial markets (or more integrated in product markets). Coeurdacier and I (2007) control for these observable characteristics of euro area countries. One could also argue that this result is not due to the euro but to some empirical regularity among European countries: For some unobservable reasons Europe is more attractive for investors than other regions in the world. However, we control for regional dummies.

Even though the percentage difference in transaction costs inside and outside the euro area is estimated to be quantitatively similar on equity and bonds, the impact is much larger on bonds. The reason is that different bonds are much closer substitutes than different equities, and this magnifies the quantity impact of any reduction in transaction costs on bond holdings. These results hold once Coeurdacier and I (2007) control for a relatively large set of variables that might be correlated with being part of the euro area (trade linkages, geography, and exchange rate volatility). They confirm the results of Lane (2006) on the positive role of the euro on bond holdings between countries of the euro area, but quantitatively, our estimated effect on bond holdings is smaller. The estimates also confirm that two eurobonds are more substitutable than other bonds: The elasticity of substitution is around three times as much. No such difference exists for equity, though.

Contrary to the literature on the euro's effect on trade in goods (Baldwin 2006, Flam and Nordstrom 2003), Coeurdacier and I (2007) find no evidence that the euro decreases the transaction cost for euro area countries of purchasing equity outside the euro area. In fact, for equities we find evidence that substantial diversion takes place, in the sense that euro area countries buy less equity from outside the euro area than what is predicted by financial gravity equations.

The diversion effect does not come from an absolute increase in transaction costs to buy non-euro assets but from a change in the relative cost of buying euro- versus non-euro-based assets. This evidence is based on comparing asset trade between euro area countries and the Nordic countries in (Finland) and outside (Sweden, Norway, and Denmark) the euro area. Interestingly, no diversion effect seems to operate for bonds. This may be because a significant portion of bonds in these countries is issued in euros.

The evidence of a diversion effect for cross-border asset trade, which has not been found in the case of goods trade, is also important because it suggests that the euro affected financial flows through a different mechanism than goods trade. In the latter case, Baldwin (2006) argues that the absence of a diversion effect suggests that the introduction of the euro has in effect brought down the fixed cost of trading in the euro area, not transaction costs. The diversion effect Coeurdacier and I (2007) find in the case of financial assets points to a transaction cost story where the relative—not absolute—transaction cost for a euro-based investor to buy assets from the rest of the world has increased with the euro. Also, we find that the euro effect is larger for flows than for stocks in the case of equities and loans. This suggests again that the euro has generated a fall in transaction costs.

I return to our empirical analysis to answer the following questions: Did larger financial markets benefit more from the creation of the euro? Did the United Kingdom, the largest financial center of the European Union but outside the euro area, disproportionately benefit from it? The answer to the first question is yes: Larger financial markets—in terms of market capitalization—both inside and outside the euro area benefited from a more pronounced fall in transaction costs to buy euro-based assets. From this point of view, the euro works as any process of financial integration in a world where economies of scale also matter for financial markets. This suggests that the euro certainly reinforces the process of concentration of financial markets. However, contrary to what is often assumed, I find no particular effect on the United Kingdom: It has not benefited more than other countries from lower transaction costs on euro-based assets.

One of the messages of Baldwin (2006) on the euro trade effect is that countries do not need to be inside the euro area to benefit from most of its economic gains. This has some intriguing political economy implications on the future dynamics of monetary integration with potential free-rider problems. For the financial side of the euro story, this message does not hold fully, however. Outsiders do benefit from lower transaction costs to diversify risk when purchasing euro assets, but the gain is around half what the insiders get.

Even if one accepts the orthodox view that financial integration brings welfare benefits, the Coeurdacier-Martin (2007) results suggest that the welfare implications of an asymmetric financial liberalization process such as the EMU are complex. Our empirical results suggest that the euro has three main effects: (1) a unilateral financial liberalization that makes it cheaper—for all countries—to buy euro area assets; (2) a diversion effect due to the fact that lower transaction costs inside the euro area lead investors there to purchase relatively fewer non-euro assets; and (3) an increase in cross-border asset holding inside the euro area, which is the counterpart of the diversion effect and corresponds to a preferential financial liberalization.

In theoretical models such as Martin and Rey (2004, 2006), where the supply of assets is endogenous and assets are imperfect substitutes, this surge in the demand for euro-based assets leads to an increase in the supply of euro-based assets, which indeed has also taken place. Also, if the location of financial markets is itself endogenous, these theoretical models predict that an asymmetric decrease in transacting financial assets across borders (the way we interpret the impact of the EMU on financial markets) leads to two effects. On the one hand, financial activity of the smallest markets outside the euro area should migrate toward euro area countries. This is so except if the outsiders issue assets in euros, which has been the case with Scandinavian bonds, for example. On the other hand, the creation of an integrated financial market should also lead to the concentration of financial activities in the largest financial markets of the euro area.

In the orthodox view, the fact that the euro has led to lower transaction costs in buying euro assets should benefit all countries, as it implies that they pay less to diversify risk. The diversion effect is clearly detrimental to non-euro area countries. If assets are imperfect substitutes, the lower demand for non-euro equity (the only asset for which some diversion is suggested by the Coeurdacier-Martin [2007] empirical analysis) implies a lower price of non-euro assets relative to euro assets. This implies an increase in the cost of capital for firms outside the euro area. Overall, non-euro area countries should benefit from more and cheaper (in terms of transaction costs) opportunities to diversify financial risk but with a deterioration in their financial terms of trade.

Euro area countries benefit from an improvement in their financial terms of trade and from lower transaction costs to diversify risk. In a monetary union where asymmetric shocks cannot be stabilized with monetary policy, such diversification may be all the more valuable. Of course, these days, one can have a less positive view of the systemic risk generated by the increased supply of new financial assets that results from euro-driven financial integration.

References

Aviat, A., and N. Coeurdacier. 2007. The Geography of Trade in Goods and Asset Holdings. *Journal of International Economics* 71: 22–51.

Baldwin, Richard E. 2006. *In or Out: Does It Matter? An Evidence-Based Analysis of the Euro's Trade Effects*. London: Centre for Economic Policy Research.

Coeurdacier, Nicolas, and Philippe Martin. 2007. *The Geography of Asset Trade and the Euro: Insiders and Outsiders*. CEPR Discussion Paper 6032. London: Centre for Economic Policy Research.

De Santis, R., and B. Gerard. 2006. *Financial Integration, International Portfolio Choice and the European Monetary Union*. European Central Bank Working Paper 626. Frankfurt: European Central Bank.

Flam, H., and Nordstrom, H. 2003. Trade Volume Effects of the Euro: Aggregate and Sector Estimates. Institute for International Economic Studies, Stockholm. Photocopy.

Lane, Philip R. 2006. Global Bond Portfolios and EMU. *International Journal of Central Banking* 2, no. 2 (June): 1–24.

Lane, Philip R. 2008. *EMU and Financial Market Integration*. IIIS Discussion Paper no. 272. Dublin: Institute for International Integration Studies.

Lane, Philip R., and Gian Maria Milesi-Ferretti. 2008. The Drivers of Financial Globalization. *American Economic Review: Papers & Proceedings* 98, no. 2 (May): 327–32.

Martin, P., and H. Rey. 2000. Financial Integration and Asset Returns. *European Economic Review* 44, no. 7: 1327–50.

Martin, P., and H. Rey. 2004. Financial Super-Markets: Size Matters for Asset Trade. *Journal of International Economics* 64: 335–61.

Martin, P., and H. Rey. 2006. Globalization and Emerging Markets: With or Without Crash? *American Economic Review* 96, no. 5: 1631–51.

Portes, R., and H. Rey. 2005. The Determinants of Cross-Border Equity Flows. *Journal of International Economics* 65, no. 2: 269–96.

Rose, Andrew K. 2001. Currency Unions and Trade: The Effect Is Large. *Economic Policy 33* (October): 449–61. London: Centre for Economic Policy Research.

Currency Invoicing of International Trade

LINDA S. GOLDBERG

The tenth anniversary of the euro is an excellent opportunity to explore the role of the euro as an international currency and some consequences of this role. In this paper, I address the use of euros and dollars in international trade transactions. Specifically, I explore the extent to which export and import transactions are invoiced in dollars and the reasons for these choices. I also comment on some related consequences for international transmission of shocks and for monetary policy effectiveness. I do not, however, address the value of euros or dollars, which is a very different concept from the role and consequences discussed in this paper; nor do I turn to the extensive evidence on the extent to which dollars and euros are used in exchange rate arrangements, central bank foreign exchange reserve portfolios, or a broad range of international financial transactions. For instance, substantial changes have occurred in corporate bond issuance, particularly in the growth of the euro's use in international bond issuance. Specifics on the role of euros and dollars in international financial transactions are well exposited in an excellent report published by the European Central Bank (ECB), *Review of the International Role of the Euro*. The most recent issue of the report, published in July 2008, provides rich and extensive information on this subject.[12]

Linda S. Goldberg is a vice president at the Federal Reserve Bank of New York and visiting officer at the Board of Governors of the Federal Reserve System. The views expressed in this paper are those of the author and do not necessarily reflect the positions of the Federal Reserve Bank of New York or the Federal Reserve System.

12. See also the discussion by Coeurdacier and Martin (2007) and the paper by Philippe Martin in this volume.

Evidence on Dollar and Euro Use in International Trade

The dollar continues to be the dominant currency of choice in international trade transactions. Table 2.4 presents examples of the dollar's share and usage for invoicing of exports in various countries. Korea and Thailand use the dollar extensively, invoicing more than 80 percent of their exports in dollars. The United States represents only around 20 percent of the direct exports of these countries, while other "dollar bloc" countries (i.e., countries with currencies that have exchange rate arrangements vis-à-vis the US dollar) as export destinations account for an additional 20 to 30 percent of exports. Even beyond exports to the United States and other dollar bloc countries from Korea and Thailand, there is a clear residual use of the dollar in international transactions. France and Germany use the dollar to invoice roughly a third of their extra–euro area export transactions. While much of this activity is likely accounted for by exports to the United States and to dollar bloc countries, there is still a small residual use of dollars on exports to other locations. This description is not the case for Hungary and Poland, which use the dollar less extensively.[13] Indeed, in Goldberg (2007) I ask whether the low share of dollars used in invoicing international trade is consistent with utility maximization for these countries seeking to join the euro area, given the share of commodities in their export baskets.

A different pattern emerges in the international trade usage of the euro. The euro's role has grown over time but mainly from its inception through 2004. Initially, the growth in the role of the euro came about through its replacement of euro area legacy currencies in invoicing international trade transactions. Later, the role of the euro expanded within countries that were at that point on the periphery of the euro area. Now, euro use is broadly observed as a European phenomenon, with widespread use of euros concentrated in, but not extending broadly beyond, transactions between countries with geographical proximity to the euro area.

Table 2.5 presents examples of euro use in settling or invoicing international trade transactions, focusing on the same group of countries as in table 2.4. Korea and Thailand use the euro only minimally, despite more than 10 percent of their exports reaching euro area destinations. By contrast, Hungary and Poland use the euro on the majority of their export transactions. This use is largely accounted for by the share of the euro area and euro bloc countries in Hungarian and Polish exports. Interestingly, as suggested by the negative sign for Poland in the rightmost column of table 2.5, some exports to these regions are not denominated in euros, perhaps due to the continuing role of the dollar in invoicing commodities and reference-priced international transactions.

---

13. In Goldberg (2007) I explore the use of dollars and euros among the accession countries to the euro area.

Table 2.4   International role of the US dollar (percent)

| Country/region | Exports invoiced in dollars (1) | Share of country exports | | Residual (1) − (2 + 3) |
		To the United States (2)	To "dollar bloc" countries (3)	
Asia				
Korea	84.9	20.8	28.2	35.9
Thailand	83.9	17.8	17.5	48.6
European Union				
France	34.2	15.4	11.8	7.0
Germany	31.6	17.9	10.8	2.9
EU accession countries				
Hungary	12.2	3.5	2.7	6.0
Poland	29.9	2.7	4.9	22.3

Note: All data correspond to 2002, except for Korea (2001) and Thailand (1996). Data for France and Germany correspond to extra–euro area trade.

Source: Goldberg and Tille (2008).

Table 2.5   International role of the euro (percent)

| Country/region | Exports invoiced in euros (1) | Share of country exports | | Residual (1) − (2 + 3) |
		To the euro area (2)	To "euro bloc" countries (3)	
Asia				
Korea	1.3	10.4	1.8	−10.9
Thailand	0.5	10.5	1.6	−11.6
European Union				
France	55.8	n.a.	13.2	42.6
Germany	49.0	n.a.	21.6	27.4
EU accession countries				
Hungary	83.1	65.5	13.1	4.5
Poland	60.2	57.6	16.5	−13.9

n.a. = not applicable

Note: All data correspond to 2002, except for Korea (2001) and Thailand (1996). Data for France and Germany correspond to extra–euro area trade.

Source: Goldberg and Tille (2008).

Determinants of Invoice Currency Selection in Trade

What reasons underlie dollar or euro use in international trade? Cedric Tille and I (Goldberg and Tille, forthcoming) look carefully at data across countries and over time in order to answer this question, expanding on the insights of a range of theoretical papers and empirical case studies.[14] Empirically, the key determinants of the use of the dollar and euro in trade are (1) the issuing country/region size—so the size of the United States in dollar use or the size of the euro area in euro use; (2) the exchange rate regime, which would capture the economic importance of the countries with currencies anchored in one way or another to dollars or euros; (3) transaction costs, including costs of moving in and out of currencies, for example, captured by bid-ask spreads, although this is not the dominant force at work by any means; and (4) which currency other producers use for export and import transactions. Two other empirical determinants are the industry compositions of goods exported or imported and specific aspects of macroeconomic volatility.

Conceptually, two key types of influences dominate which currency exporters choose for their transactions. One type is a "herding" or "coalescing" force. The second is a "hedging" force. I discuss the intuition behind this choice in more detail below and conclude by noting that the currency used for invoicing international trade transactions matters for a country's susceptibility to shocks and for its monetary policy effectiveness.

In order to understand the herding or coalescing influence, consider the exporter's goal of maximizing expected profits. Part of the exporter's decision pertains to which currency he or she should use for invoicing international transactions. A very important factor is what the exporter's competition is doing. In particular, an exporter may want to stay close to the invoicing strategies of his or her competitors. The reason is that the exporter sets his or her price in advance in some currency. Ideally, the price is set in a currency that is going to keep the demand for the exporter's products relatively stable after the exchange rate realizations determine future sales. Recognizing that there will be exchange rate fluctuations, the exporter has an incentive to set a price similar to his or her competitors' prices. If the exporter chooses otherwise, and if other producers' products can substitute for his or her product, expected profits will not be maximized since exchange rate movements can lead his or her price to be very different in the destination markets from the prices charged by competitors. Expected product demand will vary, leading to higher average marginal costs.

---

14. Theoretical antecedents include Bacchetta and van Wincoop (2005), Devereux and Engel (2001), Devereux, Engel, and Storgaard (2004), and Krugman (1980). Empirical contributions are surveyed in Goldberg and Tille (forthcoming). More recently, Kamps (2006) also explores the determinants of euro use.

The herding or coalescing motive in invoice currency choice is strongest in industries where goods for sale by various producers are close substitutes. Higher degrees of substitutability make it easier for purchasers to shift among suppliers after observing the exchange rates and final local-currency prices. Indeed, this idea of herding or coalescing in currency choice is consistent with a common invoicing currency in commodity markets or in other industries where goods produced by different players are close substitutes.

Hedging motives are also important for the currency invoicing choices of exporters. Some academic literature argues that the invoice currency selected should be the currency of the country that has the most macroeconomic stability (Devereux and Engel 2001). While this is a reasonable rule of thumb, a more specific formulation for capturing the hedging benefit from invoice currency choice on exporters stems from an analysis of producer income and costs. The exporter observes his or her marginal revenues moving around with exchange rates and their underlying drivers such as demand shocks, financial conditions, and monetary policies but also observes marginal costs fluctuating. The exporter should choose an invoice currency so that marginal revenues and marginal costs move together—hedging profit risks. In countries where the price that the exporter receives (marginal revenues) is going to be lower, the exporter wants to choose an invoice currency so that his or her marginal costs are lower as well.

Foreign exchange transaction costs also matter. Bid-ask spreads, which are one proxy for transaction costs in foreign exchange markets, still often generally favor the dollar.[15] There are exceptions, however, where the euro is favored as a low transaction cost currency. These occur mostly in the context of some of the euro area periphery countries, reinforcing the idea that geographic proximity has an effect on the international reach of the euro. Inertial forces influence transaction costs, since currencies that are extensively used and have high volumes likewise have lower transaction costs (Rey 2001).

Consequences of Invoice Currency Selection for Policy

Having described the motives influencing the choices of currencies for use in trade invoicing, it is useful to consider the policy consequences of these decisions by individual exporters. For this purpose, it is useful to divide the outcomes of individual decisions along two distinct dimensions that relate to the specific counterparties in trade. These counterparties may be

---

15. Goldberg and Tille (forthcoming) use bid-ask spreads observed through the mid-2000s. Detken and Hartmann (2002) and Goodhart, Love, and Dagfinn (2002) examine bid-ask spreads over the early years of the euro.

customers in the country issuing the currency or could be located elsewhere. For example, consider the case of US dollars used as an invoice currency. Most countries use them largely in their trade transactions with the United States. This use in invoicing trade with the issuing country is the first dimension of a currency's role in international trade. The second dimension arises when a currency is used in transactions between third countries or transactions that do not involve the United States but nonetheless use the dollar. In practice, the US dollar is extensively applied in both of these roles. The euro, by contrast, is still mainly used by countries with geographic proximity to the euro area but is not extensively used elsewhere.

A well-developed literature considers the implications of invoice currency choice and pricing decisions—local-currency pricing or producer-currency pricing—for optimal monetary policy in two trading countries, as in the contributions of Obstfeld and Rogoff (2002), Devereux and Engel (2003), Corsetti and Pesenti (2005), and Devereux, Shi, and Xu (2007). These implications apply to countries directly engaged in trade with the issuer of the currency used for invoicing, which is the first dimension of the international role of a currency. The basic message is that prices in the country whose currency is used are relatively stable. By contrast, in other markets the prices of traded goods move substantially in local-currency terms when exchange rates move. As a result, it is primarily in these other countries that consumption responds to the relative price changes induced by exchange rates. The center country will have more stable prices, although this is not necessarily a good thing. It implies stable relative prices, which may be undesirable if the efficient market response instead calls for a movement in the terms of trade.

Overall, a country with high pass-through of exchange rate movements into its own prices will have local inflation rates that are more sensitive to exchange rate movements than a country that has lower exchange rate pass-through. There will also be more expenditure switching and movement in imports in response to exchange rate movements in these high pass-through countries.

The second dimension of the international role of a currency arises when countries other than the issuing country use its currency for invoicing their international trade transactions. This use of a vehicle currency on trade among "periphery" countries has fundamental implications for periphery policy effectiveness, welfare, and transmission of shocks internationally (Goldberg and Tille 2008). If the periphery countries use the center country's currency on their bilateral international trade transactions, they are more sensitive to the center country's monetary policy, and their own national monetary policies are less effective at influencing prices in local markets.

The center country's monetary policy decisions also have externalities for the periphery. Under some conditions, the second dimension can be inefficient for periphery countries in their bilateral transactions. Given such inefficiencies, in some cases periphery countries could benefit from international monetary policy cooperation with the center country. However, engaging in such cooperation would not be welfare enhancing for the center country, which otherwise would set policy only with its own welfare as criteria.

As a final point, suppose periphery countries use the center country currency on their trade transactions, and exchange rate movements between the center currency and periphery countries' currencies influence economic conditions in the periphery. Would it be better for those countries to peg against the dollar or the center country's currency? In fact, in the simplified example and setup of Goldberg and Tille (2008), pegged exchange rates do not dominate more flexible currency arrangements. The reason is that, even if countries are using the dollar in their own trade transactions, they remain better off maintaining domestic monetary policy as a tool at their disposal. This tool still presents monetary policymakers with flexibility so that monetary policy might be targeted at offsetting some adverse consequences of domestic shocks. This benefit is lost if the country fully abandons independent monetary policy and instead follows a currency peg. While certainly there may be many other reasons for choosing a pegged exchange rate regime, in this particular context, the peg is not the solution to the inefficiencies that arise from using vehicle currencies in periphery countries.

Conclusion

The dollar still is the dominant currency in international trade transactions, but the euro has gained substantial ground since its inception 10 years ago. Key commodities and goods that are close substitutes tend to be invoiced in dollars even within the euro area. Overall, one question remains, What conditions would tip currency use from dollars to euros in invoicing of international trade transactions? There would have to be very large shocks for this to occur, but the particular conditions await more research from academic and policy communities.

References

Bacchetta, Philippe, and Eric van Wincoop. 2005. A Theory of the Currency Denomination of International Trade. *Journal of International Economics* 67, no. 2 (December): 295–319.

Coeurdacier, Nicolas, and Philippe Martin. 2007. *The Geography of Asset Trade and the Euro: Insiders and Outsiders.* CEPR Discussion Paper 6032. London: Centre for Economic Policy Research.

Corsetti, Giancarlo, and Paolo Pesenti. 2005. International Dimensions of Optimal Monetary Policy. *Journal of Monetary Economics* 52, no. 2 (March): 281–305.

Detken, Carsten, and Philipp Hartmann. 2002. Features of the Euro's Role in International Financial Markets. *Economic Policy* 17, no. 35: 553–69.

Devereux, Michael, and Charles Engel. 2001. *Endogenous Currency of Price Setting in a Dynamic Open Economy Model*. NBER Working Paper 8559. Cambridge, MA: National Bureau of Economic Research.

Devereux, Michael, and Charles Engel. 2003. Monetary Policy in the Open Economy Revisited: Exchange Rate Flexibility and Price Setting Behavior. *Review of Economic Studies* 70: 765–83.

Devereux, Michael, Charles Engel, and Peter Storgaard. 2004. Endogenous Exchange Rate Pass-Through when Nominal Prices Are Set in Advance. *Journal of International Economics* 63, no. 2 (July): 263–91.

Devereux, Michael, Kang Shi, and Juanyi Xu. 2007. Global Monetary Policy under a Dollar Standard. *Journal of International Economics* 71, no. 1 (March): 113–32.

ECB (European Central Bank). 2008. *Review of the International Role of the Euro* (July). Frankfurt.

Goldberg, Linda. 2007. Trade Invoicing in the Accession Countries: Are They Suited to the Euro? In *International Seminar on Macroeconomics 2005*, ed. Jeffrey Frankel and Christopher Pissarides. Cambridge, MA: National Bureau of Economic Research and MIT Press.

Goldberg, Linda, and Cedric Tille. Forthcoming. Vehicle Currency Use in International Trade. *Journal of International Economics*.

Goldberg, Linda, and Cedric Tille. 2008. *Macroeconomic Interdependence and the International Role of the Dollar*. NBER Working Paper 13820 (February). Cambridge, MA: National Bureau of Economic Research.

Goodhart, Charles, Richard Love, and Rime Dagfinn. 2002. Analysis of Spreads in the Dollar/Euro and Deutschemark/Dollar Foreign Exchange Markets. *Economic Policy* 17, no. 35: 535–52.

Kamps, Annette. 2006. *The Euro as Invoicing Currency in International Trade*. European Central Bank Working Paper no. 665 (August). Frankfurt: European Central Bank.

Krugman, Paul. 1980. Vehicle Currencies and the Structure of International Exchange. *Journal of Money, Credit and Banking* 12, no. 3 (August): 513–26.

Obstfeld, Maurice, and Kenneth Rogoff. 2002. Global Implications of Self-Oriented National Monetary Rules. *Quarterly Journal of Economics* 117: 503–56.

Obstfeld, Maurice, and Kenneth Rogoff. 1995. Exchange Rate Dynamics Redux. *Journal of Political Economy* 103: 624–60.

Rey, Hélène. 2001. International Trade and Currency Exchange. *Review of Economic Studies* 68, no. 2 (April): 443–64.

Euro Area: Ready for the Storm?

JEAN PISANI-FERRY AND ANDRÉ SAPIR

The euro has been, is, and will remain a currency without a state. Ten or even five years ago, many in Europe would have questioned this assertion, because they saw the single currency as a stepping stone toward political union. A few treaty revisions and failed referendums later, however, this perspective has vanished. Even if the Treaty of Lisbon, which includes most of the provisions of the aborted constitutional treaty, is eventually ratified, the momentum has been lost. For all practical purposes, the euro must be regarded as an orphan currency.

The governance structure that results from this situation is complex. The choices made at the time of the Maastricht Treaty—a monetary union without a significant federal budget, limited coordination of budgetary and structural policies, no integrated financial supervision, and no strong political counterpart to the central bank—were regarded by many of its architects as temporary. Over time, it was hoped, a more federal governance structure would emerge. The main players in the negotiation, Germany and France, did not have the same views on what this structure would be, but they shared the same dream: Both expected the euro to accelerate integration.

Reforms of limited ambition are still possible and desirable, but on the whole the euro is bound to live with this governance structure in the years to come. This does not mean that it is doomed to fail. In fact it has thrived in its first ten years of existence. The euro has provided price stability to previously inflation-prone countries. It has offered a shelter against cur-

Jean Pisani-Ferry is director of Bruegel and professor at Université Paris-Dauphine. André Sapir is senior fellow at Bruegel and professor of economics at Université Libre de Bruxelles.

rency crises. It has by and large been conducive to budgetary discipline. It has attracted five new members in addition to the eleven initial ones. And many countries in Europe wish to adopt it.[16]

On the world scene, the euro has also been successful. Even though research presented in this volume confirms that it has not rivaled the dollar's world currency status, it has certainly become a strong regional currency in Europe and the Mediterranean region. Some countries in the region have de facto adopted it, several peg to it, and many have become at least partially euroized.[17]

The question we address in this paper is whether the governance structure of the euro area is a handicap to further gains in international role and influence. Is the incomplete character of European integration bound to be perceived as a lingering weakness? Or is the rest of the world likely to accept, and adapt to, the sui generis character of the European currency?

This could have remained an abstract and unsolvable question. In fact, while governance had long been a topic for discussion among European scholars and policymakers, the rest of the world understandably paid limited attention to it. However, the advent of the crisis has put European governance to an unexpectedly demanding test. While the euro was introduced in the midst of the "great moderation" period and benefited from it in the first 8.5 years of its existence, the following 12 months were more agitated, and the last six months of its first decade were especially stormy. This limited experience has shown that there is a sharp contrast between what can be expected from a governance system in fair weather conditions and in stormy weather conditions. At the time of writing (early 2009), several lessons from this experience can be drawn. Many more will certainly come.

To address this question, we start by briefly laying out our conceptual framework. Section two is devoted to assessing the euro area's fair weather record. Stormy weather governance is reviewed in section three. We draw lessons for governance in section four and conclude in section five with the implications for the international role of the euro.

Conceptual Framework

Citizens generally do not expect their political leaders to exhibit the same qualities when the country is at peace and when it is at war. Similarly, one does not expect the same from economic governance in normal and in crisis times.

---

16. Accounts of the first ten years of the euro can be found in European Commission (2008) and Pisani-Ferry et al. (2008).

17. See especially György Szapáry's contribution to this volume in chapter 3.

In normal times, the key properties are stability, predictability, and incentive compatibility:

- After the damages of inflation and the stop-and-go policies of the 1970s, the vast majority of countries have converged on policy regimes that give high priority to macroeconomic stability. Clarity of objectives and transparent matching between policy objectives and policy instruments, including through assigning price stability to an independent central bank, have proved to be key technologies in this respect.

- In a world of forward-looking expectations, predictability of the policy course and of its responses to shocks has become regarded as an essential property. Policy rules that inform the public about the policymakers' reaction function have gained increasing support, either in the primitive form of instrument rules or in more sophisticated forms like flexible inflation targeting.

- Finally, incentive properties are of major importance in a system like the European one that heavily relies on decentralization. With monetary policy centralized but budgetary and structural policies decided at the national level, it is important that actions taken at one level influence those taken at another level in a way that is consistent with the overall objective. A key issue is whether or not actions taken centrally create incentives for stability-oriented actions by decentralized players. For example, important questions are whether the system is able to make budgetary policies consistent with the overall goal of price stability and whether labor- and product-market reforms introduced at the national level are conducive to swift adjustment in response to shocks.

However, different properties are needed in crisis times. Stability remains the objective in the medium term, but in the short term speed in countering the effects of the crisis is rather the overriding goal. Instead of predictability, policymakers aim at maximum discretion to address problems as they emerge and have recourse to innovative, previously untested solutions if needed. Finally, centralization with a view to ensuring swift implementation has precedence over incentives for good behavior at the decentralized level. Hence the qualities that are expected from a policy system in crisis times are clearly different from, and to some extent even contradictory to, those expected from the same system in normal times.

Fiscal and monetary policies tellingly illustrate this tension. The consensus view among economists is that in normal times the two instruments should be managed separately and that interaction between the two should be minimized. But in crisis times there can be a need for considerable interaction between monetary and budgetary policies.

The criteria for assessing the performance of the euro area therefore need to be specific to the situation. Instead of analyzing performance in normal times and assuming that this record informs us about performance across the entire distribution of probable events, we draw a sharp distinction between the two situations and analyze performance accordingly.

The Fair Weather Record

The record of the euro area was extensively assessed on the occasion of the tenth anniversary of the common European currency (see especially European Commission 2008 and Pisani-Ferry et al. 2008, on which this section draws).

It is widely agreed that the transition to the euro was remarkably smooth and that in spite of the disparity of the participating countries' previous inflation record, price stability has on the whole been achieved. Figure 2.3, which gives the break-even measure of inflation expectations for the United States and the euro area, indicates that they have remained low and stable over the 2004–08 period, including during the 2008 commodities-induced price hike. This has been a major contribution to macroeconomic stability.

Though still positive, the record is less satisfactory as regards budgetary discipline. Overall, the aggregate budgetary deficit of the euro area was brought down from 2.3 percent of GDP in 1998 (the year before the euro was introduced) to 0.6 percent in 2007, and gross public debt as a percentage of GDP was reduced by five percentage points. This performance was better than in the United States, where the deficit increased over the same period and where the debt ratio remained roughly constant. But there have been two shortcomings: First, in spite of the elaborate apparatus put in place to prevent and punish excessive deficits, one country (Greece) still had a deficit above 3 percent in 2007 and two (France and Portugal) were perilously close to the threshold. To say the least, this indicates uneven effectiveness of the Stability and Growth Pact. Second and more importantly, the budgetary framework overlooked the potential for quickly transforming private debt into public debt through bailouts of insolvent private institutions and agents—and more generally through giving rise to sharp boom-and-bust cycles that can make the budgetary situation look artificially sound before it sharply deteriorates in a downturn. Ireland and Spain were regarded as paragons of fiscal virtue at end-2007, but their debt ratios are now projected by the European Commission to deteriorate by 20 and 30 percentage points, respectively, between end-2007 and end-2009.[18] This suggests that the focus on national account data, the absence of stress test, and the neglect of off–balance sheet liabilities have been significant weaknesses of the European budgetary discipline framework.

European surveillance was even less effective in addressing nonbud-

---

18. On the basis of EU Commission forecasts released in January 2009.

Figure 2.3   Inflation expectations in the United States and the euro area, 2004–08

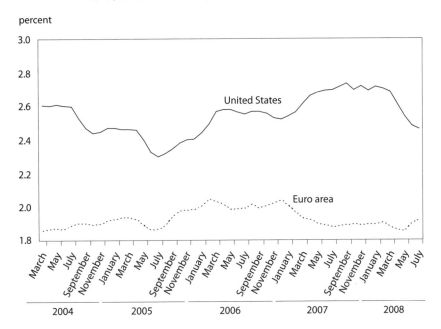

Note: The figure shows three-month moving average of monthly break-even rates.
Source: Bank for International Settlements, *Quarterly Review*, September 2008.

getary sources of instability. Article 99 of the EU Treaty mandates the European Union to monitor economic developments in the member states and to ensure that they remain mutually consistent. Little effort was devoted to macroeconomic surveillance in part because the provisions of this article are markedly weaker than those regarding excessive budgetary deficits and in part because of the misguided belief that there is little macroeconomic instability to fear when monetary policy is geared toward price stability and budgetary policy toward the avoidance of excessive deficits. The validity of the assumption that by controlling budgetary deficits one is able to control risks of instability was already questioned in Pisani-Ferry et al. (2008) and European Commission (2008) reports. Especially, it was noted that enduring divergences in price developments could be observed within the euro area, which possibly resulted in real exchange rate misalignments (figure 2.4). In other words, the so-called competitiveness channel was too slow and too weak to prevent boom-and-bust cycles fueled by excessively low real interest rates (which themselves resulted from above-average inflation). As the boom ended, Spain and Ireland, the two champions of the euro's first decade, plunged into deep and probably long recessions.

Figure 2.4   Real exchange rate and export performance divergence in the euro area, cumulative change between 1999 and 2007

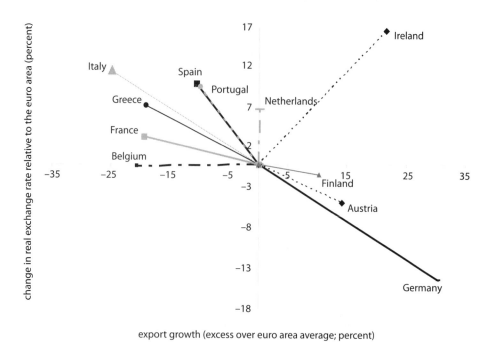

export growth (excess over euro area average; percent)

Source: Bruegel calculations based on Eurostat and DG ECFIN (European Commission).

With the benefit of hindsight, the obsession with budgetary numerology and the failure of surveillance to trigger appropriate policy responses can be regarded as a major flaw in the policy system. Even in the absence of a global crisis, they would likely have resulted in significant adjustment difficulties. To undergo this adjustment in the context of a worldwide recession is a major challenge for the countries affected and the euro area as a whole.

In spite of the success of its currency, euro area governance has been disappointing in the field of external monetary and financial relations. The relationships among immediate neighbors and potential candidates to membership have been marred with controversies about euro area entry criteria. While several countries in the region quickly adopted the euro as an external anchor and/or became largely euroized, the attitude of euro area authorities has been extremely guarded. The Commission, the European Central Bank (ECB), and the Eurogroup insisted on sticking to the letter of entry criteria defined at Maastricht and used in 1998 at the time of the creation of the euro area, even though to take as a benchmark the three EU countries with the lowest inflation rate for assessing the inflation performance of a candidate country amounted to ignoring the very existence of the euro area and the fact that the ECB has adopted a definition of price stability. There was a failure to adopt a criterion that preserves the spirit of the treaty while being adaptable to changing conditions, and this was widely interpreted as indicating reluctance toward a comprehensive enlargement.

The relation with international partners developed positively as a growing number of countries recognized the emergence of the euro as a major change in the international landscape, but it has been made unduly complex by the fragmented nature of the area's external representation. Table 2.6, from Pisani-Ferry et al. (2008), gives an overview of the external representation of the euro area. Even in normal times, such a degree of fragmentation and unevenness is bound to be a source of ineffectiveness.

Stormy Weather Experience

The weather in the euro area, which had been mostly fair since 1999, quickly turned grey and windy in the summer of 2007, when Europe suddenly faced a liquidity crisis detonated by tensions in the US subprime mortgage market. Remarkably, the ECB was the first central bank to react, with an injection of €95 billion ($130 billion) on August 9 aimed at ensuring orderly conditions in the euro money market. Later the same day the Federal Reserve provided $24 billion of liquidity. The next day, the ECB and the Federal Reserve intervened again to the tune of €61 billion ($84 billion) and $38 billion, respectively, with other central banks around the world injecting a total of roughly $20 billion.

During the next 13 months, the ECB continued to apply three measures to alleviate tensions in the euro money market. First, it continued to frontload the supply of liquidity over the reserve maintenance periods. Second, it maintained the increased share of longer-term operations in its refinancing operations, which it had gradually built up since the start of the crisis. Third, the ECB continued to conduct US dollar-term auction facilities in cooperation with the US Federal Reserve and other central banks, thereby providing US dollar liquidity to euro area banks. Altogether these measures proved that the ECB was as capable as the US Federal Reserve to contain the liquidity crisis, thus reassuring the euro area that its policy framework was robust to stressful conditions.

Then, on September 14, 2008, another, significantly more severe shock came from the United States: Lehman Brothers had gone bankrupt. The same day, credit default swaps ratcheted up, stock markets plummeted, central banks injected billions of dollars into money markets, and Bank of America agreed to buy Merrill Lynch. The liquidity situation deteriorated further on both sides of the Atlantic, and spreads between short-term in-

Table 2.6 Overview of external representation of the euro area

Forum	European Central Bank	Eurogroup Presidency	EU Presidency	European Commission	EU member states
Organization for Economic Cooperation and Development	Participates in economic and development review committee, economic policy committee, and committee on financial markets	Participates in economic and development review committee examination of the euro area		Quasi-membership (no voting rights and does not contribute to OECD budget but participates in all meetings)	19
IMF Executive Board	Observer status		Euro area position represented by executive director holding EU/euro area presidency		27
Financial Stability Forum	Full participation				5
International Monetary and Financial Committee	Observer status		Full participation depending on the constituency agreement	Observer status	27
IMF Multilateral Consultations	Full participation	Full participation	No	Full participation	
G-7 Finance Ministers	Nearly full attendance	Nearly full attendance		Partial attendance (not involved in preparatory work)	4
G-20	Full participation		Full participation	Attends meetings as part of EU Presidency delegation	5

IMF = International Monetary Fund

Note: Shaded cells denote no representation.

Source: Pisani-Ferry et al. (2008).

terbank interest rates and swap rates on government securities reached unprecedented levels. Two days later, AIG Corporation, the world's biggest insurance company, was bailed out by the US Federal Reserve. The next day, the banking crisis spread to the United Kingdom: Halifax Bank of Scotland (HBOS) merged with Lloyds TSB in an emergency rescue plan.

On September 29 the Belgo-Dutch bank Fortis was bailed out by Belgium, Luxembourg, and the Netherlands, and the next day the Belgo-French bank Dexia was bailed out by Belgium, France, and Luxembourg.

The rapid rescue of Fortis and Dexia was hailed as a success and led nearly all observers to believe that the previously untested capacity of euro area governments to cooperate in times of crisis was real. However, the mood changed rapidly. On September 30 the Irish government unilaterally guaranteed safety of all deposits, bonds, and debts in Irish banks for the next two years. On October 3 the Dutch government nationalized the Dutch activities of Fortis, forcing the Belgian government to take over its Belgian activities. Rather than continuing to cooperate and splitting the bill to maintain the Belgo-Dutch bank, the two governments simply decided to split the bank along national lines. On October 4 a meeting of the heads of state of the four major euro area countries ended in empty words as Germany refused to agree on a concerted bank rescue and stabilization plan. Finally, on October 5 the German government issued a unilateral guarantee of all deposits in German banks. The weather in the euro area had now definitely turned dark and stormy.

For a while, it looked as if the European Union, or even the euro area, was unable to coordinate the response to the crisis. A group of prominent economists rightly worried that "The current approach of rescuing one institution after another with national funds will lead to a Balkanization of the European banking sector. Agreeing on a harmonized level for deposit insurance would also be important" (Alesina et al. 2008).

At the Eurogroup and Ecofin meetings on October 6–7, finance ministers agreed that the economic situation "calls for a coordinated response at the EU level" but failed to adopt anything beyond broad principles and did not even discuss the rescue plan that the UK government would announce the following day. On October 8, the ECB reduced its policy rate by 50 basis points and changed its tender procedure, moving to fixed-rate refinancing. However, this step failed to impress money markets. At the end of the week, financial markets throughout the world suffered one of their worst days in history ("Black Friday"), which prompted the French president of the European Union to convene the first-ever meeting of the heads of state or government of the euro area. This emergency summit, held in Paris on October 12, is viewed as the turning point in the efforts to bring about a concerted European response to the financial crisis.

The Paris summit was a success on many fronts. Firstly, it sent an important message to the markets. European governments abandoned the prevailing uncoordinated case-by-case approach in favor of a series of national plans based on a common template and pledged a total of nearly 2 trillion euros to shore up their financial sectors, sparking sharp rallies across the continent's stock markets.

Secondly, the summit demonstrated that the euro area is governed not only by the ECB but also by political leaders. The Eurogroup could not have sent that message for two reasons. One, finance ministers lack the public recognition that heads of state or government enjoy. Moreover, despite being prime minister of his country, Jean-Claude Juncker, president of the Eurogroup, clearly lacks the kind of European public recognition that President Nicolas Sarkozy enjoys. Two, because the Eurogroup meets routinely and in the drab building of the EU Council, it could not have conveyed the sense of emergency and importance that was tacked to the first meeting of euro area leaders held in the Elysée Palace.

Thirdly, by inviting UK Prime Minister Gordon Brown to the Paris meeting, President Sarkozy succeeded in building a bridge between the euro area and not only the most important EU country outside the euro area, which is important politically, but also the area's main financial centre, which is equally important. Indeed, the financial crisis has exposed a fundamental issue of economic governance for the euro area. While members of the euro area clearly share common financial interests owing to the fact that they share a common central bank, they also have common financial interests with the other members of the European Union, and the United Kingdom in particular, by virtue of the Single Market in financial services. This fundamental issue also has implications for the United Kingdom, since any remedy to the euro area's financial governance that did not include the United Kingdom—for instance, a euro area banking supervision mechanism—would risk jeopardizing the role of London as the euro area's de facto financial center.

Lastly, the show of unity among all EU leaders at the European Council meeting that was held a few days after the Paris summit enabled the European Union to assume a role of global leadership in the crisis at two levels. First, the United States adjusted its banking rescue plan to make room for capital injections, thereby bringing it closer to the European template, itself based on the UK plan. Second, and more crucially, immediately after the European Council meeting, President Sarkozy and European Commission President José Manuel Barroso flew to Washington to meet with President George W. Bush, carrying with them the proposal, originally put forward by Prime Minister Brown and adopted by the European Council, for a global summit to be held before the end of 2008 to reform the world financial system. The European proposal laid the foundation for a series of G-20 leaders' summits on financial markets and the global economy, the first of which was held in Washington on November 20, 2008, and the second to be held in London on April 2, 2009.

Despite the undeniable success of the Paris summit and the decisions taken at the ensuing European Council meeting, many problems have lingered. Not only did a number of important policy issues remain unsolved but also an economic crisis soon came on top of the financial one, bringing new challenges to euro area governance.

Several major policy issues still remain unsettled. The first concerns the treatment of pan-European banks. After Fortis and Dexia (whose bailouts by national governments were only a first step and whose fates have not been settled at the time of writing), a number of other banks with pan-European operations needed to be rescued. Fortunately, however, none of these institutions are quite as multinational in their governance structure as Fortis was and Dexia remains. Their bailouts were therefore purely national. Had a bank required bailing out by several states (or should it require it in the near future), the lack of burden-sharing rules among European countries would inevitably have created a problem.

The second issue concerns the situation of small countries with relatively large financial institutions. Clearly small countries have suffered more than large countries. The bailouts in France and Germany account for less than 2 percent of each country's GDP and even in the United Kingdom, they barely reach 3 percent. By contrast the bailouts represent around 4 percent of GDP for Ireland and Belgium and 6 percent for the Netherlands and Luxembourg. Austria, a small country whose banks are heavily exposed in Central and Eastern Europe, has already committed some 5 percent of GDP. Judging from spreads and credit default swaps on government bonds, markets are already pricing the risk that public finances in small countries like Austria or Ireland could pay a high price for rescuing their banking sectors. With no common EU or euro area chest, some small countries may have to rethink their financial-sector strategies and even question the very principle of specializing in the provision of financial services.

The third issue is the situation in Central and Eastern Europe. Until September 15 the crisis hardly affected countries in the region. There were difficulties in some countries but they were mostly national. However, after the bankruptcy of Lehman Brothers, all changed: Interbank markets have been strained, there have been capital flow reversals, several currencies have depreciated sharply, and the recession has suddenly hit the region. Against this background, the euro area's response has been slow. It first overlooked the potential consequences of its decisions on the neighboring countries—be they capital outflows in response to the issuance of better guarantees in Western Europe or credit curtailments in response to demands made to banks to extend credit further in their home countries. It was then reluctant to formulate an overall policy response, beyond the financial assistance provided to countries under an International Monetary Fund (IMF) program, for fear of taking some form of responsibility for what was perceived as national policy issues. These hesitations have tended to overshadow the participation by the European Union in IMF financial assistance programs for Hungary and Latvia.

The fourth issue is the fragmentation of the Single Market. Despite the common framework put in place to facilitate the funding of banks, to provide financial institutions with additional capital resources, and to allow the recapitalization of distressed banks, it appears that uneven implementation of commonly agreed rules is the norm rather than the exception.

Not a day goes by without a measure being taken by an EU country that seems to favor national financial institutions and/or requires these institutions to provide credit to national customers.

The final issue concerns the design and implementation of a fiscal stimulus. While governments were trying to respond to the banking crisis, it became clear that it would soon unleash an economic crisis that would risk further deteriorating the financial situation and create a downward spiral resulting in economic depression. In order to avoid this eventuality, several voices on both sides of the Atlantic came out in favor of a stimulus package. On both sides, there were natural concerns about fiscal sustainability.

Even among the vast majority who supported the idea of a fiscal stimulus, two additional issues were raised in Europe, both relating to the absence of a euro area (or EU) federal state. The first is the lack of a euro area fiscal instrument to support economic activity and the necessity to rely on national instruments without being able to rely on an effective coordination mechanism. The second is the fact that euro area members entered the crisis in very different fiscal conditions, rendering the decision to set in motion national fiscal instruments all the more difficult. The European Recovery Programme put forward by us and Jakob von Weizsäcker in mid-November 2008 was precisely designed to counter these two issues. It envisaged a harmonized indirect tax (value-added tax) cut in all EU countries and the creation of a mechanism to ensure medium-term fiscal sustainability in countries with unfavorable starting conditions.

The European Economic Recovery Plan proposed by the European Commission a couple of weeks later also recognized the difficulty of engineering a European fiscal stimulus without a proper European instrument and with diverse national situations but fell short of proposing the use of common mechanisms. Instead, it simply called on EU member states to adopt national measures. The Commission proposal was adopted by the December 2008 European Council and has been implemented in various ways by EU members states. However, by essentially ignoring the two issues flagged above, the implementation of the European plan suffers from two problems.

First, because countries were allowed wide discretion in the choice of fiscal instrument, many have adopted measures that tend to favor national producers at the expense of foreign producers, thereby reintroducing barriers in the Single Market.

Second, because no new mechanism to ensure the sustainability of public finances was introduced, a number of euro area countries soon began suffering great difficulties. For many years, markets seemed not to pay attention to differences in public finance conditions across euro area countries. For instance, up to June 2007, the 10-year government spread over German bunds was as low as 20 basis points for Greece despite a public debt of around 100 percent and persistent deficits. One year later, in spite of the liquidity crisis, its spread was still reasonably low at 60 basis points.

Since then, the crisis has left a heavy mark. Greek bond spreads jumped to 150 basis points in October 2008 and reached 250 points in early January 2009. Other euro area countries whose spreads have dramatically increased since October 2008 and were above 100 basis points at the beginning of 2009 are Ireland (212 points), Italy (128 points), Slovenia (126 points), Portugal (123 points), and Spain (109 points). As a result, several of these countries have already seen their S&P ratings downgraded by one notch. In January 2009 Spain's went down from AAA to AA+, Portugal's from AA– to A+, and Greece's from A to A–, the lowest of any euro area country. This situation is worrisome because the euro area has neither a common funding scheme nor a well-specified mechanism to assist members facing a potential national funding problem.

Lessons

In a report on the euro's first years, written and published before the crisis developed, Pisani-Ferry et al. (2008) warned: "A policy framework should not only be judged by its agility in fair weather conditions, but also by its resilience in storm conditions—not only financial but also economic and political storms.... In this respect, it should be recalled that...the last eight years have been benign. The policy framework of the euro area has thus not yet been tested under stress. It remains to be seen how well EMU is set up to deal with events like disruptive global shocks or internal crises."

The experience since the start of the crisis confirms that the euro area governance system was well conceived to deal with normal conditions—even though the scope, priorities, and methods of surveillance need to be improved—but lacks the properties required to operate in crisis times enumerated in the first section, namely speed of reaction, policy discretion, and centralized action. At the center of the problem is the absence of a euro area political body capable of making appropriate financial and fiscal decisions in difficult times. Ad hoc coordination has indeed substituted for institutional responses, and this was welcome. There are, however, limits to what this type of coordination can achieve.

The Eurogroup could, one day, evolve into such a political body, but it is far from there at the moment. For the time being, the Eurogroup is simply an informal body without a defined mission, whose role had developed in two directions prior to the crisis: as an enforcer of EMU rules and as the venue for addressing the collective action problems faced by euro area members. Although it was always better in the first direction (because it could rely on treaty-based mechanisms for implementation), the latter has simply disappeared since the beginning of the crisis, despite the fact that it should have assumed precisely this role.[19] Were it not for the

---

19. The move in 2005 to a fixed presidency of the Eurogroup, instead of a rotating one, was

October 2008 euro area summit in Paris, the governance of the euro area during the crisis would have been assumed by the ECB alone, thereby underscoring the fact that the euro is a currency not only without a state but also without political governance.

The governance of the euro area has been, since the launch of the euro, the subject of difficult discussions between its members, especially between France and Germany. Whether or not these countries will draw the lessons from the crisis will largely depend on their ability to agree on a diagnosis of the problem and on remedies.

Conclusion

What are the implications of our analysis of euro area governance for the international role of the euro, as both a regional and a global currency?

As already indicated, the euro had become a successful international currency during the relatively calm years that preceded the crisis. Even though it had not rivaled the dollar's world currency status, it had certainly become a strong regional currency and has been adopted as an anchor, as a reference, or as a vehicle for financial transactions in the countries neighboring the euro area.

Is there reason to believe that the management of the crisis so far will dramatically alter this state of affairs? We feel that the governance of the euro area in the current stormy weather conditions has not enhanced the international status of the euro.

Within the euro area, rising bond spreads and falling ratings in some members, and the absence of a common funding scheme and a well-specified mechanism to assist those facing funding problems, have done nothing to improve the image of the euro with global investors. Although we regard recent remarks on the possible exit or expulsion of those members from the euro area as pure fantasy, we acknowledge that the lack of clarity on how to resolve their debt problems is a source of worry.

The treatment by the euro area of regional partners that are facing severe economic and financial difficulties and rely on the euro as their reference currency has not been satisfactory either. Such partners include primarily new EU member states, but also countries outside the European Union, like Ukraine. These countries have typically suffered from the drying up of capital flows from the euro area and from the lack of assistance by euro area institutions, including the ECB (Darvas and Pisani-Ferry 2008). Although this divide between countries inside and outside the euro area may accelerate the adoption of the euro by some outsiders, the vast majority are unlikely to join before the end of the crisis. In the meantime, there-

---

intended to give it the means to take initiative and exercise leadership, but initiatives and leadership have been remarkably absent.

fore, the weak crisis governance of the euro area is likely to be a burden on these countries, which may affect their choice of reference currency.

In conclusion, the euro has proved to be attractive as a fair weather currency for countries and investors well beyond its borders. But it remains to be seen whether it is equipped with strong enough governance to also succeed as a stormy weather currency.

References

Alesina, Alberto, Richard Baldwin, Tito Boeri, Willem Buiter, Francesco Giavazzi, Daniel Gros, Stefano Micossi, Guido Tabellini, Charles Wyplosz, and Klaus F. Zimmermann. 2008. Open Letter to the European Leaders on Europe's Banking Crisis. *Economist's View* (October 1).

Darvas, Zsolt, and Jean Pisani-Ferry. 2008. *Avoiding a New European Divide*. Bruegel Policy Brief 2008/10 (December). Brussels: Bruegel.

European Commission. 2008. EMU@10: Successes and Challenges after 10 Years of Economic and Monetary Union. *European Economy*, no. 2 (June).

Pisani-Ferry, Jean, Alan Ahearne, Philippe Aghion, Marek Belka, Jürgen von Hagen, Lars Heikensten, and André Sapir. 2008. *Coming of Age: Report on the Euro Area*. Bruegel Blueprint Series no. 4 (January). Brussels: Bruegel.

Pisani-Ferry, Jean, André Sapir, and Jakob von Weizsäcker. 2008. *A European Recovery Programme*. Bruegel Policy Brief 2008/09 (November). Brussels: Bruegel.

Geopolitical Limits to the Euro's Global Role

ADAM S. POSEN

"Hillel used to say: If I am not for myself, who will be for me? Yet, if I am for myself only, what am I? And if not now, when?"
—Mishnah Pirke Avot (Ethics of the Fathers), 1:14.

Rav Hillel could have been posing questions to the euro area's leadership today about its vision for the euro at ten. If the governments of the euro area are unwilling to combine forces and representation to shape the global environment in which they operate, will any other government feel compelled to take their views into account? If the euro area's response to the financial crisis hitting Eastern European economies, including some EU member states, is to make future euro area membership less attainable and to fearfully run from "bailouts," can it be seen as broadly attractive to potential members? If the euro is neither eagerly promoted by its issuers nor widely adopted by market participants as the alternative to the dollar at a time of the greatest postwar decline in the United States' relative economic credibility, will the euro ever become a global currency? The answer to all three questions is clearly no. For all the euro's indisputable success as a monetary regime for member economies, euro area institutions' and member countries' leadership has failed to advocate for the area's long-term international interests, failed to extend its internal stability to its neighbors and potential members, and failed to seize the moment for the euro when US policy is widely perceived to have been destabilizing.

These failures reflect an often overlooked fundamental determinant of a currency's global role: the currency issuer's geostrategic role. Economic factors alone, such as countries' relative size and inflation rates and their

Adam S. Posen is deputy director and senior fellow at the Peterson Institute for International Economics. The author is grateful to Fred Bergsten, Marco Buti, Doug Dowson, Kristin Forbes, Jeff Frankel, Marc Hinterschweiger, Jacob Kirkegaard, Ken Kuttner, Charles Maier, Richard Portes, Benn Steil, Ted Truman, and especially Jean Pisani-Ferry for helpful discussions. He is solely responsible for the opinions expressed and any errors herein.

trade patterns, are insufficient to explain the pattern of reserve currency or exchange rate peg choices seen in the world—if these were together sufficient, the euro would already be a truly global currency in every sense. For obvious reasons of diplomacy among monetary officials, and of specialization among economic researchers, there is little incentive to take the geostrategic factor into account. Yet, the national security capabilities and foreign policy projection more broadly of the government behind a potentially global currency do heavily influence the extent to which other countries take up that currency. National security relationships between governments, especially but not only where explicit military guarantees are relevant, put pressure on both sides of the relationship to link their pursuit of stability, including monetary stability.

The currency-issuing government that also provides foreign policy guarantees, let alone stations troops in and provides arms to another country, has the leverage to get some of its credit needs funded by that recipient country. This leverage results in the anchor country having its own currency–denominated debt kept as foreign reserves by the security-dependent economy and also in deepening of two-way financial transactions. The recipient country generates in turn an interest for the currency anchor country to support integration of the recipient's political and economic elites with its home economy. That integration of educational and business relationships will tend to increase the share of trade invoiced in the home country's currency, as well as the overall amount of bilateral investment and trade in the long run. In short, the various ways in which a currency is used globally by other countries are going to be more heavily and exclusively used where a national security relationship exists. Additionally, as seen in the flight to the dollar as a safe haven during the height of the 2008–09 financial crisis, having a currency backed by a leading power provides a comfort to fearful investors, further reinforcing the feedback between geostrategic and monetary integration.

Thus, for all its economic virtues, there is a limit to the degree to which the euro can become a truly global currency. The euro area is certainly not a hard power. It includes countries with differing stances on international affairs, and there is no common foreign and security policy as yet. So long as the United Kingdom keeps its national currency, the euro area does not include the country with the largest military projection capacity in the European Union. The few nonbordering countries that have pegged to the euro tend to be those with security ties to euro area members (notably African states to France, the one hard power in the euro area membership to project force); in contrast, a number of countries pegged to the dollar have geopolitical ties with the United States that outweigh their trade and financial linkages to the euro. So there will continue to be a slow increase in euro usage in trade invoicing, financial investment, and reserve holdings of third countries commensurate with those countries' deepening of real economic ties to Europe—but nothing to rival the dollar on any of these counts. Over time, this trend, too, will diminish as the size of the euro area economy shrinks relative to the rest of the world (Posen 2004). In fact, recent developments obscure the reality that the euro is at a temporary peak of influence, while the dollar will continue to benefit from the geopolitical sources of its global role, which the euro cannot yet or soon, if ever, match.

The limited and defensive response of euro area policymakers to the impact of the financial crisis on neighboring countries—including on some EU members and major trading partners of the euro area—brings home this fundamental geostrategic weakness, despite the euro's success in easier times to date. Failure to respond adequately to the financial crisis in Eastern Europe is itself the greatest threat to the future growth and stability of the euro area. The strictly economic rules-based treatment of crisis-hit Eastern European countries may actually weaken the euro's global role by demonstrating the limits of political commitment, especially if growth in the East declines persistently following the crisis. Ironically, while most EU members outside the euro area have found the goal of euro adoption more attractive in light of the crisis, they have simultaneously seen euro area membership pulling farther away because of the euro area leadership's short-sighted response.

Geostrategic Relationships Drive Exchange Rate Arrangements and Reserve Accumulation[20]

A key determinant of a country's public-sector demand for a foreign currency is the existence or not of an exchange rate peg to that foreign currency. The existence or not of an explicit official currency peg, however, understates the influence of this relationship on the dollar's global role along three dimensions. First, the vast majority of emerging markets and smaller economies run monetary policies that involve highly managed floats, if not de facto pegs, primarily against the dollar (Calvo and Reinhart 2002, IMF 2007), so the list of official peggers understates the customer base for dollars from this source. Second, to the degree that currency ties endogenously encourage trade links, capital flows, and economic integration between economies (in the spirit of Frankel and Rose 1996), private-sector demand for the anchor currency and currency of intervention will also rise. Third, countries that take on exchange rate pegs, in part as a means of monetary stabilization or credible commitment to price stability, will be extremely reluctant to alter a peg arrangement for fear of inducing instability, even if that means turbulence in the course of anchor currency movements (Eichengreen and Masson 1998).[21] In short,

---

20. This section is based on the research presented in Posen (2008).

21. Eichengreen (1999, 106) puts it well: "If the country, having brought down inflation, can

the decision to orient a country's currency and exchange rate policy to the dollar as an anchor accounts for a large and persistent share of the dollar's global role.

But what determines a country's choice of peg? The workhorse baseline for evaluating currency affiliations remains the Mundell-McKinnon optimal currency area (OCA) criteria, which emphasize the direction of trade and the relative synchronization of shocks. Given the rise of the euro area and Asia as sources of international trade and global growth, and the still important role of geographical proximity in determining trade patterns, there would seem to be a strong argument for a large number of currencies to peg (or managed float) against the euro or even the yen or renminbi, rather than against the dollar (as discussed in McKinnon 2004). These optimal criteria are offset in part by the aforementioned reluctance to change preexisting pegs and in part by increasing cyclical synchronization and deepening trade ties over time arising from those pegs. Even so, the seemingly unavoidable occurrence of financial crises and divergences that break such pegs, or force changes of their valuations, would be expected to overcome these inertial forces over time. The argument that the euro exists as an alternative to the dollar thus arises in a different form. If undervaluing the exchange rate for export success is important, then it is another argument for the target currency to shift to a basket or change anchor as export markets shift.

Thus, the question of the euro's global role requires an assessment of what is keeping export-oriented emerging markets from switching their pegs to the euro, or at least to a euro-dollar basket, when many have greater proximity to and growth in trade volumes with the euro area than with the United States. Recent cyclical divergences have been insufficient to prompt such a switch, even when the Federal Reserve has been rapidly cutting interest rates while many of the pegging countries face far less incentive and room for monetary accommodation.[22] The actual inflation differential of the euro area and the United States, current or expected, is a minor factor.[23] Nonetheless, if a number of countries did switch their

---

then smoothly exit the currency peg before being forced to do so in a crisis, the peg will have been worth the candle. The problem is the same as with using heroin or morphine to treat a patient in pain; once the suffering subsides, the patient is still hooked.... Smooth exits from currency pegs, whatever the original rationale for the peg, are very much the exception to the rule."

22. For example, the decision of Kuwait to leave its dollar peg in May 2007 was explained in these terms; see also the discussion in Setser (2007). Mohsin Khan in chapter 3 of this volume points out that even after Kuwait left the peg, it still keeps its reserves primarily in dollars and of course its oil and gas exports are invoiced in dollars.

23. The maximum difference between US and euro area headline inflation rates since the end of Bretton Woods was 1.3 percent at an annualized rate, and the latest data have come in well below that amount.

exchange rate pegs, official and de facto managed floats, away from the dollar toward the euro, many of the inertial forces mentioned above would tend to lock in the change. That, in turn, would increase the euro's role in those countries' private sectors as well.

Foreign policy and national security ties, however, play a significant role in countries' decisions about exchange rate relationships. On that count, the conditions continue to favor the dollar's global use as an anchor currency over that of the euro. The ability of such relationships to overcome even strong economic pressures to change a peg can be seen in the response of Germany and Japan when their fixed exchange rates against the dollar during the 1960s led to significant imported inflation and macroeconomic overheating. As recounted in detail in Gavin (2003), West Germany repeatedly confronted the explicit linkage of its security commitment to maintain US troops in country as a deterrent to the Warsaw Pact to Germany's commitment to maintain its part in the gold pool. The linkage of the German-US security relationship to use of the dollar culminated in the so-called Blessing Memo of 1963, which locked in the quid pro quo and which, even though politically repudiated by the subsequent West German government, was maintained in spirit. Despite the United States' relative inflation and economic failings of the 1970s, no meaningful official sales of German dollar holdings took place until 1979. That, in turn, was when the Exchange Rate Mechanism (ERM) began, which involved a one-time shift away from dollar reserves to other European currencies to enable intra-ERM interventions and was not indicative of any ongoing shift out of dollars. Moreover, it was hardly a coincidence that concrete steps toward Economic and Monetary Union (EMU) with German encouragement began in earnest only in 1992, 13 years after the ERM began, once the Cold War had clearly ended, Germany had been successfully unified, and thus American troop withdrawals were imminent and the sense of security dependence diminished.[24]

Japan, which has never significantly reduced its sense of external threat from China and other regional powers and thus its perceived need for US troop presence on Japanese territory, has also never diversified its official reserves towards the euro to any meaningful degree. This reflects a dollar focus of yen policy, which continues 40 years after Japan began importing higher inflation from the United States, despite trade with the euro area and Asia growing faster than with the United States, and despite repeated bouts of asynchronous monetary policy from the Federal Reserve (see Volcker and Gyohten 1992). The security relationship be-

---

24. The popular notion in some places that EMU was a payoff of reduced German autonomy on monetary issues for French and other nations' acceptance of reunification is unsupported by the historical evidence on the motivations of the officials involved. This geopolitical consideration, that Germany no longer needed to keep Europe from creating a potential rival to the dollar, was far more evident.

tween the United States and Japan has contributed to this conservatism in Japan's exchange rate policy, though obviously export motivations also played a role to varying degrees in keeping the yen undervalued against the dollar. The security concerns, for example, overcame the Nixon Shock, when the 1971 Nixon-Connally decision to close the gold window hit Japan the hardest in macroeconomic terms and Japan did nothing then to diversify out of dollars or to target other currencies with its exchange rate. The recurring vague proposals by some ambitious Japanese officials that the yen could be internationalized or become a rival currency to the dollar always ran aground on Japan's security-driven desire not to offend the United States, right up through the Asian Monetary Fund fiasco of the mid-1990s.

Meanwhile, it was not a coincidence that Gaullist France, being far more interested than Germany or Japan in asserting its foreign policy independence from the United States and NATO, was the loudest and most demanding member in challenging the gold pool and the fixed dollar price of gold during the 1960s—although France actually faced both a far smaller amount of imported inflation from the United States than West Germany or Japan and a far greater domestic inflation risk from unanchoring the franc than the deutsche mark and yen would have faced.

The security motivations of France's currency arrangements also were primary in its management of relations with the Central African CFA Franc Zone, as detailed in Helleiner (2003) and Stasavage (2003a, 2003b). For example, "Countries such as Guinea and Mali, which sought to break away from the CFA zone [in the early 1960s], found their broader security, trade, aid, and other economic links to France severed by the French government in ways that were very costly" (Helleiner 2003, 75).[25] Mali exited the CFA zone in 1962, when it sought closer ties with the Soviet Union and separation from France. It returned to the zone in 1984 as part of the package of returning to the Western fold and reestablishing ties with France, with full reintegration only after a coup d'etat that credibly changed the leaning of the Malian regime. Similar political breaks regarding the orientation of foreign policy precipitated exits from the currency bloc by Madagascar and Mauritania in the 1970s. Thus, the security-driven arrangement of French CFA relations—driven by postcolonial foreign policy ties rather than any economic determinants—led to the significant share of euro peggers coming from that zone in Africa. In fact, the only non-EU membership candidate countries to have a euro peg are the CFA

---

25. Stasavage (2003a, 81) similarly "suggest[s] that calculations of Francophone African leaders [regarding CFA zone membership] have had as much to do with preserving the stability of their regimes.... Fear of losing privileged aid and security arrangements has raised the cost of exit for a number of governments that otherwise would have sought to establish their own currencies" in subsequent decades.

Franc Zone, the French Overseas Territories, Cape Verde, and Comoros (ECB 2007, 41).

Another substantial share of today's euroized or euro-pegging countries are the successor states to the former Republic of Yugoslavia, which is, of course, the scene of postwar Europe's largest and most geographically contiguous military intervention. So Kosovo and Montenegro have unilaterally euroized, Bosnia-Herzegovina has a euro-based currency board, and Croatia, Macedonia, and Serbia all have managed floats with reference to the euro. Other candidate and would-be candidate countries for EU membership, notably Turkey, have chosen not to peg to the euro, even as integration has deepened between the Turkish and euro area economies.

Looking at the list of current exchange rate arrangements in European economies (ECB 2007, IMF 2007), one sees a surprisingly large number of economies for which the economic case for euro pegging seems to be clear—and which have the legal obligation from EU membership to enter into ERM2 en route to the euro area—but which choose to do otherwise. These include Poland, which followed Sweden and the United Kingdom in refusing to formally tie in to the euro; Hungary, which had maintained a wide-band float tied to the euro outside of ERM2 and in late February 2008 exited that arrangement; and the Czech Republic and Romania, which float with a euro reference but nowhere close to a peg by the European Central Bank's own description.

The question is, why has membership in the euro area, which has delivered price stability, increasing financial depth, and trade linkages with these economies, not been attractive to economies that were already EU members before the crisis hit? It would appear that these countries' pre-crisis voluntary absence from the euro area or ERM2 is consistent with their strong desire for national autonomy and for foreign relations somewhat independent of the European Union—all of which was amply demonstrated by these countries' reluctance to ratify the Treaty of Nice and related constitutional measures for the European Union—rather than for lack of economic linkages. As European officials have stressed for the last nine years, the euro area is not just an economic club, and so it should be no surprise that those EU members feeling the most politically rather than economically distant are the ones to remain outside it.

Such decisions are hardly rare or limited to the euro area and its neighbors. Looking a little further back in time, it is worth considering the breakup of the ruble zone following the collapse of the Soviet Union in December 1991. Initially, 15 post-Soviet states were sharing a common currency, and the leading experts at the time, including the IMF, advised members against leaving the ruble zone on economic grounds (Åslund 1995). Given the trade ties between these economies, the spectre of hyperinflation or at least rapid devaluation, and the putative network externalities of continued ruble usage—as well as the absence at that time of a euro with hope of membership to latch on to—the advice was sensible. Yet, the ruble zone fell apart less than two years later.

Abdelal (2001, 2003) provocatively points out that there was a clear cross-sectional difference in the monetary goals and strategies of the post-Soviet states and thus in their readiness to exit the currency union, which ran opposite to what economic criteria would predict. The Baltic states had some of the highest intraregional shares of total commerce within the ruble zone, and would suffer the largest negative terms-of-trade shock by exiting the zone (Michalopoulos and Tarr 1992), and yet were the first and most eager to exit. In contrast, the "Stans," which had similar or lower trade shares within the zone than the Baltic states but (as resource exporters) had the most to gain in terms of trade from exiting—as well as (ex post) the biggest risk of inflation from losing a credible anchor—were the most reluctant to exit. They in fact tried to keep the zone going, because politically they were the most inclined to maintain close relations with Russia and within the Commonwealth of Independent States.

So what does all this mean for the global role of the euro vis-à-vis the dollar? It means that given the limited desire and ability of the euro area members to project security relationships beyond their immediate neighborhood, there is little incentive for other countries around the world to shift their pegging, formal but also informal, from the dollar to the euro. US military spending was double that of the euro area even prior to the Iraq war, and, of course, it has surged with ill use since that time. But the point is that while some economic arguments suggest that this defense spending differential would likely hasten the euro's displacement of the dollar, through eroding savings and the current account balance, the geostrategic view suggests that at least some of that spending differential supports the dollar's global role.

Of course, most of the places in Europe with large US troop deployments are now in the euro area, but they all have seen significant declines in US troops stationed there since the pre-euro days. There are countries in Latin America and especially in Northeast Asia and the Persian Gulf where US security presence leads to dollar pegging—in contrast to the euro, dollar peggers are not limited to contiguous areas. While Kuwait indeed abandoned its dollar peg in March 2007, despite the huge troop buildup there, it is difficult to see Saudi Arabia and the other Gulf states following suit—in the extreme, one can imagine them revaluing against the dollar and/or moving to a highly managed float against the dollar, but the dollar would remain the reference currency for them. The continued prominent role of the dollar in Egypt and Turkey, when their trade and financial ties have shifted so strongly toward the euro area relative to the United States, is also consistent with their security priorities—represented by the large US troop deployments in those countries. In this context of ongoing military deployment, is it credible to think that Japan or South

Korea (or Taiwan) would move voluntarily to a renminbi peg, were such an option meaningful? Would anyone outside the potential members of the European Union and some Mediterranean neighbors consider initiating a euro peg?[26] No and no.

Even in the purely economic realm of foreign policy, the euro area leadership does not assert itself in a way that induces other countries to affiliate with its membership. The fragmented external representation of the euro area membership at the IMF and other international financial institutions reveals the constraints on the euro area's ability to respond to global developments—and thus to influence the environment of countries outside the euro area itself. This situation is likely driven by the perception of some member states that direct participation in the G-20 or representing a constituency in the IMF serves their national interest better than yielding that individual role for a stronger promotion of common euro area positions. Whatever the reason, the euro area leadership's inability to present a forceful common position means that it acts to maintain the status quo rather than to exert influence over the global agenda. It also shows the leadership's revealed preference for internal economic issues over global ones. "If I am not for myself, who will be for me?" If the euro area countries do not stand up for themselves together in international economic decisions, let alone in geopolitics more broadly, which outside countries will stand with them and be more inclined to take up their currency?

The Euro Area Response to Eastern Europe

The global financial crisis has if anything clearly displayed the geopolitical limitations on the euro's global role because the euro area authorities have failed to show leadership even as a regional anchor currency. A successful regional currency role for the euro would entail fulfilling responsibilities toward countries in the region that have adopted the euro as a monetary anchor or whose financial systems are partially euroized. Doing so would require correctly treating the current crisis as different from any one for which the Maastricht criteria were designed and flexibly interpreting those rules for the current challenges. Fulfilling the regional responsibilities toward Eastern Europe would also require actively trying to export stability from the euro area to potential and future members, rather than concentrating solely on the maximum protection of current members.

In a nutshell, however, the instinctive reaction of euro area policymakers has been to go into a defensive crouch when a number of Eastern European economies ran into significant difficulties as a result of the crisis.

---

26. Tunisia and Morocco do have basket pegs that de facto include both the euro and the dollar, where on an economic basis it would seem straightforward for them to peg solely to the euro if not to euroize.

While some adjustment funds have been provided via financial support of IMF programs for particular countries, the main response of the euro area has been to make sure that no country could conceive of accelerating the process of attaining euro area membership, of swapping or repoing assets in national currencies for euros, or of receiving any transfer of a meaningful amount of funds rather than a loan. The loud volume at which these self-imposed limits on euro area action were rapidly proclaimed conveyed clearly that euro area policymakers are insecure about the stability of the euro and treat that stability as hugely fragile. The impression given is hardly one to inspire confidence in the currency, and overrides any expectations by potential euro members of European solidarity or that the euro might entail a broader political commitment.

Thus, ironically, while most EU members outside the euro area have found the goal of euro adoption more attractive in light of the crisis, they have simultaneously seen euro area membership move farther away because of the euro area leadership's short-sighted response. Counting the sudden huge depreciation of all Eastern European currencies in autumn 2008—irrespective of their economic fundamentals—as strict observance of the ERM2 "waiting area" criterion for exchange rate stability is outright punitive. Similarly the literal enforcement of the debt and deficit criteria for euro membership without some out for crisis mitigation or bank recapitalization expenditures will be horribly contractionary, above and beyond anything enforced on euro member countries under the Stability and Growth Pact. György Szapáry's paper in chapter 3 documents the mounting difficulties for new member states of meeting the fiscal deficit and long-term interest rate criteria as a result of this exogenous shock from the crisis. As Jean Pisani-Ferry and I argue in the introduction to this volume, new members should be given a "more sensible, not easier, path [to euro entry]. At a minimum the Commission and Eurogroup should offset the ways in which the crisis has made euro accession more distant even for countries with good policies."

Yes, some Eastern European EU members—notably Hungary, Latvia, and Romania—pursued ill-advised policies leading to currency mismatched borrowing, unsustainable current account deficits, and eroding fiscal balances, while others did not. Some would say that one of their policymakers' reasons for misbehaving was the belief that they had a commitment from the euro area, at least regarding monetary stability. Since other new member states had at least as much of a plausible commitment, though, most of them had relatively better chances of meeting the criteria for membership, and they did not go on such binges, so that cannot be the whole story.[27] For purposes of this paper, the point is that disregard

---

27. We should probably be even more skeptical of this claim. Italy, Greece, and to a lesser degree Portugal all were brought into the euro area on the basis of some dubious measures and flexible interpretation of the criteria. The run-up to the launch of the euro did not credibly

for the losses suffered by the new member states in favor of what seems to maximize the stability for the current euro area members only unravels the elite ties and decreases the leverage that build up incentives for currency affiliation. Add in deep disappointment of expectations about intra-EU solidarity, as well as ever receding goal posts for euro entry, and we should expect some Eastern European countries to want to self-insure and diversify on the monetary front, much as East Asia did after feeling ill-served by the IMF in 1997–98.[28]

The euro area's narrowly economic and internally focused approach to the Eastern European situation actually raises a significant geopolitical risk for the European Union. The emphasis on country by country programs (when the IMF is needed) and strict assessment by fixed criteria (even for the exemplar governments) may be economically motivated, but it sets member state against member state in trying to distinguish themselves. The Czechs insist they are not the Hungarians, the Estonians that they are not the Latvians, the Bulgarians that they are not the Romanians, and that each must be treated accordingly. In a narrow rules-based mindset, such a separating equilibrium seems to make sense, for all that matters are the standards of the current euro area. In the current crisis, such inflexible discipline will inevitably lead to bad outcomes for some member states. At worst, the euro area would be pushing a number of Eastern member states down a very dangerous path economically and politically. So doing cannot but hurt the competitiveness and stability of their perhaps more economically virtuous immediate neighbors as well. Eroding intra-European solidarity thus will not just be damaging to the euro's regional role but also could eventually be harmful to European economic and political stability over the medium term.

"If I am only for myself, who am I?" The euro cannot become a global currency and an effective influence for stability, let alone one of the international financial architects, if it does not live up to its responsibilities as the world's most important regional currency.

---

deter them into more disciplined behavior any more than it induced irresponsible behavior by Ireland, Austria, or the Netherlands. So the premise that enforcing rules, even under the guise of IMF conditionality, will force Hungary or Romania to see the error of their ways is empirically suspect.

28. It would be accurate to point out that, during the crises of the 1990s, the US government did little for its closely tied countries Mexico or South Korea beyond using the IMF, much as the euro area has done for Eastern Europe at present. It also misses the point. That neglect did result in some self-insurance and some distancing from the United States by affected countries, even as the economic fundamentals of their currency orientation did not change. Furthermore, the concern here is how geopolitics determines global currency usage, and, unlike the United States, the euro area does not offer national security support or have the advantages of currency incumbency to offset US levels of self-absorption.

Is this Crisis the Last Opportunity for the Euro to Step Up Globally?

Many observers have logically expressed concern that the recent turmoil may be the big event that pushes the dollar off its pedestal as the dominant international currency. Given the euro's apparent readiness on some purely economic criteria to be an alternative to the dollar, the euro's ascent to at least comparable status with the dollar has a surface and popular plausibility. Indeed, some observers predicted before the euro's launch that the euro would some day rival the dollar as a reserve currency, if not also as a private store of value and means of account, producing a bipolar monetary system.[29]

Some analysts (notably Bergsten 2005) have argued that for the euro to overcome the dollar's incumbency and network advantages, and attain codominance, the United States would have to commit a series of significant policy mistakes or suffer a balance-of-payments crisis. These analysts assume such a process to have been operating when the pound sterling lost its role to the dollar in the 1930s, when the United Kingdom's balance of payments and monetary discipline flagged. According to this view, the dollar, however, was spared such a fate during the 1970s only because neither the deutsche mark nor the yen was a viable alternative at the time. The lack of an alternative reserve currency at that time was supposedly the key factor in the dollar's ongoing global role. Again, if one looks solely at the basic economic factors like size and financial liquidity being in place for the euro at present, then to these analysts recent events indicate that the time is ripe for an accelerated switch to the euro, if not a formal regime change.

It is overdue and correct for American and other observers to shed any remnants of the excessive doubts about the euro's viability, which prevailed in many quarters since the mid-1990s, and to recognize that the euro has been an ample success within the monetary realm (Posen 2005, DG ECFIN 2008). But to argue that this crisis is the turning point for the euro to equal the dollar in, or displace the dollar from, its global role would be misguided. The source of all this euro optimism is too narrow and deterministic a focus on simple observable economic determinants of reserve currency holdings and reserves to the exclusion of other issues.[30]

---

29. See Alogoskoufis and Portes (1992), Bergsten (1997a, 1997b), Portes and Rey (1998). Note that most of these economic analyses focus specifically on the reserve currency role, given availability (for the most part) of data on official currency holdings and the assumption that many other aspects of the dollar's or euro's usage would follow shifts in this usage. That is not to say that they dismiss other aspects such as pegging by third countries or private-sector invoicing, but they do not focus on them. They do not consider non-economic aspects of these dynamics.

30. While a large literature in political science has emerged in the last 20 years on the political

The mainstream economics literature on currency status admits as much by its repeated frustration in theoretically accounting for the observed behavior of dollar holders in the public sector. It is just as troubling in the private sector, given the apparent willingness of foreign investors to give the United States an "exorbitant privilege" via accepting low-yielding US treasuries and other dollar-denominated investments.[31]

This is why Hausmann and Sturzenegger (2006) were fully justified in invoking the physics analogy of unobservable "dark matter" to explain the gap in relative returns for dollar holders.[32] The United States' global political leadership in security, commercial, and even cultural affairs has a critical impact on dollar usage in the monetary realm and constitutes a significant share of this dark matter. The euro area does not have any of this dark matter with which to exert a gravitational pull on other countries beyond the basic economic factors. It is no coincidence that Russia, trying to tout independence from the United States and woo Europe politically, is the only one of the major emerging markets to actively move into the euro. This holds true today, even when all substantial reserve accumulators—particularly China—face substantial financial expense and risk from not reallocating their portfolios, given their dollar exposure on accumulated reserves.

The crisis itself will do nothing to increase the geopolitical significance or attraction of the euro area. In addition to the likely frustration of

---

economy of monetary policy, the focus has tended to be on monetary statecraft, the tactical use of exchange rate policy in specific instances (e.g., Henning 1994, Kirshner 1993). The few who deal with currency choice end up emphasizing the same trio of economic determinants of reserve status as typical in economics. A partial exception are the essays collected in Andrews (2006) and Kirshner (2003) and the contributions therein. More provocative are the broader historical syntheses of Maier (2006) and Strange (1996) on sources of American power, which take currency usage as part of the package.

31. As argued in Posen (2008): "The missing mass problem in pure economic explanations of currency behavior is why Chinn and Frankel (2007) have to include such a large role for imputed "network" effects via lags, even though that labeling does little work…. [It] is also why Andrew Rose (2007) in his latest research on exits from currency unions reveals that what shapes currency unions around the world is not what the received theory predicts…the most striking facts are that aggregate macroeconomic features of the economy do a poor job in predicting currency union exits…. And this gap is why Gourinchas and Rey (2007) and Curcuru, Dvorak, and Warnock (2008) debate whether a differential financial return actually exists for US holders of foreign assets versus foreign holders of US assets…. The fact that long-term holdings of US dollar assets by foreigners have been a losing proposition in relative as well as absolute terms has to be taken at face value at some point: These assets were and are held, at least in part, for nonfinancial reasons." Those reasons are primarily the geopolitical factors set out in this paper.

32. Although closer analysis indicated that Hausmann and Sturzenegger's specific contention about intangibles leading to high profits from US foreign direct investment abroad did not hold up as the source of that dark matter. See Gros (2006), Higgins, Klitgaard, and Tille (2005), and Setser (2006) for persuasive critiques of that contention.

the Eastern European economies already integrated into the euro region discussed in the preceding section, neither economic growth nor financial stability in the euro area is going to be visibly better than that of the United States over the 2008–2010 period. In fact, for a number of reasons, recovery is likely to be slower in the euro area, and most countries will have debt overhangs and asset price declines more persistent than in the United States. It is worth noting that the euro area's performance as a real economy has not been so compelling and was at least as inflated by unsustainable growth of late as the United States.[33] The best available sectoral analysis of productivity developments in the euro area economies suggests that an increase in productivity growth did not drive the recent boom in Europe.[34] In fact, the boom could be cloaking a continued downward trend in productivity growth, since it came through increased input of low-skilled labor. In any event, absent improved productivity growth, the boom is not based on a sustainable source of growth. Baily (2008) comes to a similar assessment based on independent corporate studies and on the breakdown of Okun's law relationships when the recent employment increase accompanied rather slow growth.

Why does this matter for the present moment as the opportunity for the euro to rise to global currency status? Because it indicates that the current relative parity in the sizes of the euro area and US economies is unlikely to last. The demographics continue to favor the United States, both on birth rate and on immigration. Even allowing for a decline in the US productivity growth trend, the gap between euro area and US productivity growth rates will remain sizable for the coming years as well. Thus, as in Posen (2004), the US economy will gain in size relative to the euro area, even as it shrinks relative to China and world GDP as a whole—and we know that relative size of economies is an important determinant of currency status. Add demographic trends to relative economic size, and the potential for the euro area to project power in geostrategic affairs is also on a downward trend, even if its members committed to so doing. There may be even less appetite for consolidated external EU or euro area representation now than before the crisis. This is the natural, if unfortunate, result of political pressures to look after a nation's parochial interests in times of hardship.

---

33. Among monetary accomplishments beyond maintenance of price stability are good management to date of the financial turmoil, the exertion of greater unity and voice by the ECB Governing Council vis-à-vis the member central banks, the (slight) consolidation of chairs and shares in the international financial institutions, and the successful support of continued financial deepening in euro area bond markets. See DG ECFIN (2008), Posen (2005), and Pisani-Ferry et al. (2008) for summary positive assessments of the euro in its own terms.

34. See the official discussions of the EU-KLEMS database research in ECB (2008) and DG ECFIN (2008).

"If not now, when?" If the euro cannot expand its global role through political initiative when the gap in economic factors and relative performance between the euro area and the United States has temporarily narrowed, and the demand for monetary leadership is high, it is unlikely to ever do so.

* * * * * *

To reiterate a point made by others in this volume, competition with the dollar for monetary leadership should not be a motivation for euro area policies.[35] The message of this paper is not that the euro area policymakers should pursue an expanded regional strategy, let alone more assertive behavior in foreign and security policy for the sake of having the euro become a more global currency. The message is an empirical one about the noneconomic fundamentals limiting the euro's role internationally: Because the euro area is not offering to the states behind potentially associated currencies a broader range of security relationships in general, it will not attract as many adherents as the economic factors would seem to suggest. The defensive rather than affirmative response of the euro area leadership to the crisis in Eastern Europe, and the poor (or worse) economic performance of most of the euro area compared with that of the United States as a result of the crisis, will reinforce this limitation.

But this positive argument that the euro is unlikely to become a global currency and real alternative to the dollar does not say that US monetary hegemony is automatic. In fact, I argue that the causality runs at least as much from security leadership to economic leadership as in the other direction; there need not be a ready alternative currency for the dollar to lose its global leadership. Given the euro's limitations, fragmentation of the global monetary system, rather than a smooth shift to a viable dollar rival, is more likely to emerge, should the US mistakes lead to dollar failure. In such a situation, there would be an erosion of easy currency convertibility between currency zones, a shift of reserves toward gold and other "hard" commodities, and lesser cross-border flows of capital, all inducing greater macroeconomic instability. This scenario is, of course, along the lines of Kindleberger's (1986) interpretation of the 1930s, when there was no monetary leadership to be had and the world trading system collapsed as a result. While things are unlikely to get that bad, since we are emerging from the worst of the crisis already, no one should view the failure of the euro to rise to global currency status as costless—either for Europe or for the world.

The ECB's founding chief economist, Otmar Issing (2009), claims on the basis of the euro's experience that you can have a currency without

---

35. See the contributions to this volume by Bini Smaghi (chapter 1), Liikanen (chapter 4), Pisani-Ferry and Posen (introduction), and Summers (chapter 4).

a state. Perhaps, at least in good times. But the euro's record also demonstrates that you certainly cannot have a *global currency* without a state. And if no other nation-state is dominant enough in geopolitics to provide a global currency, and the international framework behind it, that stateless currency may not do very well even for its own region.

References

Abdelal, Rawi. 2001. *National Purpose in the World Economy: Post-Soviet States in Comparative Perspective*. Ithaca, NY: Cornell University Press.

Abdelal, Rawi. 2003. National Strategy and National Money: Politics and the End of the Ruble Zone, 1991–1994. In *Monetary Orders: Ambiguous Economics, Ubiquitous Politics*, ed. Jonathan Kirshner. Ithaca, NY: Cornell University Press.

Alogoskoufis, George, and Richard Portes. 1992. European Monetary Union and International Currencies in a Tripolar World. In *Establishing a Central Bank: Issues in Europe and Lessons from the U.S.*, ed. Matthew Canzoneri, Vittorio Grilli, and Paul Masson. Cambridge, UK: Cambridge University Press.

Andrews, David, ed. 2006. *International Monetary Power*. Ithaca, NY: Cornell University Press.

Aslund, Ånders. 1995. *How Russia Became a Market Economy*. Washington: Brookings Institution Press.

Baily, Martin. 2008. Productivity and Potential Growth in the US and Europe. Presentation at the European Central Bank, Frankfurt, Germany, January 17.

Bergsten, C. Fred. 1997a. The Dollar and the Euro. *Foreign Affairs* 76, no. 4: 156–80.

Bergsten, C. Fred. 1997b. The Impact of the Euro on Exchange Rates and International Policy Cooperation. In *EMU and the International Monetary System*, ed. Paul Masson, Thomas Krueger, and Bart Turtelboom. Washington: International Monetary Fund.

Bergsten, C. Fred. 2005. The Euro and the Dollar: Toward a "Finance G-2"? In *The Euro at Five: Ready for a Global Role?* ed. Adam Posen. Washington: Institute for International Economics, 27-39.

Calvo, Guillermo A., and Carmen M. Reinhart. 2002. Fear of Floating. *Quarterly Journal of Economics* 107, no. 2: 379–408.

Chinn, Menzie, and Jeffrey Frankel. 2007. Will the Euro Eventually Surpass the Dollar? In *G7 Current Account Imbalances: Sustainability and Adjustment*, ed. Richard H. Clarida. Chicago, IL: University of Chicago Press.

Curcuru, Stephanie E., Tomas Dvorak, and Francis E. Warnock. 2008. *Cross-Border Returns Differentials*. International Finance Discussion Paper no. 921 (February). Washington: Federal Reserve Board.

DG ECFIN (Directorate-General for Economics and Finance). 2008. *EMU@10—Successes and Challenges after Ten Years of Economic and Monetary Union*. Brussels: European Commission. Available at http://ec.europa.eu.

ECB (European Central Bank). 2007. *Review of the International Role of the Euro*. Frankfurt.

ECB (European Central Bank). 2008. Productivity Developments and Monetary Policy. *Monthly Bulletin* (January): 61–73. Frankfurt.

Eichengreen, Barry. 1999. *Towards a New International Financial Architecture: A Practical Post-Asia Agenda*. Washington: Institute for International Economics.

Eichengreen, Barry, and Paul Masson. 1998. *Exit Strategies: Policy Options for Countries Seeking Greater Exchange Rate Flexibility.* IMF Occasional Paper no. 168. Washington: International Monetary Fund.

Frankel, Jeffrey A., and Andrew K. Rose. 1996. *The Endogeneity of the Optimum Currency Area Criteria.* NBER Working Paper no. W5700 (August). Cambridge, MA: National Bureau of Economic Research.

Gavin, Francis. 2003. Ideas, Power, and the Politics of US International Monetary Policy during the 1960s. In *Monetary Orders: Ambiguous Economics, Ubiquitous Politics*, ed. Jonathan Kirshner. Ithaca, NY: Cornell University Press.

Gourinchas, Pierre-Olivier, and Hélène Rey. 2007. From World Banker to World Venture Capitalist: U.S. External Adjustment and the Exorbitant Privilege. In *G7 Current Account Imbalances: Sustainability and Adjustment*, ed. Richard H. Clarida. Chicago, IL: University of Chicago Press.

Gros, Daniel. 2006. Why the US Current Account Deficit Is Not Sustainable. *International Finance* 9, no. 2: 241–60.

Hausmann, Ricardo, and Frederico Sturzenegger. 2006. Why the US Current Account Deficit Is Sustainable. *International Finance* 9, no. 2: 223–40.

Helleiner, Eric. 2003. The Southern Side of Embedded Liberalism: The Politics of Postwar Monetary Policy in the Third World. In *Monetary Orders: Ambiguous Economics, Ubiquitous Politics*, ed. Jonathan Kirshner. Ithaca, NY: Cornell University Press.

Henning, C. Randall. 1994. *Currencies and Politics in the United States, Germany, and Japan.* Washington: Institute for International Economics.

Higgins, Matthew, Thomas Klitgaard, and Cedric Tille. 2005. The Income Implications of Rising U.S. International Liabilities. *Current Issues in Economics and Finance* 11, no. 12. New York: Federal Reserve Bank of New York.

IMF (International Monetary Fund). 2007. *Annual Report on Exchange Arrangements and Exchange Restrictions.* Washington.

Issing, Otmar. 2009. The Euro: Does a Currency Need a State? *International Finance* 11, no. 3: 297–310.

Kindleberger, Charles P. 1986. *The World in Depression, 1929–1939*, 2d. ed. Berkeley: University of California Press.

Kirshner, Jonathan. 1993. *Currency and Coercion: The Political Economy of International Monetary Power.* Princeton, NJ: Princeton University Press.

Kirshner, Jonathan, ed. 2003. *Monetary Orders: Ambiguous Economics, Ubiquitous Politics.* Ithaca, NY: Cornell University Press.

Maier, Charles. 2006. *Among Empires: American Ascendancy and Its Predecessors.* Cambridge, MA: Harvard University Press.

McKinnon, Ronald. 2004. Optimum Currency Areas and Key Currencies: Mundell I versus Mundell II. *Journal of Common Market Studies* 42, no. 4: 689–715.

Michalopoulos, Constantine, and David Tarr. 1992. *Trade and Payments: Arrangements for States of the Former USSR.* Studies of Economies in Transition no. 2. Washington: World Bank.

Pisani-Ferry, Jean, Philippe Aghion, Marek Belka, Juergen von Hagen, Lars Heikensten, Andre Sapir, and Alan Ahearne. 2008. *Coming of Age: Report on the Euro Area.* Blueprint no. 4. Brussels: Bruegel.

Portes, Richard, and Hélène Rey. 1998. *The Emergence of the Euro as an International Currency.* NBER Working Paper no. 6424 (February). Cambridge, MA: National Bureau of Economic Research.

Posen, Adam. 2004. *Fleeting Equality: The Relative Size of the US and EU Economies to 2020*. US-Europe Analysis Series (September). Washington: Brookings Institution.

Posen, Adam, ed. 2005. *The Euro at Five: Ready for a Global Role?* Washington: Institute for International Economics.

Posen, Adam. 2008. Why the Euro Will Not Rival the Dollar. *International Finance* 11, no. 1: 75–100.

Rose, Andrew. 2007. Checking Out: Exits from Currency Unions. *Journal of Financial Transformation* 19 (April): 121–28.

Setser, Brad. 2006. On the Origins of Dark Matter. Brad Setser's Blog, January 13, 2006, www.rgemonitor.com/blog/setser/113810 (accessed April 3, 2008).

Setser, Brad. 2007. *The Case for Exchange Rate Flexibility in Oil-Exporting Economies*. Policy Briefs in International Economics 07-8. Washington: Peterson Institute for International Economics.

Stasavage, David. 2003a. *The Political Economy of a Common Currency: The CFA Franc Zone since 1945*. Aldershot: Ashgate Publishers.

Stasavage, David. 2003b. When Do States Abandon Monetary Discretion? Lessons from the Evolution of the CFA Franc Zone. In *Monetary Orders: Ambiguous Economics, Ubiquitous Politics*, ed. Jonathan Kirshner. Ithaca, NY: Cornell University Press.

Strange, Susan. 1996. *The Retreat of the State: The Diffusion of Power in the World Economy*. Cambridge: Cambridge University Press.

Volcker, Paul, and Toyoo Gyohten. 1992. *Changing Fortunes: The World's Money and the Threat to American Leadership*. Pittsburgh, PA: Three Rivers Press.

3

Regional Perspectives

East Asia

C. RANDALL HENNING

East Asia provides a crucial test of the euro's attractiveness as an international currency outside Europe's own neighborhood. This paper compares the roles of the euro and dollar in the region and their prospects. Although I consider myself an early and consistent supporter of the Economic and Monetary Union (EMU), I do not predict a rapid increase in the role of the euro in East Asia. The international role of its currency is not the most important test of the success or failure of a monetary union. Such a role for the euro would not necessarily benefit Europe, moreover, because it carries costs as well as benefits. However, examining the international role of the euro is important to understanding the operation and stability of the international monetary system. The following sections address the overall prospects for the euro, approaches to understanding currency use in East Asia, the recent empirical record, and the relevance of Asian regionalism. These treatments are followed by a brief conclusion.

Overall Prospects for the International Role of the Euro

The advent of the EMU created an alternative to the dollar that is potentially more attractive than any of the European "legacy" currencies or the Japanese yen. When asked about this in the 1990s, Lawrence Summers,

C. Randall Henning is visiting fellow at the Peterson Institute for International Economics and a member of the faculty at American University. He has written on international monetary cooperation, Asian regional integration, and Europe's monetary union, including most recently articles on the exchange rate policy of the euro area (Henning 2007a, 2007b). He wishes to acknowledge Marko Klasnja for excellent assistance on this paper.

then at the US Treasury Department, was fond of saying, "The fate of the dollar is still largely in our own hands" (US Senate 1997). This statement was reassuring, but in a diplomatically evasive way. In previous decades, the United States could make macroeconomic mistakes—which it did on monetary policy in the 1970s and fiscal policy in the 1980s—with relative impunity. Because the currency alternatives were limited to the Deutsche mark, Japanese yen, and Swiss franc—currencies backed by economies and capital markets that were nowhere near the size, diversity, and liquidity of those of the United States—such mistakes produced diversification out of the dollar only at the margin. I argued that the United States would pay a greater cost in terms of diversification out of dollar assets if it made such mistakes after the creation of the euro (Henning 1997, 2000). At least until relatively recently, though, the United States has avoided high inflation or large fiscal deficits since the advent of the euro.

The euro's encroachment on the international role of the dollar has so far been on the margin, rather than game-changing. This is true across most measures—foreign exchange reserves, trade invoicing, vehicle function in foreign exchange markets, and international financial assets. In its most successful arena, as the currency of denomination of international bond issues, the euro plays a role that approaches but remains slightly less than that of the dollar. Rather than a continuous trend increase in the euro's share by this measure, however, we have seen a leveling off in recent years (ECB 2008, box 1, 15–16). Extrapolating from prior experience, therefore, prospects for the euro seemed more hopeful at its fifth anniversary (Posen 2005) than at its tenth. The euro has become widely used in its own regional neighborhood but not a global currency seriously challenging the dollar in other regions—a conclusion well documented by the European Central Bank's annual report on the subject (ECB 2008; see also Cohen [forthcoming] and Cohen and Subacchi 2008).

Asian countries hold most of the world's foreign exchange reserves and are therefore especially relevant to the euro's global future (table 3.1). Seven Asian countries, including India, rank among the top 10 holders of official foreign exchange reserves and 9 Asian countries rank among the top 15. The reserves of ASEAN+3+2 (that is, the member countries of the Association of Southeast Asian Nations plus China, Japan, and Korea, and then adding Hong Kong and Taiwan) amount to almost $4 trillion, more than 54 percent of world foreign exchange reserves (as of April 2008). Moreover, East Asia represents almost 20 percent of world product, at current exchange rates—25 percent when calculated at purchasing power parity—and 27 percent of world exports. Philip Lane and Gian Maria Milesi-Ferretti (2007) calculate that the region holds more than 12 percent of international financial assets. Moreover, these percentages are growing. For the euro to break out of the European neighborhood into a global role, it would have to capture "currency market share" in East Asia.

Table 3.1   World's major foreign exchange reserve holders

Rank	Country	Amount (billions of US dollars) 2001	2005	April 2008	Percent share of world total, April 2008
1	**China**	212	819	1,757	24.02
2	**Japan**	388	829	978	13.37
3	Russia	33	176	519	7.09
4	**India**	45	131	304	4.16
5	**Taiwan**	122	253	289	3.96
6	**Korea**	102	210	260	3.55
7	Brazil	36	53	195	2.66
8	**Singapore**	75	116	175	2.40
9	**Hong Kong**	111	124	160	2.18
10	Algeria	18	56	126	1.72
11	**Malaysia**	29	69	123	1.69
12	**Thailand**	32	51	107	1.47
13	Mexico	44	73	92	1.26
14	Libya	14	38	87	1.20
15	Poland	25	40	76	1.04

Note: Asian countries are highlighted in bold.

Sources: International Monetary Fund, *International Financial Statistics,* September 2008; Central Bank of Taiwan.

Alternative Approaches to Currency Use in Asia

Two alternative views provide a useful context in which to situate analysis of international currency usage in East Asia. Let us call them the "dollar standard" school and the "dollar pessimist" school.

Ronald McKinnon (2006) has written most lucidly on the East Asian dollar standard and his book on the subject is a key point of reference. The concept of "conflicted virtue" plays a central role in his analysis. Asian countries with high domestic saving rates, capital outflow, and current account surpluses accumulate foreign assets but are not able to lend in their own currencies; they choose to accumulate dollar assets. Growing current account surpluses place them in a dilemma: They must appreciate their currencies to avoid foreign protectionism but suffer losses on their dollar portfolios if they do so. Conflicted virtue for creditor countries involves the same currency mismatch, but with opposite effects, as "original sin" for debtor countries. Given his assumptions and orientation, McKinnon concludes that East Asian reliance on the dollar is both desirable and likely to continue.[1] The so-called revived Bretton Woods interpretation offered by Michael Dooley, David Folkerts-Landau, and Peter Garber (2003) is closely related to the dollar standard view. Although they are less concerned about the role of the dollar as a nominal anchor for Asian countries, the revived Bretton Woods advocates also defend heavy Asian foreign exchange intervention, currency undervaluation, and accumulation of large piles of dollar reserves.

Counterpoised to the dollar standard view are many who believe this pattern of intervention and reserve accumulation to be unsustainable. Barry Eichengreen expects that, when faced with continued US current account deficits, trend depreciation of the dollar, and an intractable collective action dilemma among reserve holders, Asian central banks will at some point sell dollars for other currencies (Eichengreen 2006). That point could be the euro's historic moment of opportunity to broaden its international role to East Asia.

Though their argument is not specific to East Asia, Menzie Chinn and Jeffrey Frankel (2008) are particularly bullish on the euro in the long term. The concept of a "tipping point" in currency usage is one of the contributions of their recent article. They argue that the underlying determinants can change incrementally over a considerable period without causing equivalent changes in reserve currency shares. But once these changes cumulate to a certain threshold, the reserve portfolio can be redistributed relatively rapidly. Chinn and Frankel believe that such a threshold could be reached as early as 2015. While the concept is intriguing, the existence and location of the tipping point are, of course, hypotheses.

Present Role of the Dollar and Euro in East Asia

As of the tenth anniversary of the creation of the euro, the dollar continues to play the dominant role in East Asia. To get a sense of the relative standing of the two currencies—and the distance that the euro must cover to play a role equal to that of the dollar in the region—consider their shares in foreign exchange reserves, exchange rate regimes, foreign currency markets, bond markets, and trade invoicing, in that order.

Foreign Exchange Reserves

With respect to shares in world foreign exchange reserves, the dollar's share is about 62.5 percent in value terms and 68 percent in quantity terms.[2] Most East Asian countries do not publicly disclose the currency composi-

---

1. McKinnon discusses alternatives to the dollar in his 2006 book, but the euro is not one of them.

2. I thank Edwin M. Truman and Daniel Xie for providing this calculation.

Table 3.2 Estimated composition of Asian reserves, selected countries (percent)

Country	Estimate			Source	Date
	Dollar	Euro	Yen		
Australia[a]	46	37	8	Reserve Bank of Australia[c]	July 2008
China	65 to 70	—	—	Brad Setser[d]	April 2008
Hong Kong	73[b]	—	—	Hong Kong Monetary Authority[e]	June 2007
Japan	83 to 89	—	—	Truman and Wong (2006)	End of 2004
Korea	65	—	—	Bank of Korea[f]	March 2008
New Zealand	85	12	2	Reserve Bank of New Zealand[g]	June 2007
Philippines	83	10	4	Truman and Wong (2006)	End of 2004

a. The Reserve Bank of Australia's "benchmark composition" is 45, 45, and 10 percent for dollar, euro, and yen, respectively.
b. Reported as "dollar bloc" currencies, possibly including Canadian, Australian, and New Zealand dollars.
c. IMF Monthly Data—Reserve Bank of Australia, International Reserves and Foreign Currency Liquidity, October 2008, available at www.rba.gov.au.
d. Brad Setser, "Estimating the Currency Composition of China's Reserves," RGE Monitor, May 2008.
e. Hong Kong Monetary Authority, *Annual Report 2007*.
f. *Korea Times*, "Assets in Dollars Take 65% of Reserves," March 23, 2008, available at www.koreatimes.co.kr.
g. Reserve Bank of New Zealand, *Annual Report 2006–2007*.

Note: In the cases of China, Hong Kong, Japan, and Korea, estimates of the breakdown of the non-dollar share into euro and yen shares are not provided.

tion of reserves, so we have to be content with the estimates of various authors who have closely examined reserve management policies. Table 3.2 compiles these estimates for seven countries in the region. Although the country coverage is incomplete, the largest reserve holders are represented. Some of these guesses are fairly well educated, and the numbers for Australia and New Zealand are known rather than estimated. Because the holdings of China, Japan, and Korea are large relative to their partners in Southeast Asia, the dollar share of the reserves for ASEAN+3 as a whole can be estimated at about 74 percent, with reasonable confidence that the dollar's true share lies within 5 percent of this figure.

It thus appears that the role of the dollar is greater in East Asian holdings than in world reserve holdings. Given that the Japanese yen would be expected to play its small remaining role (3.4 percent of world reserves) in its own regional neighborhood, the share of the euro must be correspondingly smaller in this region than worldwide.

Two observations about this measure are noteworthy. First, Edwin M. Truman and Anna Wong (2006) find that reserve diversification has generally been "passive" rather than "active"—that is, effected through the depreciation of the dollar relative to the euro and other reserve currencies rather than through conversions. To the extent that central banks actively change reserve levels, Truman and Wong find such changes to be generally stabilizing rather than destabilizing of exchange rates but also that Japan's "Great Intervention" of 2003–04 largely accounts for this finding. Over the next couple of years, it will be interesting to see whether these findings are symmetrical to movements of the dollar—that is, whether or not Asian central banks use episodes of dollar appreciation as an opportunity to *actively* diversify into the euro without accentuating downward movement of the US currency.

The second observation is a caveat: The shift of reserves into sovereign wealth funds (SWFs) could mask currency diversification. Monetary authorities that wish to diversify might well initiate that shift through the most *opaque* vehicle, especially if they are concerned that their move could prompt other dollar holders to sell their reserves—the collective action dilemma about which Eichengreen warns. The currency composition of foreign exchange reserves is disclosed on a global basis by the International Monetary Fund (IMF), whereas the composition of SWF portfolios is not—which might persuade dollar holders to use the latter as the vehicle.

Exchange Rate Regimes

The dollar also dominates as the reference currency for hard pegging, soft pegging, and managed floating in the region. Table 3.3 lists the exchange rate regimes in East Asia as classified both by the IMF and by Carmen Reinhart, Ethan Ilzetzki, and Kenneth Rogoff (2008), the latter presenting a more fine-grained classification scheme. Reinhart, Ilzetzki, and Rogoff incorporate observations through 2007, thus encompassing the shift within the region toward greater exchange rate flexibility prior to the 2007–09 financial turmoil. The table shows the degree to which rates were still pegged and managed in the region.

But the composition of the baskets against which currencies are managed is generally opaque, which has spawned a cottage industry among international monetary economists devoted to estimating them. Jeffrey Frankel and Shang-Jin Wei (1994, 2007) and Ronald McKinnon and Günther Schnabl (2006), among others, have estimated the implicit weight of the dollar to be very high, above 90 percent in the case of China after its switch to gradual appreciation in July 2005. The Malaysian ringgit shadows the renminbi very closely, gradually moving in tandem with it upward against the dollar. Hong Kong has a currency board based on the dollar. The Korean won, Singapore dollar, and Thai baht appear to give somewhat less weight to the dollar and modest weight to the yen. Masa-

Table 3.3   Asian exchange rate regimes

Country	International Monetary Fund	Reinhart, Ilzetzki, and Rogoff
Brunei	De facto peg	Crawling band, narrow[b]
Cambodia	Managed floating[a]	Crawling peg
China	De facto peg	De facto peg
Hong Kong	Currency board	Currency board
Indonesia	Managed floating	Managed floating
Japan	Float	Free float
Korea	Float	Managed floating
Laos	Managed floating	—
Malaysia	Managed floating	Crawling band, narrow
Myanmar	Managed floating	Dual market
Philippines	Float	Crawling band, narrow
Singapore	Managed floating	Moving band[c]
Thailand	Managed floating	Moving band
Vietnam	Managed floating	Crawling peg
Australia	Float	Free float
India	Managed floating	Crawling band, narrow
New Zealand	Float	Managed floating

a. The full IMF designation is "managed floating with no predetermined path."
b. The full Reinhart-Ilzetzki-Rogoff designation is "de facto crawling band that is narrower than or equal to +/−2 percent."
c. The full Reinhart-Ilzetzki-Rogoff designation is "moving band that is narrower than or equal to +/−2 percent," allowing for appreciation or depreciation over time.

Sources: Reinhart, Ilzetzki, and Rogoff (2008); Reinhart and Rogoff (2004); International Monetary Fund, De Facto Classification of Exchange Rate Regimes and Monetary Policy Framework, available at www.imf.org.

hiro Kawai (2007) observes a growing diversity of exchange rate regimes and argues that McKinnon overstates the dominance of the dollar, but nonetheless confirms that substantial weight is placed on the US currency. The weight given to the euro in these implicit baskets is generally low, and the European Central Bank lists no East Asian country among those using the euro in baskets for pegs and managed floats.[3]

Several analysts have proposed that East Asian governments peg jointly to a common basket, usually composed of the dollar, euro, and yen (see especially Williamson 1999 and 2005, Ogawa and Ito 2002; also de Brouwer 2002, Rajan 2002, Kawai 2004 and 2007). But monetary authorities in the region have declined this advice and shifted toward greater currency flexibility in the last three years without adopting a common basket—or without much coordination of exchange rates in other respects either. Asian authorities undertook this shift as the dollar depreciated against

3. Frankel and Wei (2007) specifically emphasize in their results that China appears to have assigned no weight at all to the yen and euro.

the euro. But it is not at all clear that these countries were seeking stability against the euro rather than appreciation against the dollar.

Recall that the 1997–98 crisis forced Asian currencies off their dollar pegs but that, as the crisis passed, Asian authorities reestablished those pegs in a softer form that appears to have been less vulnerable to speculative attack. Several Asian currencies have exhibited a good deal of flexibility during the present financial turmoil as well. But the previous pattern of reversion to relative stability could well be repeated when this crisis eventually recedes. Whether Asian authorities choose to restabilize their currencies and, if so, whether they peg softly against the dollar or a broader basket will serve as an indicator of the postcrisis direction of currency use in the region.

Vehicle Currency, Financial Assets, and Trade Invoicing

The general picture of dollar dominance and minimal euro encroachment is reflected in the other, remaining international roles for currencies.

Table 3.4 presents the shares of key currencies in the foreign exchange markets of Asian countries. As a vehicle currency, the dollar dominates foreign exchange markets in East Asia as it does globally—being on one side of more than 90 percent of all trades in most markets and 84.6 and 88.3 percent of all trades in Japan and Singapore, respectively. The euro is exchanged in 18.7 percent of all trades in East Asia, about half the figure for the Japanese yen.

Figure 3.1 presents information provided by the European Central Bank on the role of the euro in the outstanding stock of international bonds across regions. The euro has a modest share, 23.9 percent, in international debt securities in East Asia. Most international bonds in the region are denominated in dollars, which have a 60.1 percent share; the Japanese yen holds a 3.9 percent share (ECB 2008, table 2).

Table 3.5 presents the shares of currencies in trade invoicing in selected Asian countries. In this sample, the dollar again plays the dominant role. The US currency plays the least role in Japanese trade, where 55 percent of exports and 65.7 percent of imports are invoiced in dollars, and the yen naturally plays a substantial role. The dollar plays the largest role in Indonesian trade. The euro plays a correspondingly small role, in the single digits in percentage terms, for all countries listed. McKinnon and Schnabl (2006, 19–20) also report that trade specifically among Asian countries other than Japan is predominantly invoiced in dollars.

The shares for the euro in nearly all of these functions are smaller than Europe's shares in world GDP, trade, and capital markets. Table 3.6 presents a comparison of the size of the euro area and the European Union relative to the United States and Japan on several measures. The euro area's GDP is comparable to that of the United States, its population larger,

Table 3.4   Currency shares in foreign exchange market transactions

Country	Total[a]	Currency shares (percent)[b]				
		US dollar	Euro	Yen	Pound sterling	Other[c]
China	9.3	98.5	0.7	0.7	1.1	98.9
Hong Kong	174.6	96.1	12.8	10.4	7.4	73.2
Indonesia	2.8	93.0	11.2	8.3	2.6	84.9
Japan	238.4	84.6	18.3	71.1	6.9	19.1
Korea	33.4	92.0	6.1	11.6	4.4	85.9
Malaysia	3.4	97.1	5.9	7.0	4.9	85.1
Philippines	2.3	99.2	2.3	2.3	1.9	94.4
Singapore	230.6	88.3	27.2	25.1	13.2	46.3
Taiwan	14.6	94.6	14.5	23.7	7.5	59.6
Thailand	6.2	94.4	8.8	15.2	2.2	79.3
East Asia	715.6	89.5	18.7	35.6	8.8	47.4
Australia	169.5	91.3	17.5	10.7	7.7	72.8
India	34.1	95.8	9.3	27.7	9.7	57.5
New Zealand	12.3	94.2	10.4	4.6	3.7	87.3
East, South Asia, and Oceania	931.4	90.1	18.0	30.3	8.6	52.9
World total	3,988.1	86.8	36.8	17.0	14.4	44.9

a. Daily averages, in billions of US dollars.
b. Because two currencies are involved in each transaction, the sum of shares comes to 200 percent.
c. Includes all other participating countries' currencies, the major ones being the Swiss franc, Canadian dollar, Australian dollar, and Swedish krona.

Note: These data aggregate spot, outright forward, and foreign exchange swap transactions and adjust for local interdealer double counting (i.e., "net gross" basis).

Source: Bank for International Settlements, *Triennial Central Bank Survey 2007*.

and per capita income over 80 percent that of the United States. The size of euro area imports is comparable to that of US imports, and euro area exports are much larger than US exports. Among these measures, the euro area is substantially smaller than the United States only in the size of its capital markets.

The smaller share of the euro in East Asian trade and finance is consistent with Europe's share in East Asia's exports, however. Figure 3.2 shows that the euro area is the destination of about 12 percent of the exports of the ASEAN+3 region and the European Union as a whole is the destination of about 15 percent. The dollar's share greatly exceeds the US share in the region's exports, about 17 percent, which has declined from 32 percent in 1986. The reversal of the relative status of Japan and China—with Japan falling from 28 to 8 percent and China rising from 5 to 31 percent between the early 1980s and 2007—is the most striking message of this figure.

Figure 3.1 Share of the euro in the stock of outstanding international debt securities in selected regions, 2007Q4

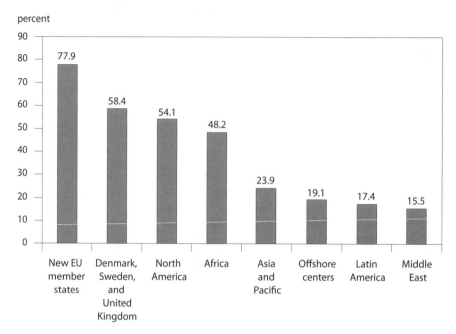

percent

Note: Narrow measure (i.e., excluding home-currency issuance) as a percent of the total amount outstanding.

Source: ECB (2008).

Asian Regionalism

Since the Asian financial crisis of 1997–98, the members of ASEAN+3 have pursued a number of initiatives to strengthen regional cooperation in international finance (see, for example, Henning 2002, Eichengreen 2002, Bergsten and Park 2002, de Brouwer 2004, Kuroda and Kawai 2004, Rajan and Sirigar 2004, Amyx 2005, and Grimes 2006). These have included the Chiang Mai Initiative (CMI), regional bond funds, bond market initiatives, and, most recently, discussion of the collectivization of the bilateral swap arrangements of the CMI. Sustained use of the dollar stands in marked contrast to the discourse within East Asia on regionalism and the desirability of "self-help mechanisms" to reduce reliance on the IMF and, by extension, the United States and Europe. Nonetheless, by providing a common point of reference for soft pegs and managed floats, the dollar helped to facilitate regional cooperation. Consider the role of the dollar and the relative absence of the euro in these regional projects.

Under the CMI, East Asian governments have concluded about

Table 3.5   Currency shares in Asian trade invoicing

Country	Exports					Imports				
	Euro	Dollar	Yen	Pound	Other	Euro	Dollar	Yen	Pound	Other
Australia, 2007	1.0	74.3	0.5	0.7	23.5[a]	8.1	52.0	1.9	1.4	36.6[a]
Indonesia, 2007	1.8	93.2	1.5	0.1	3.3	4.3	83.6	4.1	0.2	7.7
Japan, 2007	8.9	55.0	34.0	0.1	1.3	5.6	65.7	27.6	0.1	1.1
Thailand, 2007	3.5	80.7	6.2	0.5	9.1[b]	—	—	—	—	—
India, 1999	7.1	85.0	—	—	7.9[c]	8.1	84.0	—	—	7.9[c]
Korea, 2003	7.6	84.6	5.3	0.9	1.6	6.1	78.3	14.0	0.6	1.0
Malaysia, 1996[d]	4.9[e]	66.0	6.8	1.0	21.3[f]	—	—	—	—	—

— = no data provided

a. Includes Australian dollar (22.2 and 33.9 percent for exports and imports, respectively).
b. Includes Thai baht (6.7 percent).
c. Calculated as residual above the shares for euro and dollar.
d. Data refer to total trade, without the breakdown for exports and imports.
e. Share for euro is obtained by adding the share for Deutsche mark and approximated shares of other euro legacy currencies.
f. Includes Malaysian ringgit and Singapore dollar (17.8 and 3.5 percent, respectively).

Sources: Bank of Indonesia; Ministry of Finance, Japan; Bank of Korea; Australian Bureau of Statistics; Reserve Bank of India; Bank of Thailand.

Table 3.6   Comparison of Europe, United States, and Japan, 2007

Measure	EU-27	Euro area	United States	Japan
Population (millions)	495	320	302	128
GDP (billions of dollars)[a]	16,830	12,158	13,844	4,384
GDP per capita (thousands of dollars)[a]	34.0	38.2	45.8	34.3
Exports of goods and services (billions of dollars)[b]	1,750	2,064	1,163	714
Imports of goods and services (billions of dollars)[b]	1,966	2,024	2,017	622
International reserves minus gold (billions of dollars)	534	216	60	953
Stock market valuation (trillions of dollars)[c]	13.1	8.4	19.6	4.8
Bond market valuation (trillions of dollars)[c]	23.2	18.8	27.1	8.7
Bank assets (trillions of dollars)[c]	37.7	26.7	10.2	6.6

a. GDP and GDP per capita data for EU-27 and euro area converted into dollars at a rate of $1.37 per euro (average for 2007).
b. Export and import data for EU-27 and euro area exclude intragroup trade.
c. Data are for 2006.

Sources: International Monetary Fund, *International Financial Statistics* (September 2008), *Global Financial Stability Report* (April 2008), *World Economic Outlook* (April 2008), and *Direction of Trade Statistics* (August 2008); European Commission, Eurostat Database.

Figure 3.2   Destination of East Asian exports, 1980–2007

percent of total ASEAN+3 exports

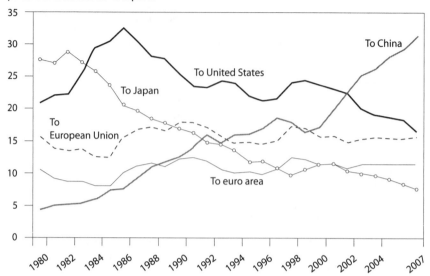

ASEAN+3 = members of the Association of Southeast Asian Nations plus China, Japan, and Korea

Source: International Monetary Fund, *Direction of Trade Statistics,* August 2008.

17 bilateral swap agreements, which are in various states of expiration, renegotiation, and renewal at any one time. Although ASEAN+3 officials sometimes advertise the total size to be $80 billion, eliminating double counting brings this figure closer to $55 billion. Thirteen of these are swaps of local currency for US dollars; four are swaps of two local currencies (see also Katada 2008). The US dollar is the only non-Asian currency that is involved. As this paper was finalized, East Asian governments were discussing transforming the CMI from a network of bilateral swap agreements into a collectively managed pool of reserves. If they decide to effectively pool a portion of their reserves in this way, East Asian governments will face decisions on, among other things, the amount of reserves to place under collective management and which currencies to pool. Given the prominence of the dollar in their foreign exchange reserve holdings, exchange rate regimes, trade, and external debt, it would be surprising if the dollar were not their main choice of currency to pool.

The bond market initiatives were launched with the intention of capturing the financial intermediation that is being done in London and New York and of possibly creating a pan-Asian bond market. The accomplishments of these initiatives are patchy, but if they are more successful in the future, these projects will more likely foster the use of currencies from within the region than use of the euro. Former Thai prime minister Thaksin Shinawatra's October 2008 proposal in the *Financial Times* to create an Asian bond, while obscure on some crucial details, appears to be a case in point (Thaksin 2008). The regional bond funds are small but intended to catalyze the creation of the legal and institutional infrastructure for bond markets. As with the bond market initiatives, the bond funds are more likely to promote local currencies than outside currencies as alternatives to the dollar as the denominator of Asian bonds.

There are, of course, several proposals for common currencies in East Asia or a subgroup within the region. Among the more thoughtful is Peter Kenen and Ellen Meade's analysis of proposals for a common currency for ASEAN (Kenen and Meade 2008, 147–78; see also Choo and Wang 2002 and Chung and Eichengreen 2007). They argue that a monetary union among the original six ASEAN members would probably be more sustainable than one that included China and/or Japan, provided that it were open to membership on the part of the other ASEAN members, Taiwan, and perhaps Korea, Australia, and New Zealand. To make a common currency viable, such a grouping would have to not only continue to liberalize trade but also unify its members' financial markets and strengthen supranational political institutions. Kenen and Meade anticipate that strengthening regional institutions will be the more difficult and lengthy of these two hurdles. In the meantime, the region might consider the proposals for common currency baskets, discussed above, in which the euro could be represented. But consideration of the more modest alternatives also includes discussion of an Asian Currency Unit (ACU) to serve as the numeraire of an "Asian monetary system" or as a parallel currency (see, for example, Kawai 2007 and Eichengreen 2007).

All this is not to suggest that various regional projects will necessarily come to fruition. Rather, it is to say that, when Asians consider reducing dependence on the United States and the dollar, their first preference is to consider alternative currencies within the region, either existing or new, rather than outside currencies such as the euro. The widespread expectation that Europe's share of world GDP will decline in the coming decades, followed a little more gradually by the United States (Wilson and Purushothaman 2003), will reinforce the temptation of officials and private actors in Asia to *bypass* the euro should they pursue any long-run shift away from the dollar. Of course, the problem in Asia is that the attractiveness of the Japanese yen has diminished and the Chinese renminbi is not yet suitable, for a host of reasons, and not likely to be so for a decade or two (see, respectively, Katada 2008 and Bowles and Wang 2008).

Conclusion

This paper surveys the respective roles of the euro and dollar in East Asia, finding that the dollar continues to play a strong role in the region and that the challenge presented by the euro remains moderate. The dollar pessimist view cannot be dismissed, but the evidence to date is more consistent with dollar optimism. To the extent that East Asian monetary authorities and private markets wish to shift away from the dollar, they are more interested in using local currencies or new regional currencies than in using the euro more heavily. The prospects for the euro and the dollar hinge on the existence and proximity of a "tipping point." Those wishing to increase the euro's role as an international currency will want such a point to come soon rather than after the emergence of other currencies as alternatives to the dollar.

Could the present financial crisis prove to be such a historic moment of opportunity for the euro? As this paper was completed, the financial crisis that began in mid-2007 precipitated a deep recession in the advanced economies and substantially reduced the growth outlook for emerging markets. This crisis and the response to it could well profoundly change economies and government institutions but in ways that were difficult to foresee at that juncture. As of the second half of 2008, though, the crisis did not seem to be providing an advantage to the euro in its competition against the dollar. Although the crisis had originated in the US subprime mortgage market, and the George W. Bush administration's response had been reactive and changing, it had not become a balance-of-payments crisis for the United States. To the contrary, investors around the globe sought safe haven in US Treasury securities and the exchange value of the dollar surged after July 2008. Foreign monetary authorities and financial institutions sought dollar liquidity, opening swap lines with the US Federal Reserve System. East Asia, along with much of the rest of the world, appeared to be embracing rather than rejecting the dollar at that juncture.

The 2007–09 crisis afflicted Europe as well as the United States, of course. European efforts to rescue failing banks contained damage to the financial system, but financial regulation remained fragmented in the European Union and the fiscal response of the member states remained at best loosely coordinated. On the whole, therefore, the European response to the crisis did not appear substantially more decisive, proactive, or strategic than the US response. The crisis made euro area membership more attractive to several EU member states that were not yet part of the monetary union. If the economic size of the euro area grows with its membership in coming years, the euro could become generally more attractive. But this might simply offset the effects of the expected decline in the relative size of the European economy, incomplete integration of its financial markets, and fragmented governance of the euro area (Ahearne and Eichengreen 2007, Coeuré and Pisani-Ferry 2007).

If the 2007–09 crisis does not give a decisive boost to the euro, what other scenarios might create a "rosy future" for the international role of the European currency and how probable might they be? One possibility would be the revival of the European economy, an increase in its potential growth rate through structural reform and full integration of the European financial and capital markets. Another possibility would be a sustained rise in inflation in the United States, undermining the dollar's roles as a nominal anchor and a reliable store of private wealth. These scenarios are not impossible, but they do not appear to be more likely in the face of the recession beginning in 2008.

The scenario that offers the best chance for the euro probably rests on the historically low rate of private savings in the United States, large fiscal deficits, continued current account deficits, accumulation of external debt, and a trend depreciation of the dollar. If unchecked, this pattern could eventually reach a tipping point. However, the crisis will probably raise US private savings during the recession and might be just the sort of transformative event that changes saving behavior over the long term as well. If US private savings were to increase permanently and the federal government were to solve the long-term fiscal problem posed by entitlement spending, the tipping point could be averted or postponed until after currencies within Asia emerge as alternatives to both the dollar and the euro.

References

Ahearne, Alan, and Barry Eichengreen. 2007. External Monetary and Financial Policy: A Review and a Proposal. In *Fragmented Power: Europe and the Global Economy*, ed. André Sapir. Brussels: Bruegel.

Amyx, Jennifer. 2005. What Motivates Regional Financial Cooperation in East Asia Today? *Asia Pacific Issues* 76. Honolulu: East-West Center.

Bergsten, C. Fred, and Yung Chul Park. 2002. *Toward Creating a Regional Monetary Arrangement in East Asia*. Research Paper 50. Tokyo: ADB Institute.

Bowles, Paul, and Baotai Wang. 2008. The Rocky Road Ahead: China, the US and the Future of the Dollar. *Review of International Political Economy* 15, no. 3 (August): 335–53.

Chinn, Menzie, and Jeffrey Frankel. 2008. Why the Euro Will Rival the Dollar. *International Finance* 11, no. 1: 49–73.

Choo, Han Gwang, and Yunjong Wang, eds. 2002. *Currency Union in East Asia*. Seoul: Korean Institute for International Economic Policy.

Chung, Duck-Koo, and Barry Eichengreen, eds. 2007. *Toward an East Asian Exchange Rate Regime*. Washington: Brookings Institution Press.

Coeuré, Benoît, and Jean Pisani-Ferry. 2007. The Governance of the European Union's International Economic Relations: How Many Voices? In *Fragmented Power: Europe and the Global Economy*, ed. André Sapir. Brussels: Bruegel.

Cohen, Benjamin J. Forthcoming. Toward a Leaderless Currency System. In *Whither the Key Currency? American Policy and the Global Role of the Dollar in the 21st Century*, ed. Eric Helleiner and Jonathan Kirshner.

Cohen, Benjamin J., and Paola Subacchi. 2008. "A One-and-a-Half Currency System," *Journal of International Affairs* 62, no. 1: 151–64.

de Brouwer, Gordon. 2002. Does a Formal Common-Basket Peg in East Asia Make Economic Sense? In *Financial Markets and Policies in East Asia*, ed. Gordon de Brouwer. London: Routledge.

de Brouwer, Gordon. 2004. Institutions to Promote Financial Stability: Reflections on East Asia and an Asian Monetary Fund. Available at www.weforum.org.

Dooley, Michael P., David Folkerts-Landau, and Peter Garber. 2003. *An Essay on the Revived Bretton Woods System*. NBER Working Paper 9971 (September). Cambridge, MA: National Bureau of Economic Research.

ECB (European Central Bank). 2008. *The International Role of the Euro* (July). Frankfurt.

Eichengreen, Barry. 2002. What to Do with the Chiang Mai Initiative. *Asian Economic Papers* 2: 1–52.

Eichengreen, Barry. 2006. *Global Imbalances and the Lessons of Bretton Woods*. Cambridge, MA: MIT Press.

Eichengreen, Barry. 2007. Parallel Process? Monetary Integration in Europe and Asia. In *Toward an East Asian Exchange Rate Regime*, ed. Duck-Koo Chung and Barry Eichengreen. Washington: Brookings Institution Press.

Frankel, Jeffrey, and Shang-Jin Wei. 1994. Yen Bloc or Dollar Bloc? Exchange Rate Policies of the East Asian Economies. In *Macroeconomic Linkages: Savings, Exchange Rates and Capital Flows*, ed. Takatoshi Ito and Anne O. Krueger. Chicago, IL: University of Chicago Press.

Frankel, Jeffrey, and Shang-Jin Wei. 2007. Assessing China's Exchange Rate Regime. *Economic Policy* 51 (July): 575–614.

Grimes, William W. 2006. East Asian Financial Regionalism in Support of the Global Financial Architecture? The Political Economy of Regional Nesting. *Journal of East Asian Studies*, no. 6: 353–80.

Henning, C. Randall. 1997. *Cooperating with Europe's Monetary Union*. Policy Analyses in International Economics 49. Washington: Institute for International Economics.

Henning, C. Randall. 2000. U.S.-EU Relations after the Inception of the Monetary Union: Cooperation or Rivalry? In *Transatlantic Perspectives on the Euro*, ed. C. Randall Henning and Pier Carlo Padoan. Washington: Brookings Institution and European Community Studies Association.

Henning, C. Randall. 2002. *East Asian Financial Cooperation*. Policy Analyses in International Economics 68. Washington: Institute for International Economics.

Henning, C. Randall. 2007a. Democratic Accountability and the Exchange Rate Policy of the Euro Area. *Review of International Political Economy* 14, no. 5 (December): 774–99.

Henning, C. Randall. 2007b. Organizing Foreign Exchange Intervention in the Euro Area. *Journal of Common Market Studies* 45, no. 2 (June): 315–42.

Katada, Saori N. 2008. From a Supporter to a Challenger? Japan's Currency Leadership in Dollar-Dominated East Asia. *Review of Political Economy* 15, no. 3 (August): 399–417.

Kawai, Masahiro. 2004. The Case for a Tri-Polar Currency Basket for Emerging East Asia. In *Economic Linkages and Implications for Exchange Rate Regimes in East Asia*, ed. Gordon de Brouwer and Masahiro Kawai. London: Routledge.

Kawai, Masahiro. 2007. Dollar, Yen, or Renminbi Bloc? In *Toward an East Asian Exchange Rate Regime*, ed. Duck-Koo Chung and Barry Eichengreen. Washington: Brookings Institution Press.

Kenen, Peter B., and Ellen E. Meade. 2008. *Regional Monetary Integration*. New York: Cambridge University Press.

Kuroda, Haruhiko, and Masahiro Kawai. 2004. Strengthening Regional Financial Cooperation in East Asia. In *Financial Governance in East Asia: Policy Dialogue, Surveillance and Cooperation*, ed. Gordon de Brouwer and Yunjong Wang. London: Routledge.

Lane, Philip R., and Gian Maria Milesi-Ferretti. 2007. The External Wealth of Nations Mark II: Revised and Extended Estimates of Foreign Assets and Liabilities, 1970–2004. *Journal of International Economics* 73, no. 2 (November): 223–50.

McKinnon, Ronald I. 2006. *Exchange Rates under the East Asian Dollar Standard: Living with Conflicted Virtue*. Cambridge, MA: MIT Press.

McKinnon, Ronald I., and Günther Schnabl. 2006. The East Asian Dollar Standard, Fear of Floating, and Original Sin. In *Exchange Rates under the East Asian Dollar Standard: Living with Conflicted Virtue*, ed. Roland I. McKinnon. Cambridge, MA: MIT Press.

Ogawa, Eiji, and Takatoshi Ito. 2002. On the Desirability of a Regional Currency Basket Arrangement. *Journal of Japanese and International Economies* 16: 317–34.

Posen, Adam. 2005. *The Euro at Five: Ready for a Global Role?* Special Report 18. Washington: Institute for International Economics.

Rajan, Ramkishen, and Reza Sirigar. 2004. Centralized Reserve Pooling for the ASEAN+3 Countries. In *Monetary and Financial Integration in East Asia: The Way Ahead* 2. Asian Development Bank. Basingstoke: Palgrave.

Rajan, Ramkishen. 2002. Exchange Rate Policy Options for Southeast Asia: Is There a Case for Currency Baskets? *The World Economy* 25: 137–63.

Reinhart, Carmen, and Kenneth Rogoff. 2004. The Modern History of Exchange Rate Arrangements: A Reinterpretation. *Quarterly Journal of Economics* 119, no. 1: 1–48.

Reinhart, Carmen, Ethan O. Ilzetzki, and Kenneth S. Rogoff. 2008. Exchange Rate Arrangements Entering the 21st Century: Which Anchor Will Hold? Photocopy.

Thaksin, Shinawatra. 2008. "How an Asian Bond Could Save Us from the Weak Dollar," *Financial Times*, October 7, 11.

Truman, Edwin M., and Anna Wong. 2006. *The Case for an International Reserve Diversification Standard*. Working Paper 06-2. Washington: Institute for International Economics.

US Senate, Committee on the Budget. 1997. *Europe's Monetary Union and Its Potential Impact on the United States Economy*. 105th Congress, 1st Session. Washington: GPO.

Williamson, John. 1999. The Case for a Common Basket Peg for East Asian Currencies. In *Exchange Rate Policies for Emerging Asian Countries*, ed. Stefan Collignon, Jean Pisani-Ferry, and Yung Chul Park. London: Routledge.

Williamson, John. 2005. *A Currency Basket for East Asia, Not Just China*. Policy Briefs in International Economics 05-1. Washington: Institute for International Economics.

Wilson, Dominic, and Roopa Purushothaman. 2003. *Dreaming with BRICs: The Path to 2050*. Global Economics Paper 99 (October). New York: Goldman Sachs.

Euro Area Neighboring Countries

GYÖRGY SZAPÁRY

This paper assesses the rising role of the euro in euro area neighboring countries: the Central and Eastern European countries that joined the European Union in 2004 (new member states, or NMS),[4] the Southeastern European countries,[5] Russia, and Ukraine. The international role of the euro has been analyzed and discussed extensively in the academic literature and is also the subject of an annual review by the European Central Bank (ECB). Ewe-Ghee Lim (2006) reviews the relevant literature and discusses the factors that facilitate international currency status, such as the issuing country's large economic size, its well-developed financial system, its political stability, confidence in its currency as a store of value, and network externalities.

While the euro has clearly overtaken the European legacy currencies as a reserve currency, at the *global* level the shares of the dollar and the euro in international reserves have stabilized since 2003 at roughly 64 and 27 percent, respectively. It is difficult to judge whether this is some sort of equilibrium diversification, since confidence and perceptions can change. The ECB itself maintains a neutral position with regard to the role of the euro as an international currency: It will neither seek to promote that role

György Szapáry is a visiting professor at the Central European University, Budapest, a member of the Board of Directors of OTP Bank Hungary, and former deputy governor of the National Bank of Hungary. He is grateful for assistance and comments from Zsolt Darvas, Gergely Tardos, and former colleagues at the National Bank of Hungary.

4. Bulgaria, Cyprus, the Czech Republic, Estonia, Hungary, Latvia, Lithuania, Malta, Poland, Romania, Slovakia, and Slovenia.

5. Albania, Bosnia and Herzegovina, Croatia, Macedonia, Kosovo, Montenegro, and Serbia.

nor do anything to counteract it (Issing 2008). History teaches us that there is a natural tendency to keep the incumbent global reserve currency as the vehicle, hence for a newcomer to seriously challenge that role is a slow process at best.

At the *regional* level, the situation is quite different from that at the global level. If the economies of countries neighboring a large single-currency area—such as the euro area—are strongly integrated with the member countries forming that area, there are powerful incentives for the countries on the periphery to use the single currency as vehicle and nominal anchor. Since the euro area plays a dominant role in the trade, capital flows, labor movements, and financial systems of the NMS (Darvas and Szapáry 2008), the role of the euro as a vehicle has naturally significantly increased in the NMS. In the Southeastern European countries, similar trends have prevailed, but the economic ties of Russia and Ukraine with the euro area are not as strong.

The rising role of the euro in the region can be assessed by looking at exchange rate arrangements (pegging relationships and the anchoring role of the euro for floaters); currency composition of foreign exchange reserves; and the euro's use in bank lending and deposits, in settling and invoicing foreign trade, and in domestic contracts. The following sections review each of these elements of the use of the euro.

Exchange Rate Arrangements

Pegging Relationships

An increasing number of countries have pegged their exchange rate to the euro over time. Figure 3.3 shows the evolution of the exchange rate regimes in the euro area neighboring countries. Four of the 12 NMS—Cyprus, Malta, Slovakia, and Slovenia—have already joined the euro area. Three countries peg their currencies to the euro under currency board arrangements—Bulgaria, Estonia, and Lithuania—while Latvia maintains a conventional peg to the euro. Among non-EU members, Croatia and Macedonia peg their currencies de facto to the euro under managed floating, Bosnia-Herzegovina pegs its currency to the euro under a currency board arrangement, while Montenegro has unilaterally adopted the euro as its currency and so has Kosovo. (Macedonia and Kosovo are not shown in figure 3.3.)

Thus, all the countries in Southeastern Europe except the floaters Albania and Serbia have either adopted the euro as their domestic currency or pegged their currencies to the euro. This is evidence of the role of the euro as a nominal anchor in the euro area neighboring countries that are currently not members of the European Union but are potential candidates.

Figure 3.3 Exchange rate arrangements in the euro area neighboring countries, 1996–2008

Country	1996	1997	1998	1999	2000	2001	2002	2003	2004	2005	2006	2007	2008
Bulgaria	Floating	Currency board, Deutsche mark	Currency board, Deutsche mark	Currency board, euro									
Cyprus	Peg to ECU +/– 2.25%			Peg to euro				Peg to euro, +/– 15%				ERM2, +/– 15%	Euro
Czech Republic	Peg, 65% Deutsche mark and 35% US dollar	Floating											
Hungary	Crawling peg, +/– 2.25%, 30% US dollar (70% ECU / 70% Deutsche mark)			Crawling peg, euro +/– 2.25% (70% euro)			Peg to euro, +/– 15%						Floating
Estonia	Currency board, 8 EEK = 1 Deutsche mark								ERM2, currency board				
Latvia	Peg to special drawing rights, +/–1%								Peg to euro	ERM2, +/–1%			
Lithuania	Currency board to US dollar						Currency board to euro			ERM2, currency board			
Malta	Peg (US dollar, euro, pound sterling)								Peg to euro	ERM2, pegged			Euro
Poland	Crawling peg (US dollar, Deutsche mark, pound sterling, French franc, Swiss franc) (55% euro and 45% US dollar)				Floating								
Romania						Floating							
Slovakia	Managed floating									ERM2 narrow band	ERM2, +/–15%		Euro
Slovenia	Managed floating									Euroization			
Albania	Floating (since July 1992)												
Bosnia and Herzegovina	Currency board, 1 KM = 1 Deutsche mark						Currency board, 1 KM = 0.51113 euro						
Croatia	Managed floating						Managed floating, de facto peg to euro						
Montenegro	Peg to Deutsche mark						Euroization						
Serbia	Peg to Deutsche mark				Managed floating								
Russia	Peg to US dollar				Managed float (de facto peg to US dollar)					Managed float against a basket of US dollar and euro			
Ukraine	Peg or de facto peg to US dollar												Floating

Legend:
- Pegged to euro
- Pegged to US dollar
- Floating
- ERM2 member
- Pegged to the Deutsche mark or a basket of currencies
- Euro legal tender, through either euro area membership or unilateral euroization

ECU = European Currency Unit
ERM2 = Exchange Rate Mechanism
EEK = Estonian kroon
KM = convertible mark

Note: Slovakia adopted the euro on January 1, 2009.

Source: International Monetary Fund, www.imf.org.

The Anchoring Role of the Euro for Floaters

The euro's rise as nominal anchor is also evident among the floaters. Figure 3.4 shows the minimum variance basket for domestic currencies, where an increase in the value indicates an increase of the weight of the euro in the minimum variance basket and hence a greater stability vis-à-vis the euro than against the dollar. Among the EU-member inflation targeters (figure 3.4, panel A), the weight of the euro has significantly increased in all countries. In most countries, it has taken place more or less continuously since 1995. In Poland, however, it has substantially increased only with some lag after the removal in 2000 of the exchange rate band within the framework of inflation targeting. It seems that this action was needed to change the markets' perceptions about the behavior of the zloty's exchange rate, which had been mostly perceived as anchored to the dollar. In Romania, too, the share of the euro in the minimum variance basket of the lei's exchange rate suddenly increased only in 2003. This occurred under managed floating and continued following the adoption of inflation targeting in 2005. In the non-EU members, a similar development occurred in Albania, a floater, and in Serbia after abandonment of the exchange rate peg to the Deutsche mark and the introduction of the managed floating system in 2001 (figure 3.4, panel B).

The Russian ruble was de facto pegged to the US dollar until 2005, but since then it has been managed against a basket of currencies composed of the dollar and the euro. Hence the weight of the euro in the minimum variance basket has increased (panel B). Among the countries considered, only the Ukrainian hryvnia has been pegged to the dollar, but following the recent financial crisis, the hryvnia depreciated by about 90 percent by mid-December 2008.

Implications of the Choice of Exchange Rate Regime

The above review of exchange rate arrangements and developments clearly points to the increasing role of the euro as nominal anchor not only in the EU member countries but also among the non-EU countries in the region. Among the euro peggers and managed floaters, this is a deliberate choice by the authorities, which reflects a recognition of the close economic ties with the euro area economy and hence a desire to use the euro as a stabilizing nominal anchor. In the case of floaters, the greater stability of their currencies against the euro is the result of market forces and reflects the high degree of trade and financial integration with the euro area and the associated perceptions. These perceptions are anchored by the fact that the interest rate reactions of these countries' monetary authorities are influenced and tend to be guided by the steps taken by the ECB, a natural behavior given the close financial integration. Euro adoption expectations also strengthen these market perceptions.

Figure 3.4   Minimum variance baskets, 1995–2008

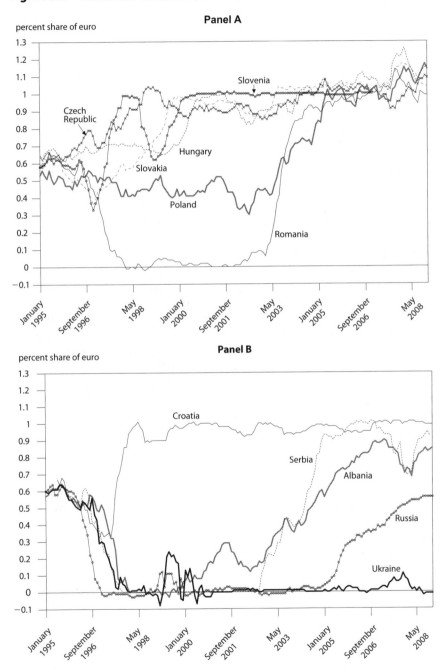

Panel A

percent share of euro

Czech Republic

Slovenia

Hungary

Slovakia

Poland

Romania

Panel B

percent share of euro

Croatia

Serbia

Albania

Russia

Ukraine

Note: Values shown correspond to the weight of the euro in the minimum variance portfolio, where the portfolio consists of the logarithmic exchange rate changes against the euro and the dollar. For every month shown, weights were calculated using daily data from the most recent year; outliers were removed from the data before the calculations.

Source: Author's calculations using data from Datastream.

At this point the full impact of the current global financial crisis on the economies of the euro area neighboring countries is not yet known. It might well bring changes in the exchange rate arrangements of some countries, but such changes would not diminish the anchoring role of the euro, since the fundamentals underpinning that role—i.e., the trade and financial integration with the euro area—will not change. The expected timing of euro adoption might be altered: delayed in some countries, expedited in others. However, joining the euro area is not only the stated goal of the countries' authorities but also an obligation under the EU Treaty. Therefore, euro adoption expectations will continue to guide market perceptions in the medium to long run.

The choice of exchange rate regime has implications for the likely inflation performance and indebtedness in foreign currency. With a fixed exchange rate, the price level convergence associated with the catching-up process can take place only via higher inflation, while in the floaters, it can also take place via nominal appreciation of the exchange rate. In the fixers, therefore, inflation will tend to be high, and while borrowing in euros is encouraged because of the low perceived exchange rate risks, real interest rates become very low or negative, leading to rapid growth of credit and to large current account deficits and indebtedness in foreign currency. This has occurred in the Baltic States and Bulgaria. In the floaters, there is the possibility of letting the nominal exchange rate appreciate, which can help to keep down the inflation rate and domestic interest rate, thereby reducing the likelihood of large borrowing in foreign currency. This has been the experience in the Czech Republic and Slovakia.[6] The risks for the banking systems associated with the large share of foreign-currency borrowings in some of the euro area neighboring countries in the wake of the current global financial crisis are discussed below.

Currency Composition of Foreign Exchange Reserves

Most central banks consider the currency composition of foreign exchange reserves as confidential data, so published data for individual countries are scant. Using information from the International Monetary Fund's database on the currency composition of foreign exchange reserves (COFER) reported on a voluntary basis by some 115 countries, Lim (2006) publishes aggregate data for the currency composition of reserves for the "dollar area" and the "euro area." The latter is defined as "all the European countries immediately surrounding EMU and countries worldwide that largely peg to the euro." This, of course, does not include the euro area

---

6. Darvas and Szapáry (2008) provide a detailed analysis of the effects of price level convergence on inflation, interest rates, and credit growth under different exchange rate regimes in the catching-up economies of the new EU member states.

proper, where the euro is the domestic currency, but includes several African countries that peg their currencies to the euro.

Using Lim's data, figure 3.5 shows the share of euro in foreign exchange reserves for the dollar area and the "euro area" (as defined above) during the period 1999–2005. Two observations can be made about these data: first, that the share of euro reached close to 60 percent in the "euro area" in 2005, while it was only about 25 percent for all reporting countries; and second, that the share of euro had increased fairly rapidly during 1999–2002 (from about 40 percent) but stagnated between 2002 and 2005. While these data point to the increasing role of the euro in the larger set of "euro area" countries that these data refer to, the share of euro in the euro area neighboring countries that we are looking at is likely to be significantly higher than the 60 percent shown in the 2005 IMF data. This is confirmed by those few individual countries that publish data on the currency composition of their reserve holdings (figure 3.6). In Bulgaria and Lithuania, the share is over 90 percent, while in Croatia, Romania, and Slovakia, it is 70 to 85 percent.

The dominance of the euro in foreign exchange reserves in Central and Eastern Europe is a direct result of the euro's role as a nominal anchor, either through the existing pegging relationships or simply due to the financial integration with the euro area. This makes the euro the currency of choice for intervention by the monetary authorities. Countries generally also consider the currency composition of foreign debt when deciding on the composition of reserves. If a country holds a relatively high share of debt denominated in dollars, it will tend to hold a relatively high share of reserves in dollars. Table 3.7 shows the currency composition of external debt for a selected number of countries in the region that report such data. In Romania, for instance, only 68 percent of the external debt is denominated in euros, which may explain why it holds only about 70 percent of its reserves in euros, while in Lithuania, where 99 percent of the external debt is denominated in euros, close to 100 percent of its reserves are held in euros (figure 3.6). However, Lithuania has a currency board arrangement pegged to the euro, which is probably the stronger reason to hold a high proportion of reserves in euros, as is the case for Bulgaria, where only 67 percent of the external debt is denominated in euros but over 90 percent of reserves is held in euros.

Share of the Euro in Bank Loans and Deposits

A characteristic of the countries neighboring the euro area is the large share of foreign-currency loans in bank lending and, though to a lesser extent, the large share of foreign-currency deposits (figures 3.7a and 3.7b). The euro dominates foreign-currency loans and deposits, except in Hungary, where Swiss franc loans dominate, and Ukraine, where dollar

Figure 3.5   Share of euro in foreign exchange reserves, 1999–2005

percent

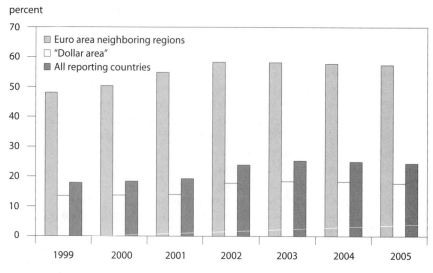

Source: Lim (2006).

Figure 3.6   Currency composition of foreign exchange reserves in selected countries, 2007

percent

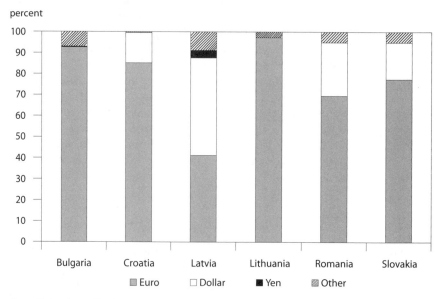

Source: National central banks.

Table 3.7   Currency composition of external debt in selected countries, 2003–07 (percent)

Country	2003	2004	2005	2006	2007
Bosnia					
Euro	18.7	21.4	22.5	25.5	28.2
US dollar	21.0	18.8	19.6	18.3	16.7
Special drawing rights	32.7	33.6	33.7	33.3	32.6
Other	27.6	26.2	24.2	22.9	22.5
Bulgaria					
Euro	37.0	44.4	55.7	63.1	67.3
US dollar	47.2	39.4	29.5	25.7	25.7
Other	15.8	16.3	14.8	11.2	7.0
Estonia					
Euro	100.0	100.0	100.0	100.0	100.0
US dollar	0.0	0.0	0.0	0.0	0.0
Special drawing rights	0.0	0.0	0.0	0.0	0.0
Other	0.0	0.0	0.0	0.0	0.0
Lithuania					
Euro	80.4	88.2	n.a.	n.a.	99.4
US dollar	13.3	6.7	n.a.	n.a.	0.0
Special drawing rights	0.0	0.0	n.a.	n.a.	0.0
Other	6.3	5.1	n.a.	n.a.	0.6
Romania					
Euro	53.7	54.4	54.8	61.7	68.4
US dollar	36.0	35.7	34.8	28.6	23.0
Special drawing rights	4.9	3.2	2.0	0.8	0.0
Other	5.4	6.7	8.4	9.0	8.6
Slovenia					
Euro	n.a.	n.a.	n.a.	n.a.	99.6
US dollar	n.a.	n.a.	n.a.	n.a.	0.4
Other	n.a.	n.a.	n.a.	n.a.	0.0

n.a. = not available

Sources: National central banks and ministries of finance.

loans prevail. In 2007 the share of foreign-currency loans was generally 50 percent or more of total outstanding loans and reached 80 percent or more in some countries operating currency boards where the perceived exchange rate risk had been low (Estonia and Lithuania). In countries with floating exchange rates, the shares were also high: 72 percent in Albania, 59 percent in Hungary, and 55 percent in Romania. In these countries, foreign-currency borrowing was encouraged by the positive spreads between the domestic and the relevant foreign interest rates. In the Czech Republic, where interest rate spreads are negative, the share was only 9 percent in 2007. Foreign-currency borrowings were facilitated by the

Figure 3.7a   Composition of bank loans, 2007

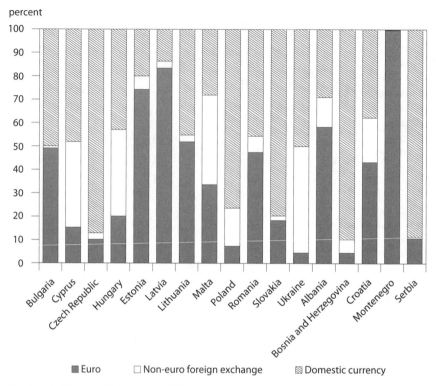

percent

Note: Data for Albania and Serbia are from 2006.

Source: European Central Bank.

dominant role of foreign-owned banks in Central and Eastern Europe. With the exception of Cyprus, Malta, and Slovenia, the share of foreign-owned banks in the total assets of the banking system ranges from 60 to 90 percent in the NMS (Darvas and Szapáry 2008, 33–34).

Lenders and borrowers underestimated the dangers in foreign exchange loans, as the risks had been masked by rapid real convergence in the countries under consideration and the expectation that this trend would continue uninterrupted, increasing the salaries toward euro area levels and keeping the exchange rates stable or on an appreciating trend. However, the high share of foreign-currency loans has exposed these countries to serious exchange rate risks when there is a sudden change in market conditions, as became evident during the current global financial crisis. Since mid-2008, the exchange rates of the currencies of Hungary, Poland, Romania, Russia, and Ukraine have depreciated considerably, in Ukraine by as much as 90 percent. The consequent increase in the bur-

Figure 3.7b   Composition of bank deposits, 2007

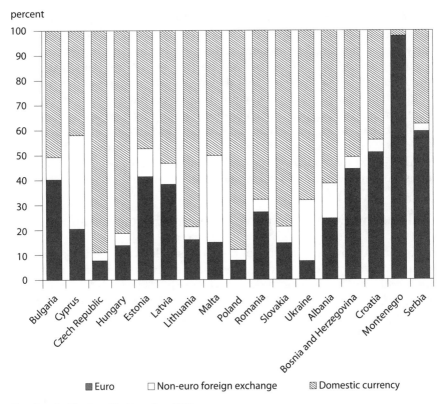

percent

Note: Data for Albania and Serbia are from 2006.

Source: European Central Bank.

den of debt servicing strains the payment capabilities of the borrowers, particularly of households. Combined with the sharp economic downturns in these countries, this situation is likely to lead to an increase in the volume of nonperforming loans and erode the banks' capital. In response, banks are cutting back on their lending, further exacerbating the economic downturn.

The bank bailout packages introduced in Western Europe and the United States help the mother banks to continue to finance their subsidiaries in Central and Eastern Europe, although many of them have reduced the flow of financing and have shortened the maturities. The IMF's standby credit arrangement for Hungary has two funds, one for recapitalizing banks and the other for providing liquidity to banks that wish to take advantage of these facilities. All these measures are useful, but the banking systems in several Central and Eastern European countries remain exposed to significant risks due to the high volume of foreign-currency obligations, and the situation needs to be monitored carefully.

A main lesson from this situation is that the authorities should take measures to slow down the growth of foreign-currency lending, particularly to the unhedged household sector. Many measures have been used around the world with more or less effectiveness (World Bank 2007). The problem with most of them is that they distort the markets and can be circumvented. The most effective would be a tax on interest payment on foreign-currency credit (possibly combined with higher reserve requirements on the banks' foreign currency liabilities), which would effectively raise the cost of borrowing in foreign currency and slow its growth. This can be reinforced by a mandatory maximum limit on the loan-to-value ratio for household mortgage loans, which has been growing especially fast.[7]

Role of the Euro in Settling/Invoicing Foreign Trade

Another way to assess the role of the euro is to look at the euro's share in settling/invoicing foreign trade. The share of the euro in trade invoicing and settlement has increased over the years (ECB 2008, 42–44), and as can be seen from figures 3.8a and 3.8b, it is higher than the share of exports to and imports from the euro area, which points to the importance of euro-denominated trade transactions with third countries.

Using data for 2000 and 2002, Linda S. Goldberg (2005) calculates an optimal invoicing choice for the EU accession countries (now new member states) based on the observation that invoicing practices depend largely on macroeconomic volatility (hedging) and on the vehicle currency in goods that are reference priced and traded on organized competitive markets (herding). She concludes that some of these countries might be pricing too much of their trade in euros rather than in dollars and thus might be taking on excessive risks in international markets. However, the pegging relationships and the increased role of the euro as a nominal anchor in these countries since the time to which her data refer provide compelling reasons for traders to invoice in euros, as the domestic currency will tend to be less volatile vis-à-vis the euro than the dollar, at least in normal times.

Role of the Euro in Domestic Contracts and Cash Holdings

A feature for which there is no readily available data is the use of the euro in domestic contracts in the euro area neighboring countries. It can be observed, however, that the euro is frequently used in contracts for

---

7. The shortcomings of the existing institutional architecture in Europe to deal with the current financial crisis are discussed in Darvas and Pisani-Ferry (2008).

Figure 3.8   Euro's share in settling/invoicing foreign trade, 2006

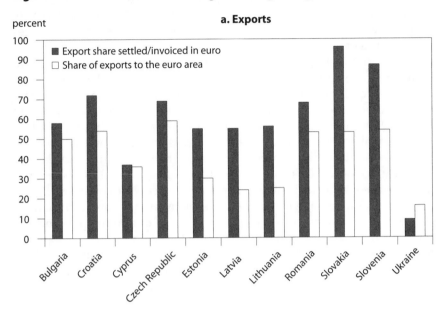

a. Exports

percent

- Export share settled/invoiced in euro
- Share of exports to the euro area

Bulgaria, Croatia, Cyprus, Czech Republic, Estonia, Latvia, Lithuania, Romania, Slovakia, Slovenia, Ukraine

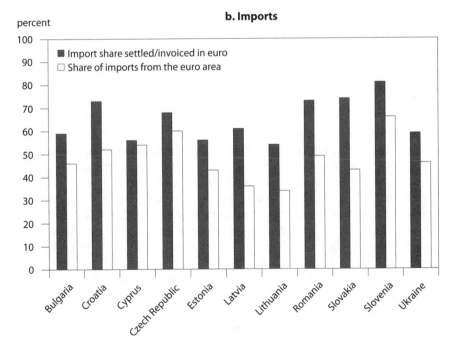

b. Imports

percent

- Import share settled/invoiced in euro
- Share of imports from the euro area

Bulgaria, Croatia, Cyprus, Czech Republic, Estonia, Latvia, Lithuania, Romania, Slovakia, Slovenia, Ukraine

Source: European Central Bank.

renting out office space and residential property, mostly when the renters are foreign companies or individuals. Hotel room rates are also typically tied to the euro in several countries. The motivation for such practices may be the same as for invoicing in euros for trade.

Euro cash holdings outside the euro area can be gauged by euro banknote trade figures. The ECB (2008, 51) estimates that Eastern Europe accounted for 37 percent of euro banknote purchases from and 24 percent of sales to countries outside the euro area in 2007. A survey commissioned by the Oesterreichische Nationalbank in 2007 revealed that the holding of euro banknotes varies considerably across countries and tends to be higher in Southeastern European countries than in Central and Eastern European countries. This may be a reaction to the high inflation experience of the former Yugoslavia and of some of its successor countries (Backé, Ritzberger-Grünwald, and Stix 2007). The relatively high euro cash holdings in the euro area neighboring countries are also due to the proximity of these countries to the euro area, which is the main business, shopping, and tourism destination for people traveling from these countries. There is also some evidence that high-denomination euro banknotes are used in these countries for large cash transactions in the informal economy.

The Global Financial Crisis and Prospects for Euro Area Enlargement

Before the current financial crisis, it looked like the greatest challenge for countries hoping to adopt the euro was to satisfy the Maastricht inflation criterion. In December 2008 only Slovakia met this criterion (table 3.8). Inflation was especially high, far exceeding the criterion, in the NMS with fixed exchange rates. While inflation is now abating in the NMS due to the sharp economic downturn, the pressures on the fiscal deficits and government debt due to the slowdown in growth and the rise in interest rates are rising. Furthermore, with the inflow of foreign portfolio investments that had previously kept the long-term interest rates low now drying up, some countries will also have difficulties in meeting the interest rate criterion. Indeed, among the non–euro area members, only the Czech Republic and Slovakia met the criterion for long-term interest rates in December 2008, while in July 2008, only Hungary and Romania had not met that criterion. With regard to the fiscal deficit, at least four countries will not meet the criterion, based on the EU Commission's January 2009 forecast. More countries might fail to meet the criterion by the end of 2009. It now looks like satisfying the criteria for fiscal deficit and long-term interest rate will be equally challenging and perhaps even more difficult than meeting the inflation criterion.

Recent events on global financial markets have convincingly demonstrated that membership in the euro area provides protection against

Table 3.8 Fulfillment of the Maastricht criteria in the new member states

Country	Harmonized indices of consumer prices, December 2008 (12-month average rate of change)	Country	Long-term government bond yields, December 2008	Country	General government surplus (+) or deficit (−), 2009[a]	Country	General government gross debt, 2009[a]
Average of three lowest EU members	2.6	Average of three lowest-inflation countries	3.57				
Reference value	4.1	Reference value	5.57	Reference value	−3.0	Reference value	60.0
Euro area	**3.3**	**Euro area**	**3.71**	Bulgaria	2.0	Estonia	6.1
Slovakia	3.9	Malta	4.17	Cyprus	−0.6	Bulgaria	12.2
Poland	4.2	Czech Republic	4.30	Czech Republic	−2.5	Lithuania	20.0
Cyprus	4.4	Slovenia	4.56	Malta	−2.6	Romania	21.1
Malta	4.7	Cyprus	4.60	Slovakia	−2.8	Slovenia	24.8
Slovenia	5.5	Slovakia	4.72	Hungary	−2.8	Czech Republic	29.4
Hungary	6.0	Poland	5.70	Lithuania	−3.0	Slovakia	30.0
Czech Republic	6.3	Bulgaria	7.76	Estonia	−3.2	Latvia	30.4
Romania	7.9	Hungary	8.31	Slovenia	−3.2	Cyprus	46.7
Estonia	10.6	Romania	8.38	Poland	−3.6	Poland	47.7
Lithuania	11.1	Lithuania	9.00	**Euro area**	**−4.0**	Malta	64.0
Bulgaria	12.0	Latvia	9.03	Latvia	−6.3	**Euro area**	**72.7**
Latvia	15.3	Estonia	n.a.	Romania	−7.5	Hungary	73.8

n.a. = not available

a. January 19, 2009 forecast of the European Commission, Directorate General for Economic and Financial Affairs (DG ECFIN).

Note: Grey indicates countries that did not meet criterion.

Source: European Commission, Eurostat Database.

exchange rate risks at times of financial crisis. As a result, the authorities of many NMS now want to accelerate the process of joining the euro area. Paradoxically, the challenges may now be more difficult than they were before the crisis. The unambiguous lesson to be drawn from this is that countries should make progress toward preparing for euro adoption and satisfying the Maastricht criteria in a sustainable manner during good times.

Conclusion

All indicators point to the very important role of the euro as a vehicle currency and nominal anchor in the euro area neighboring countries. At this regional level, the role of the euro far exceeds its role at the global level. This is true not only for the new EU member states but also for the non-EU member countries in Southeastern Europe. The driving forces behind this rising role are the close trade and financial integration of these countries with the euro area and the expectations that these countries will one day join the currency union, even if not all of them are members of the European Union yet. These considerations do not apply to Russia and Ukraine, although the former has included the euro next to the dollar in the currency basket against which it manages the exchange rate of the ruble.

The close integration with the euro area also presents challenges. The widespread borrowing in euros or other foreign currencies at low interest rates by domestic residents has led to rapid growth of credit, fueling inflation and leading to large current account deficits and exposure to foreign exchange risks in many countries of the region. The rapid depreciations of the currencies in a number of these countries in the wake of the global financial crisis has brought to the fore the dangers that this situation can present for the domestic financial systems. The authorities will have to pay more attention to this problem in the future and take effective actions to rein in foreign-currency lending. The current financial crisis is not expected to alter the anchoring role of the euro in these countries, because the fundamentals underpinning that role will not change.

References

Backé, Peter, Doris Ritzberger-Grünwald, and Helmut Stix. 2007. The Euro on the Road to East: Cash, Savings and Loans. *Monetary Policy and the Economy* Q1/107: 114–27. Vienna: Oesterreichische Nationalbank.

Darvas, Zsolt, and György Szapáry. 2008. Euro Area Enlargement and Euro Adoption Strategies. 2008. *European Economy, Economic Papers* 304 (February). Brussels: European Commission.

Darvas, Zsolt, and Jean Pisani-Ferry. 2008. *Avoiding a New European Divide*. Bruegel Policy Brief 2008/10 (December). Brussels: Bruegel.

ECB (European Central Bank). 2008. *The International Role of the Euro* (July). Frankfurt.

Goldberg, Linda S. 2005. Trade Invoicing in the Accession Countries: Are They Suited to the Euro? *Federal Reserve Bank of New York Staff Reports* 222 (October). New York: Federal Reserve Bank of New York.

Issing, Otmar. 2008. *The Birth of the Euro*. Cambridge: Cambridge University Press.

Lim, Ewe-Ghee. 2006. *The Euro's Challenge to the Dollar: Different Views from Economists and Evidence from COFER (Currency Composition of Foreign Exchange Reserves) and Other Data*. IMF Working Paper WP06/153 (June). Washington: International Monetary Fund.

Oesterreichische Nationalbank. 2007. *The Euro in Central, Eastern and Southeastern Europe*. Vienna, Austria.

World Bank. 2007. *Credit Expansion in Emerging Europe: A Cause for Concern?* Regular Economic Report, Part II: Special Topic (January). Washington.

Middle East and Oil Exporters

MOHSIN S. KHAN

The Middle East region is a US dollar zone. The euro's role remains very much secondary to that of the dollar in foreign trade, holdings of reserve assets, and exchange rate regimes. Indeed, on the trade side the role of the euro is now less than that of the pre-euro European currencies. At the same time, however, there is considerable discussion in the region about reducing the dominance of the dollar and increasing the relative importance of the euro.

This paper describes the euro's current role in the Middle East and North Africa (MENA) region[8] and in the Middle East oil exporters, specifically the Gulf Cooperation Council (GCC) countries.[9] I focus on three main areas: the direction of imports and exports; the growth in official reserve assets; and the exchange rate regime. The discussion on the MENA region essentially serves as a backdrop to a more detailed look at the GCC countries, which now represent more than one-half of MENA's GDP, over 60 percent of exports and over 50 percent of the region's imports. Over

Mohsin S. Khan has been a senior fellow at the Peterson Institute for International Economics since March 2009. Before joining the Institute, he was the director of the Middle East and Central Asia department at the International Monetary Fund from 2004 to 2008. He is grateful to Taline Koranchelian and Gene Leon for their suggestions and helpful inputs and to participants in the conference for their comments. The views expressed are the sole responsibility of the author.

8. MENA comprises Algeria, Bahrain, Djibouti, Egypt, Iran, Jordan, Kuwait, Lebanon, Libya, Mauritania, Morocco, Oman, Qatar, Saudi Arabia, Sudan, Syria, Tunisia, the United Arab Emirates, and Yemen.

9. The GCC countries are Bahrain, Kuwait, Oman, Qatar, Saudi Arabia, and the United Arab Emirates.

the last decade or so, the economic epicenter of the region has clearly shifted from Eastern Mediterranean countries to the GCC countries; what happens in the Persian Gulf countries has an important bearing on what happens in the region, and because they are major oil exporters and large financial investors, they also play a systemic role in the world economy.[10]

Since the debate on the dollar versus the euro has been most active in the GCC, any changes in favor of the euro will have been led by the choices made in these countries. In fact, with the GCC Monetary Union planned for 2010, the choice of an appropriate exchange rate regime for the single currency is going to be one of the most critical decisions for the GCC and the MENA region. As mentioned, the paper starts with the MENA region as a whole and then looks more closely at the GCC countries. The final section draws some conclusions about the future role of the US dollar and the euro.

Role of the Euro in MENA

Trade Patterns

Overall, US dollar transactions dominate MENA exports and imports. Although MENA exports to the United States represent only about 9 percent of total exports, less than half of the exports going to the European Union (figure 3.9), it is estimated that over 60 percent of exports are denominated in US dollars for two primary reasons. First, about 70 percent of MENA exports are oil, which is priced in dollars in international markets. And second, exports to Asia, which in 2007 represented 44 percent of MENA exports, are also largely denominated in US dollars. Interestingly, the share of exports going to Europe has been on the decline, falling from 26 percent in 2000 to 21 percent in 2007, while the share of exports to the United States has remained virtually constant. Even if oil exporters are excluded, the share of exports to Europe has fallen from 50 percent in 2000 to less than 40 percent in 2007.

On the import side, the role of Europe, and therefore the euro, is much greater. Imports from the European Union account for the largest share of MENA imports (33 percent), with Asia at 30 percent and the United States around 8 percent (figure 3.9). But here again, as with exports, the share of Europe in MENA imports has fallen from 39 percent in 2000 to 33 percent in 2007. This decline has been mostly offset by the increase in the share of imports from Asia, which rose from 22 percent in 2000 to 30 percent in 2007.

---

10. A useful description of the GCC by the European Central Bank is available in Sturm et al. (2008).

Figure 3.9   Direction of MENA trade, 2007 (percent)

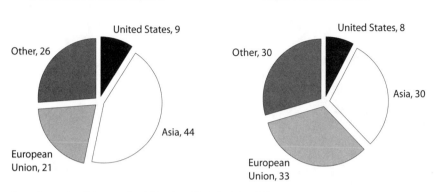

Source: International Monetary Fund, *Direction of Trade Statistics,* 2008.

Figure 3.10   MENA's gross official reserves, 1998–2007

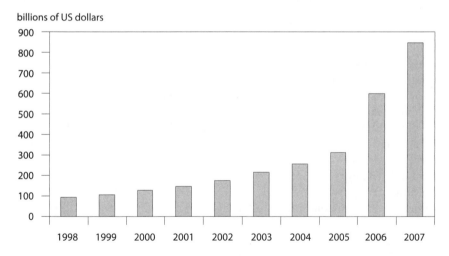

Source: International Monetary Fund, *International Financial Statistics,* 2008.

Official Reserve Assets

The large current account surpluses generated by oil-exporting countries have dramatically increased MENA's official international reserves. Gross official reserves of the region averaged about $180 billion during 2000–2004 and rose more than fourfold to $830 billion by 2007 (figure 3.10). Despite the sharp decline in world oil prices in the second half of 2008, gross in-

Figure 3.11   Exchange rate arrangements in MENA

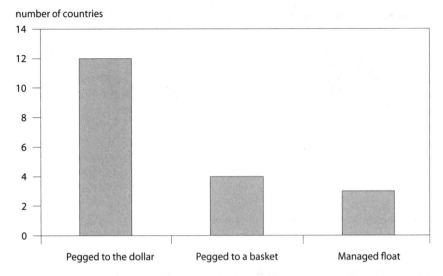

number of countries

Source: International Monetary Fund, *Classification of Exchange Rate Arrangements and Monetary Frameworks,* 2008.

ternational reserves of MENA were well over $1 trillion by end-2008. The foreign assets managed by special-purpose government funds, commonly known as sovereign wealth funds (SWFs), are not included in official central bank reserves. SWFs in MENA are estimated to hold over $1 trillion.[11]

The currency distribution of MENA official reserves is undisclosed. While the International Monetary Fund (IMF) does receive the currency composition of reserves from some MENA central banks, it publishes the data only in aggregate form. Anecdotal evidence suggests that while euro holdings are growing, particularly in the oil exporters, the bulk of official reserve assets are held in US dollar financial assets.

Exchange Rate Regimes

Virtually all MENA countries maintain a pegged exchange rate regime, with the exception of Algeria, Sudan, and Tunisia. Twelve countries are pegged to the US dollar, four are pegged to a basket, and three operate a managed float (figure 3.11). However, two of those countries that classify

11. Accurate figures on the assets of SWFs, in particular the larger ones in MENA, such as the Abu Dhabi Investment Authority (ADIA) and the Qatar Investment Authority (QIA), are difficult to obtain as they are not made publicly available. A variety of unofficial estimates place the assets of the GCC SWFs anywhere from $1 trillion to $2 trillion.

themselves as managed floaters—Algeria and Tunisia—operate as if they were pegged to a basket.

In the countries that are pegged to a basket, the euro has a higher weight than the US dollar in North Africa. For example, in Morocco the relative weights are 80 percent euro and 20 percent US dollar; in Tunisia the euro has a weight of 55 percent and the dollar 45 percent. This is not surprising because North African countries, and particularly Morocco and Tunisia, have close historical trade links with Europe. Algeria's basket is made up of 60 percent dollar and 40 percent euro, basically in line with exports and imports. Libya and Syria are pegged to special drawing rights (SDR), in which the US dollar has a 45 percent weight and the euro 29 percent.

Overall, therefore, MENA countries currently maintain a peg to the US dollar, although there is growing interest in some of them to move to a basket peg. Any move to peg to a basket will undoubtedly lead to a significantly greater role for the euro, particularly if the basket is constructed using trade shares. On the export side, aside from the fact that oil is priced in US dollars, the euro would have a weight of about 20 to 25 percent. Using imports gives the euro about a 30 to 35 percent share in the basket.

Oil Exporters' Perspectives

The MENA region has 11 oil exporters, of which the GCC is the largest as a group.[12] It is primarily in the six GCC countries that there has been a very active discussion on diversifying away from the US dollar and having the euro take on a greater role in foreign asset holdings and exchange rate policy.[13]

The GCC was established in May 1981 with the explicit aim of forging closer ties and stronger links among the six member states.[14] A few months later (in November 1981) member states signed an agreement to establish the GCC Free Trade Area and outlined the steps for closer economic cooperation. On December 31, 2001, the GCC members agreed to a revised economic agreement to advance economic integration and lead to a common market by 2008 and a monetary union by 2010.

The GCC is a relatively homogeneous group of countries, sharing a common cultural and political history,[15] and are mainly exporters of oil,

---

12. Other large oil producers in MENA include Algeria, Iran, Iraq, and Libya. In Syria oil production is declining rapidly.

13. As mentioned in the previous section, Algeria and Libya are pegged to a basket that includes the euro. Iraq has a managed floating regime, although de facto it is a crawling peg. Iran's diversification away from the US dollar has been dictated by political factors and sanctions.

14. Initially, Iraq was also involved in the discussions to establish the GCC but in the end decided not to join.

15. Edmund O'Sullivan (2008) has a very extensive discussion of the history of the Gulf

gas, and refined products. They jointly account for over 40 percent of global oil reserves and 23 percent of natural gas reserves. Oil and gas production contributes over half of total GDP and three-quarters of total exports and government revenues. The combined GDP of the GCC countries in 2008 was over $1 trillion, and they have an average per capita income of $25,000, making them the wealthiest group in the developing world.

Much progress has been made toward the goal of a full-fledged GCC Monetary Union.[16] GCC countries have virtually unrestricted intraregional mobility of goods, national labor, and capital and full convertibility; regulations and supervision of the banking sectors are being gradually harmonized. The GCC common market was established in January 2008 and provides GCC citizens equal treatment in all economic activities. All members (except Kuwait since May 2007) have pegged their currencies to the US dollar since 2003, and a common external tariff was introduced that same year. Although the GCC currencies were de facto pegged to the US dollar for decades,[17] a single GCC currency is expected to encourage trade and financial integration and facilitate foreign direct investment.

International interest in the GCC has been increasing recently mainly because of the dramatic rise in oil prices since 2004. This led to larger current account surpluses and a massive build-up of foreign assets. Maintaining a peg to the US dollar started to be questioned on grounds that it was contributing to global imbalances. The GCC (and, of course, China) were running large current account surpluses, while the United States was experiencing large current account deficits. For example, the current account surplus of GCC countries rose from $88 billion in 2004 to $200 billion in 2007 (and nearly $300 billion in 2008), and official foreign reserves (excluding foreign assets held by SWFs) reached $420 billion. Therefore, to reduce global imbalances, the GCC current account surpluses needed to be reduced, and changing the exchange rate was considered one solution. The GCC countries were urged to abandon the US dollar in favor of a more flexible regime—either a basket peg or managed floating.[18] An appreciation of the currency against the US dollar would increase imports (exports would not be affected since oil is priced in US dollars), thereby reducing the current account surplus.

---

states. Marcus Noland and Howard Pack (2007) cover some of the Gulf countries in their study of the Arab economies.

16. Willem Buiter (2008) questions whether the political requirements for the GCC Monetary Union are met. The political commitment, however, appears firm.

17. During 1980–2002, Bahrain, Qatar, Saudi Arabia, and the United Arab Emirates (UAE) were pegged with bands to the SDR but de facto pegged to the US dollar. Oman was pegged to the US dollar and Kuwait to an undisclosed basket.

18. Maintaining the US dollar peg but changing the parity (i.e., a revaluation) was also proposed.

Figure 3.12   Direction of GCC trade, 2007 (percent)

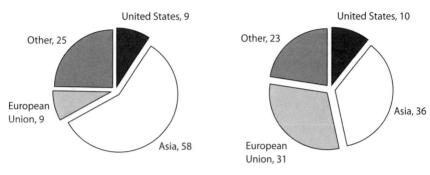

Destination of GCC exports

Origin of GCC imports

Source: International Monetary Fund, *Direction of Trade Statistics,* 2008.

With the recent drop in oil prices and the appreciation of the US dollar, calls for changing the GCC exchange rate regimes to correct global imbalances have died down. But the general question still remains—should the GCC countries continue pegging to the US dollar or move to another regime such as pegging to a basket, which would naturally include the euro, or even managed floating? While for now, the member states, except Kuwait, have stated their commitment to the dollar peg, they have also stated that all options are open for the single currency when the GCC Monetary Union is established in 2010.[19]

Following the analysis in the previous section on MENA, I now turn to GCC trade patterns, the currency composition of reserve assets, and then address the main question of the exchange rate regime.

Trade Patterns

The GCC economies have traditionally been very open to international trade in goods and services (and labor). As figure 3.12 shows, Asia has the largest share of GCC exports (58 percent in 2007), with the United States and the European Union accounting for around 9 percent each. However, since oil is priced in US dollars, even the exports to the European Union are denominated in US dollars. On the import side, the European Union accounts for about 31 percent, so the rest of the imports are priced in US dollars. As in the case of MENA, it is worth noting that the share of imports

---

19. The Kuwait government has stated that it is committed to joining the monetary union. Oman, on the other hand, while maintaining the dollar peg, intends to join only at a later stage.

Figure 3.13   GCC gross official reserves, 1998–2007

billions of US dollars

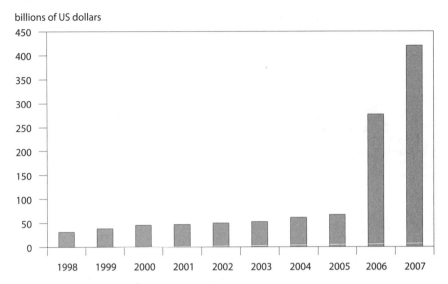

Source: International Monetary Fund, *International Financial Statistics,* 2008.

coming from the European Union has been declining—from 34 percent in 2000 to the current 31 percent. The share of the United States has also been declining while that of Asia has been growing steadily. Intra-GCC trade has been low, reflecting the dominant role of oil in these economies, but with economic diversification increasing, trade among them has been rising, albeit from a very low base.

Official Reserve Assets

The spectacular rise in oil prices from 2004 to mid-2008 led to large current account surpluses in the GCC and a corresponding increase in official foreign exchange reserves. The cumulated current account balance of the GCC from 2003 through 2007 amounted to about $725 billion (and is estimated to be over $1 trillion at end-2008). Official reserves of the GCC countries, which hold over half of MENA reserves, rose to $420 billion in 2007 (figure 3.13). Most of these reserves are held in US dollar financial assets. In 2007 the US dollar share was over 90 percent (see, for example, Setser and Ziemba 2008). Two arguments have been made to justify the holding of over 90 percent of GCC reserves in US dollars. First, the peg with the US dollar makes the United States an obvious destination for investing. Second, and related to the first point, US financial markets are able to handle very large volumes of foreign inflows without much trouble.

GCC SWFs are opaque and reluctant to reveal information about their holdings.[20] At present, there is no official information on the total value, distribution, or currency composition of their assets. Since there are no accurate numbers on holdings of SWFs, trying to obtain the currency composition of their assets is a somewhat futile task. It is quite likely that the US dollar share is lower than for official reserves and the euro share correspondingly higher because of the long-term nature of SWF assets. But SWFs also have a lot of foreign direct investment in the MENA region. In most cases, their investments and the returns on those investments are in US dollars. All in all, how much they hold in US dollars or in euros is almost impossible to say, although anecdotal evidence—mainly press reports—suggests that the share of US dollar-denominated assets far exceeds euro-denominated financial assets in their portfolios. Brad Setser and Rachel Ziemba (2008) assume that about 50 percent are in US dollars, largely on the basis of press reports that the Kuwait Investment Authority's (KIA) dollar assets are around 40 percent of its total financial assets.[21]

Exchange Rate Regimes

GCC member countries officially pegged their currencies to the US dollar on January 1, 2003, as an explicit step toward monetary integration. Although at that time the countries (except Kuwait) were already pegged to the US dollar, the decision was based on the expectation that the dollar peg would maintain stability and strengthen confidence in the economies, and the countries would go into the monetary union at those parities. As such, GCC countries have pursued macroeconomic policies consistent with fixed rates to the US dollar. The flexible factor markets in these countries, particularly the labor market, have helped them in this regard. Also, GCC members have accumulated large foreign exchange reserves, supporting the credibility of the peg and discouraging speculation against their currencies.

By and large a good case can be made for the GCC countries pegging to the dollar. Macroeconomic conditions in the GCC have been stable for the last two decades, even during periods of dollar fluctuations, and over time the cyclical synchronicity between the GCC and the United States has been increasing, despite the apparent divergence in 2008. The peg to the US dollar has helped the region avoid nominal shocks from geopolitical

---

20. An international working group of sovereign wealth funds—comprising 26 countries, including some from the GCC—has reached agreement on a draft set of voluntary, generally accepted principles and practices (GAPP) that reflects the current practices of SWFs or actions to which they aspire. The GAPP is intended to guide the conduct of investment practices of SWFs, including revealing more information on the legal framework, governance and institutional structures, risk management, and investment policies.

21. Neither the KIA nor the Kuwait government has verified this estimate of the share of US dollar assets, which appears to be on the low side.

events feeding into the economy. These geopolitical risks are likely to continue, placing a premium on the US dollar peg.

The dollar peg provides a well-understood and credible anchor for monetary policy (Abed, Erbas, and Guerami 2003). The peg has clearly anchored inflationary expectations at low levels and provides certainty about future exchange rate movements. For example, notwithstanding the jump in inflation in 2007–08 in the GCC, forward markets continue to reflect confidence in the dollar peg. The peg is obviously easy to administer and does not require the institutions necessary for implementing an independent monetary policy. Such institutions would need to be built, become effective, and establish credibility. Also, since the monetary transmission mechanism is weak in the GCC countries, given the absence of developed domestic capital markets, the shallowness of credit markets, and the limited effectiveness of interest rates, a peg seems to be the only realistic option as a monetary policy anchor.

The exchange rate peg simplifies trade and financial transactions, accounting, and business planning, as well as monetary coordination among the member countries. Exchange rate risk can be easily hedged, even in the absence of a well-developed domestic private forward exchange market, as agents can work through US dollar markets. With cross rates fixed, intra-GCC transactions benefit as traders and investors do not have to take on any exchange rate risk, thereby encouraging further integration of the individual GCC economies. Absent developed financial markets, and particularly forward markets in which to hedge, the central banks would have to provide forward cover, as is the case in most developing countries with flexible exchange rates.

Labor-market flexibility can support international competitiveness under a fixed exchange rate regime. GCC countries face a relatively elastic supply of labor (mostly unskilled) from low-income countries in the Middle East and South Asia. Non-nationals make up some two-thirds of employment in the GCC members. These countries have been applying the policy of nationalization of the labor force in a very flexible manner, to avoid labor shortages and minimize output disruptions.

Major oil exporters generally prefer pegged exchange rates. Of the 26 countries whose oil exports account for over 50 percent of their total exports, 18 (including the GCC countries) have conventional fixed pegs. Even some countries that are classified as managed floaters (for example, Algeria and Kazakhstan) keep the volatility of their exchange rates within a tight band, making them appear akin to peggers. This implies that in countries with foreign exchange coming primarily from the dominant export commodity, and subject to considerable price volatility, it is more difficult to operate a free foreign exchange market, particularly if the institutions to support it are not well developed.[22]

---

22. This is one of the main reasons that Jeffrey Frankel and Ayako Saiki (2002) argue for

Of course, the dollar peg has a number of disadvantages too. First, it imports US monetary policy, which may at times not be appropriate for local needs.[23] With an open capital account, the dollar peg requires the GCC countries to follow US interest rate policy, which has the potential to result in policies unsuited to their business cycles.[24] If the divergences between business cycles are likely to be temporary, policy tools other than interest rates or exchange rates would have to be used to influence domestic activity. In particular, fiscal policy would bear the burden of controlling aggregate demand, and to a lesser extent quantitative credit controls (for example, loan-to-deposit ratios) and tighter prudential regulations would need to be used to curb credit expansion. The peg also means that GCC countries cannot defend against imported inflation, although in the long run, higher inflation in trading partners would be offset by depreciation of their currencies against the US dollar. Furthermore, the peg forces adjustment of the real exchange rate to a new equilibrium to go through prices rather than the nominal exchange rate. Adjustment through prices is slower than through the exchange rate and may trigger price-wage spirals, generate low real interest rates, and increase the risk of asset bubbles as investors move into real estate and equity markets.[25]

Even if pegging is an appropriate choice for GCC countries, pegging to the US dollar is not the only option. Adopting a basket peg may be a useful way to introduce some flexibility in the exchange rate. The example of Kuwait is a case in point. In May 2007 Kuwait abandoned the peg to the US dollar in favor of a peg to a currency basket, reverting to the exchange rate system that existed prior to January 2003.[26] With a basket peg, the main anchor properties of an exchange rate peg could be retained but at the same time gaining some adaptability to the adverse swings among the values of the major reserve currencies. For example, with oil priced in US dollars, volatility in the price of oil is reflected, under a dollar peg, directly in volatility in oil export receipts. Under, say, an SDR peg the volatility of oil export receipts would have been much less in the past few years.

---

pegging the currency to the export price of the main export commodity for small open economies that are relatively specialized in the production and export of a particular mineral or agricultural commodity.

23. Setser (2007) has made this argument. But this can happen with a basket peg as well. For example, in the case of an SDR peg, the monetary policy needs of the GCC may be different from the monetary policy stances of the United States, Europe, and Japan.

24. For example, US monetary policy of low interest rates in 2007–08 was at odds with the booming GCC economies, as was the US policy of high interest rates in the late 1990s when oil prices and growth in the GCC were low.

25. Such bubbles have been evident in all the GCC countries over the past few years.

26. While the basket is undisclosed, the currency weights in the new basket were initially estimated to be: 50 percent US dollar, 40 percent euro, and 10 percent pound sterling. It appears now that the weight of the US dollar is much higher in the basket.

The volatility of the nominal effective rate would be reduced, benefiting foreign trade, investment, and balance sheet stability. In the short run, a basket peg can help contain imported inflation by shielding the currency against cross-rate movements among the major currencies.

But at the same time, basket pegs reduce the informational benefits of maintaining constant one bilateral exchange rate relevant for price comparisons and economic transactions. Also, they are less transparent and more difficult to explain to the public. And they tend to be less credible than single-currency pegs, especially if the currency weights are not known or are changed over time.[27] A failure to disclose the relative weights and composition of the currencies used in the basket could complicate the assessment of exchange rate risk and lead to undesirable consequences. In Kuwait, for example, the basket was undisclosed and its adoption led to a strong demand for the dinar, large capital inflows, and an increase in liquidity. This speculation complicated monetary policy management rather than simplifying it as was hoped.

More generally, pegging to a basket of currencies does not buy a country monetary independence. Under capital convertibility, interest rates would likewise have to follow a "basket" of interest rates. This will reduce somewhat the problems arising from extreme desynchronization between the monetary policy needs in the GCC and the United States, but in quantitative terms the gain is not likely to be that much. Take, for example, the case of Saudi Arabia illustrated in figure 3.14. Suppose that instead of being pegged to the US dollar, the Saudi riyal had been pegged to the SDR and the domestic interest rate had mirrored the SDR interest rate. During 2006, the Saudi rate would have been about 100 to 150 basis points lower and in 2008, about 50 to 100 basis points higher. Whether such small changes would have a significant impact on aggregate demand and inflation is questionable.

Under a basket regime, the central bank would have to actively manage foreign exchange operations and risk. The relatively low levels of financial intermediation and lack of available financial instruments would limit the scope of these operations (Roger, Restrepo, and Garcia 2008). And pegging to a basket would not fully address the management of oil price volatility or the rise in liquidity from increases in oil prices. A basket that included the price of oil, as has sometimes been suggested, would respond to the relatively higher volatility of oil prices (by the weight given to the oil price in the basket). This could have serious adverse effects on other sectors of the economy. For example, higher oil prices would lead to a real appreciation, which would raise the cost of other exports and dampen diversification efforts—the classic "Dutch disease" problem. It is also unclear that a fall

---

27. The effect is minimized in the case of pegging to the SDR, where the composition and weights of the currencies that make up the basket are public knowledge. But the SDR are not particularly well understood by the general public.

Figure 3.14   Interest rates, January 2003–August 2008

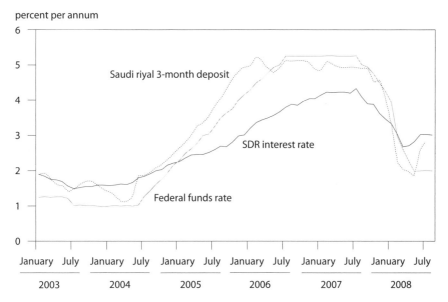

percent per annum

Saudi riyal 3-month deposit

SDR interest rate

Federal funds rate

	January	July	January	July	January	July	January	July	January	July	January	July
	2003		2004		2005		2006		2007		2008	

Sources: International Monetary Fund, *International Financial Statistics;* Saudi Arabian Monetary Agency, Monthly Reports.

in oil prices would depreciate the currency sufficiently to accommodate the adverse terms-of-trade change and stabilize export earnings. Also, one can argue that oil itself is an international currency. So for the GCC, as a major oil-exporting bloc, pegging to the price of oil would be like pegging the nominal (fiat) currencies to their own (commodity) currency. It would obviously not anchor the GCC countries' currencies to something truly exogenous.

Looking Ahead

The euro will likely become more prominent in the MENA region as trade with Europe increases and reserves are correspondingly shifted into euro-denominated assets. However, judging by history, this process will be slow, and it is difficult to see the euro overtaking the US dollar anytime soon. In the North African countries—Morocco and Tunisia—it has, but this example is unlikely to be replicated in the region. MENA will remain for the time being largely a dollar zone. The currencies will generally re-main pegged, but not necessarily just to the US dollar. While switching completely to pegging to the euro is not really in the cards, except again perhaps for isolated cases like Morocco, where the euro has an 80 percent weight, the move to a basket in which the euro has a significant weight is a more likely possibility.

Since the GCC countries are such important players in the region, a more pertinent question is what they will or should do. If pegging is an optimal strategy for the GCC countries, especially since managed floating is neither a viable nor a desirable option, what should they peg to? As long as oil continues to be priced in US dollars, switching to a euro peg is simply not going to happen. For the time being, on balance, maintaining the dollar peg is the right exchange rate policy for the GCC countries.

What about the future, and particularly when the GCC Monetary Union is established, still slated for 2010? What should be the exchange regime for the single currency? GCC governments have stated often that they intend to stay with the US dollar for now, and the choice of exchange rate arrangements under the planned monetary union has not been made. The choice comes down basically to keeping the dollar peg regime, perhaps with a change in parity if necessary, or pegging to a basket in which the US dollar would have a relatively high weight, followed by the euro.[28]

The familiarity of GCC governments, central banks, and private economic agents with the US dollar peg, as well as the preference of the GCC countries to date for a fixed exchange rate, argue in favor of maintaining the current arrangement even after the monetary union comes into being. In fact, in 2003 GCC member countries opted to fix their bilateral parities and to peg their currencies to the US dollar in the run-up to the GCC Monetary Union in 2010 precisely to benefit from the greater certainty about the parities at which they would enter the monetary union. Keeping the single GCC currency pegged to the US dollar for some time would leave the public and policymakers on already very familiar ground.

On the other hand, with increasing integration in international trade, services, and asset markets, the GCC countries can be more prone to external shocks, and a higher degree of exchange rate flexibility may become more desirable in the medium term to ensure external stability and international competitiveness. In particular, as oil reserves are depleted in some member countries, such as Bahrain and Oman, and the nonoil tradable sectors expand, the private sector will need to be competitive to function as the main source of employment opportunities for the rapidly growing national labor forces. Furthermore, policies aimed at increasing participation rates by nationals in GCC labor markets will erode over time the partial insulation flexible labor markets have provided to the peg regime.

All in all, there are strong arguments in favor of the GCC countries retaining the fixed exchange rate regime. The dollar peg seems to be the best option leading up to, and also in the short run after, the establishment

---

28. For an extensive discussion of the choice of exchange rate regime for the GCC Monetary Union, see IMF (2008).

of the monetary union. In the future, flexibility could be introduced by implementing a basket peg, following the example of Kuwait and other major oil exporters like Algeria and Libya. While capable of dampening volatility from swings among the major currencies, and avoiding monetary policy from being tied exclusively to the United States, a basket peg would not eliminate the effects of imported inflation nor would it allow the GCC countries to operate an independent monetary policy.

If a basket peg regime is chosen, what should the basket look like? Pegging to the SDR is one option. Another option could be a basket consisting only of the US dollar and the euro. Such a basket has many advantages. First, it would be simple to interpret. Second, it would cover the bulk of transactions in goods, services, and financial instruments (now in the dollar and euro area). Third, it would reduce monetary dependence of the GCC on the US Federal Reserve. And finally, it would allow for the use of dollar or euro hedging instruments to efficiently manage financial risks. A move to such a basket would help ensure the role of the euro as it would encourage trade and financial flows between the GCC and Europe.

To sum up:

- MENA and the GCC are dollar zones; while the use of the euro is growing, it is not yet posing any competition to the US dollar.

- GCC countries should remain pegged to the US dollar for now and even after adopting a single currency following the establishment of the GCC Monetary Union in 2010.

- If increased flexibility of the exchange rate turns out to be necessary or desirable in the future, pegging to a basket is more appropriate than managed floating.

- A basket consisting of the US dollar and the euro, with publicly announced weights, would be a good option since it would be relevant for most trade and financial transactions; using such a basket would undoubtedly enhance the role of the euro in the Middle East region.

References

Abed, G., N. Erbas, and B. Guerami. 2003. *The GCC Monetary Union: Some Considerations for the Exchange Rate Regime.* IMF Working Paper no. 03166. Washington: International Monetary Fund.

Buiter, W. M. 2008. *Economic, Political and Institutional Prerequisites for Monetary Union among Members of the Gulf Cooperation Council.* CEPR Discussion Paper no. 6639. London: Centre for Economic Policy Research.

Frankel, J., and A. Saiki. 2002. A Proposal to Anchor Monetary Policy by the Price of the Export Commodity. *Journal of Economic Integration* 17, no. 3: 417–48.

IMF (International Monetary Fund). 2008. *The GCC Monetary Union—Choice of Exchange Rate Regime.* Washington. Available at www.imf.org.

Noland, M., and H. Pack. 2007. *The Arab Economies in a Changing World*. Washington: Peterson Institute for International Economics.

O'Sullivan, E. 2008. *The New Gulf: How Modern Arabia is Changing the World for Good*. United Arab Emirates: Motivate Publishing.

Roger, S., J. Restrepo, and C. Garcia. 2008. Choosing a Currency Basket in a Commodity Exporting Economy. International Monetary Fund, Washington. Photocopy.

Setser, B. 2007. *The Case for Exchange Rate Flexibility in Oil-Exporting Economies*. Policy Briefs in International Economics 07-8. Washington: Peterson Institute for International Economics.

Setser, B., and R. Ziemba. 2008. *Understanding the New Financial Superpower—the Management of GCC Official Foreign Assets*. RGE Monitor. Available by registration at www.rgemonitor.com.

Sturm, M., J. Strasky, P. Adolph, and D. Peschel. 2008. *The Gulf Cooperation Council Countries: Economic Structures, Recent Developments, and Role in the Global Economy*. European Central Bank Occasional Paper no. 92. Frankfurt: European Central Bank.

Latin America

MARIA CELINA ARRAES

Over the first ten years of its existence, the euro has proved to be more than a powerful symbol of collective identity. It has proven its global importance both as a medium of exchange and as a store of value. However, its importance as a unit of account and as an anchor for pegging local currencies is yet to be established. The emergence of an internationally used currency is a very slow process. During the last decade, the euro's international role has grown gradually but steadily, which is related to the central role of the euro area in the global economy and international trade.

In fact, the euro meets a number of criteria to function as a key international currency, including its use in one of the world's largest economic entities, supported by a monetary authority committed to price stability and the emergence of euro-denominated financial instruments. According to the European Central Bank (ECB 2008), the most prominent driver of the international role of the euro remains the geographical, economic, financial, and institutional proximity to the euro area.

The euro has become the second most important international currency after the US dollar if global foreign exchange markets are included. According to the ECB, the share of the euro in international loans and deposits, merchandise trade, and global foreign exchange markets is very significant. In addition, the share of the euro in bond issuing and its use in international reserves is just as impressive. The euro accounted for 26.5 percent of the global official reserves in 2007, according to International Monetary Fund (IMF) data. Another example of the euro as an inter-

Maria Celina Arraes is the deputy governor for international affairs at the Central Bank of Brazil.

national currency is the fact that, according to the Bank for International Settlements, banks have been significantly increasing their issuance of euro-denominated debt.

In Latin America, the use of the euro is growing despite inertia and the dollar's incumbency advantages. Moreover, the main variables that determine the international use of a currency—economic size, significance of foreign trade flows, financial-market development, and the degree of price and exchange rate stability—indicate that the euro has potential to become more prominent as an international currency used by Latin American countries.

Euro's Role in Latin American Trade and Investment

From a regional perspective, the US dollar is the most used reference currency. Nevertheless, the growing weight of economic and commercial ties between Latin America and Europe is having a direct impact on the use of the euro, as well as on the overall economic performance of the region.

Although the United States is still the region's major commercial partner, Latin American countries are strengthening their ties with other regions, including the European Union. The euro area is an important commercial partner of Latin America and an important source of borrowing and foreign direct investment (FDI) in the region.

The role of the euro as a price-setting and invoicing currency in Latin America depends on international practices for invoicing and settlement of foreign trade. Commodities are traded mainly in US dollars. Change will be slow due to the high degree of standardization of the markets. For noncommodity exports, the level of competition in the market for a product should be taken into account. Nevertheless, as trade between Europe and Latin America grows, so will the use of the euro in trade invoicing and settlement.

Latin America's imports from the European Union increased from 45 billion euros in 2003 to 78 billion euros in 2007. Exports to the European Union continue to climb, rising from 40 billion euros in 2003 to 80 billion euros in 2007. Figure 3.15 shows EU shares in percent.

Among selected Latin American countries, the average share of trade flow with the euro area is about 13 percent of the total flow. If one excludes Mexico, this share goes up to 18 percent (table 3.9). Brazil is the major commercial partner of the euro area, being the biggest importer in relative terms and the second-largest exporter after Chile. Mexico directs a comparatively small part of its exports to euro area countries. While the share of euro area imports is higher in the bigger Latin American economies, the share of exports to euro area countries is higher in the smaller economies. These figures show there is room for improvement in the trade relationship.

Figure 3.15   Latin American trade with the European Union, 2003–07

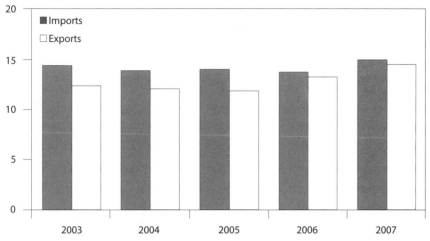

EU share in percent

Source: International Monetary Fund, *Direction of Trade Statistics.*

Table 3.9   Selected Latin American countries' merchandise trade with the eurozone, 2007 (percent share)

Country	Exports	Imports	Trade flow
Brazil	19.8	20.1	19.9
Argentina	15.4	17.5	16.3
Uruguay	16.6	11.5	13.5
Mexico	4.9	10.3	7.6
Chile	21.0	11.3	17.2
Peru	15.2	9.4	12.8
Subtotal	12.8	13.5	13.1
Subtotal (excluding Mexico)	18.8	16.9	18.0
Eurozone in world merchandise trade[a]	28.3	27.2	27.8

a. 2006 World Trade Organization data. Includes intra-area trade.

Source: International Monetary Fund, *Direction of Trade Statistics.*

According to the latest data from the Economic Commission for Latin America and the Caribbean (ECLAC 2008), in 2007 global FDI flows reached US$1.8 trillion, with Latin America and the Caribbean receiving 7 percent of these global flows. Latin America's largest FDI recipients in 2007 were Brazil, which received US$34.5 billion, Mexico (US$23.2 billion), and Chile (US$14.4 billion).

Table 3.10 EU outward and inward foreign direct investment, by geographic region, 2006

Region	Outward flows Billions of euros	Percent	Inward flows Billions of euros	Percent
Extra–European Union	260.2	100.0	157.1	100.0
Europe	66.8	25.7	25.8	16.4
Africa	11.8	4.5	1.9	1.2
North America	102.5	39.4	82.7	52.6
Asia	30.6	11.8	29.5	18.8
Oceania	7.6	2.9	4.5	2.9
Central and South America	39.5	15.2	19.7	12.5

Source: European Commission, Eurostat Database.

The euro area has been a very important source of borrowing and FDI to Latin American countries. For these countries, there is a clear benefit from access to EU markets and from EU investments. Closer ties with the European Union are beneficial because they are a useful diversification. Many European companies operate either on their own or in joint ventures in Latin America. In particular, the presence of European banks in the region has increased considerably.

According to the latest data from the European Commission (2008), EU outward FDI stocks increased over the 2002–06 period by 42 percent and by 11 percent between 2005 and 2006. The geographical distribution of EU FDI outflows in 2006 also shows the American continent as the main destination with a share of 55 percent.

EU FDI outflows to Latin America averaged 12 billion euros during the 2002–06 period. The year 2004 saw a surge in EU FDI flows to Latin America, reaching an unprecedented level of 20 billion euros, but then falling to 12 billion euros in 2005 and 2006.

In the last decades, the outward investment flows generated by Latin American firms have increased as a result of their intensified international expansion efforts. Direct investment from the South and Central American countries in the European Union accounted for 12.5 percent of the global investment there in 2006 (table 3.10).

From 2001 to 2008, euro area countries were the source of an average of 21.5 percent of total external borrowing and about 44.6 percent of FDI inflows to Brazil (figure 3.16). However, the share of Brazilian FDI directed to the euro area is small, well below the share of other important areas. From 2007 to July 2008, Brazil's direct investment in the euro area reached 7.7 percent of total Brazilian direct investment abroad, approximately half of the Latin American average of 15 percent.

Figure 3.16   Euro area countries' investments in Brazil, by category, 2001–08

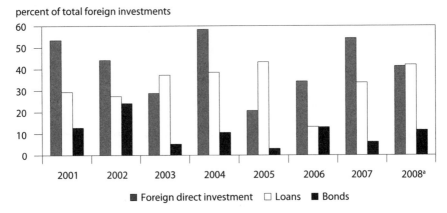

percent of total foreign investments

■ Foreign direct investment   □ Loans   ■ Bonds

a. January to July.

Source: Banco Central do Brasil.

Euro in Latin American External Assets and Liabilities

With respect to the euro's share in international debt markets, net issuance of euro-denominated debt securities, according to the narrow measure, increased from the equivalent of US$261.8 billion in 2004 to US$340 billion in 2007, based on data from the ECB (2008). In the third quarter of 2008, net issuance of euro-denominated bonds and notes reached US$464 billion.

It is well known that countries have to decide their own levels, composition, and maturity structure of foreign debt. In general, the currency composition of foreign debt should be related to the composition of earnings from foreign trade. Agnes Bénassy-Quéré, Lionel Fontagne, and Amina Lahreche-Revil (1999) argue that the question that should be asked is what would be the optimum anchor basket that would make it possible to minimize the losses arising from fluctuations between international currencies, given a geographic structure of foreign trade and a borrowing structure inherited from past decisions. Thus, as trade between Europe and Latin America grows, euro-denominated debt may account for a larger share of Latin America's total foreign debt. Table 3.11 shows current share of euro-denominated debt in selected Latin American countries.

In recent years, the amount of international bond issues in Latin America has increased. However, the average size of euro-denominated issues is still smaller than that of US dollar-denominated issues. Nonetheless, the share of euro-denominated issues in total sovereign external bonds is significant, with Argentina and Mexico representing the highest shares among selected countries (table 3.12).

Table 3.11 Euro-denominated external debt in selected Latin American countries

Country	Classification	Period	Percent share of total debt
Brazil	Total	2007	6.1
Argentina	Public	2008Q2	10.6
Uruguay	Total	2007	5.2
Peru	Public	2008Q2	12.9
Chile	Total	2006	3.6

Note: Total debt according to classification.

Sources: Central banks of Brazil, Uruguay, Argentina, and Chile; Ministry of Economy and Finance of Peru.

Table 3.12 Sovereign euro-denominated bonds, September 2008
(percent of total sovereign external bonds)

Country	Share
Brazil	14.0
Argentina	28.4
Uruguay	6.1
Mexico	18.4
Peru	15.5

Note: Sovereign external bonds face value.

Source: Bloomberg.

The external debt of Latin American countries is issued mainly in the US dollar. These countries are little exposed to the euro, as less than 10 percent of the regional debt on average is denominated in euros. However, the share of the euro in the structure of external bonds may increase with more international borrowing instruments denominated in euros.

On the asset side, the currency composition of foreign exchange reserves depends on several factors such as market liquidity, country's exchange rate regime, diversification strategies, and matching trade partners. Exchange rate volatility could lead as well to portfolio shifts both into and out of a currency. The policies and credibility of the ECB have an important influence on the euro's international value and its use in international price setting and as anchor for monetary and exchange rate policies.

A recent ECB study and data from the IMF suggest that the share of the euro in global foreign exchange reserves has reached 26.5 percent (table 3.13). The share has gradually increased over the years but recently stabilized.

The magnitude of the euro's use as a reserve of value currency by

Table 3.13 Official foreign exchange reserves in euros

Country/grouping	Percent of total reserves
All countries, 2007	26.5
Developing countries, 2007	28.4
Selected Latin American countries, 2006[a]	
Chile	24.7
Peru	17.8
Uruguay	1.3

a. Data reported by countries' authorities.

Sources: International Monetary Fund; European Central Bank for selected countries.

Latin American countries is not so clear. According to the ECB, developing countries have relatively more international reserves in euros than the global average, but the overall composition of Latin American countries' reserves remains largely unknown. Only three countries in the region make public the currency allocation of their international reserves: Chile, Peru, and Uruguay. Chile's case is worth noticing since almost one-quarter of its reserves is invested in euro-denominated assets. In July 2008, the Brazilian government introduced a bill in congress proposing the creation of a sovereign wealth fund. The proposal's two main features are funding by budget resources (not involving use of international reserves under Banco Central do Brasil management) and investing in both external and internal financial assets. The fund when implemented will probably have different benchmarks from those of international reserves. On currency composition, a new scenario should arise in the Brazilian case for international sovereign assets as a whole, favoring the euro.

Euro as a Peg

The US dollar still keeps its place as the world's preferred currency for pegging and exchange rate arrangements. This is mostly because the use of a currency as anchor is linked with issues such as trade and financial integration level. Most of the countries that have some arrangement with the euro also have historical or geographical relationships with the euro area. In this sense, no Latin American economies currently have any kind of exchange rate arrangements using the euro as a peg (figure 3.17).

The choice of the exchange rate regime is very important for the monetary policy of a country. It involves the implementation and monitoring of instruments to maintain the stability of the currency value and, simultaneously, keep enough flexibility in order to absorb external shocks. Nowadays, many factors contribute to the search for alternatives for exchange rate regimes, notably larger financial-market integration and growth of

Figure 3.17   Exchange rate regimes in selected Latin American countries, 2003–06

percent of countries

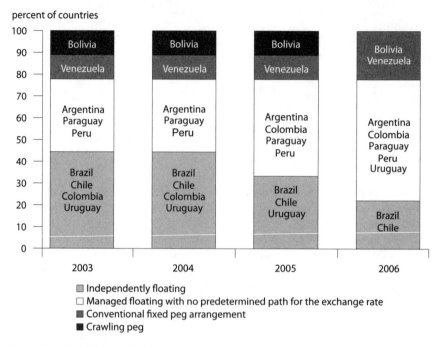

■ Independently floating
□ Managed floating with no predetermined path for the exchange rate
■ Conventional fixed peg arrangement
■ Crawling peg

Source: International Monetary Fund.

international trade. One of the alternatives is monetary integration, and the symbol of this mechanism is the European continent's adoption of a single currency.

Conclusion

Despite the increase in trade and financial linkages between Latin America and the euro area during the last decade, Latin America's strongest relationship is still with the US dollar. It is also important to note that in the past decade new players have emerged in the global economy. Thus, these linkages have diversified as a result of the growing importance of trade between Latin America and Asia and of national policies favoring intraregional trade agreements.

The rise of the euro is a unique, outstanding event and is an unparalleled model for Latin American countries' monetary integration ambitions. The European Payments Union inspired the creation in the 1960s of the Convênio de Pagamentos e Créditos Recíprocos (CCR), a regional payments system with multilateral settlement in South America under the aegis of the Latin American Integration Association. More recently, the central banks of Argentina and Brazil put in place on October 3, 2008, the Payment System on Local Currency (SML). This system allows the invoicing and settlement of exports by each country in its own currency. Both systems can continue to benefit from European lessons on monetary integration.

On interregional cooperation, the Strategic Partnership between the European Union and Brazil is an example of how the two continents can work together. The partnership was established at the first EU-Brazil Summit in July 2007. It constitutes a political commitment of the European Union and Brazil to engage in political, regional, economic, and social developments. The next step toward improved commercial and financial ties clearly seems to be to close an agreement between the European Union and the Mercosur already under discussion.

Given the current economic scenario, the dollar's dominance does not seem to be threatened, but there is room for a larger role for the euro as now it does not reflect the strength of the economic ties between the two regions. In this sense, the performance of the European economy will be a key factor.

In a nutshell, the Latin American commercial and financial relationship with euro area countries seems to be much more significant than the relationship with the euro itself. The euro is an alternative currency for Latin America and is both instrumental and essential to increase investment flows to the region. The importance of the euro for Latin America will depend on the intensification of trade and financial links between Latin America and the euro area and on the global economic structure that will emerge after the current global financial crisis is resolved.

References

Bénassy-Quéré A., L. Fontagne, and A. Lahreche-Revil. 1999. *Exchange-Rate Strategies in the Competition for Attracting FDI*. CEPII Working Paper 99-16. Paris: Centre d'études prospectives et d'informations internationales.

ECB (European Central Bank). 2008. *The International Role of the Euro*. Frankfurt.

ECLAC (Economic Commission for Latin America and Caribbean). 2008. *Foreign Investment in Latin America and the Caribbean 2007*. Santiago.

European Commission. 2007. *European Union Foreign Direct Investment Yearbook 2007*. Brussels.

European Commission. 2008. *European Union Foreign Direct Investment Yearbook 2008*. Brussels.

Market View

THOMAS MAYER

During the 10 years of its existence, the euro has turned into a resounding success. Price stability, defined by the European Central Bank (ECB) as inflation of "less than but close to 2 percent" over the medium term, was largely maintained, and increasing financial integration promoted economic integration and supported economic growth. Between 1999 and 2008, euro area GDP growth averaged a little more than 2 percent per year compared with just about 1¾ percent in 1992–98. Success at home was accompanied by success abroad. Over the years, the euro has gained in importance in international securities markets and as an international reserve currency. Somewhat surprisingly, the present financial crisis seems to have even added to the attractiveness of the euro as many countries have come to see the Economic and Monetary Union (EMU) as a shield against the economic damage caused by the plunge in confidence in stand-alone financial systems and currencies of smaller countries. Thus, several EU accession countries have raised early EMU entry in their list of economic policy priorities, and previously EMU-skeptical long-time EU member countries, such as Denmark and Sweden, appear to be warming up to the euro.

However, it would be misleading to simply extrapolate into the future the success of the euro during its first decade. Looking ahead, the euro is likely to face at least two important challenges: real economic adjustment within the euro area and maintenance of fiscal and financial stability without a central fiscal authority. Hence, while the euro enjoyed a happy

Thomas Mayer is a managing director and chief European economist at Deutsche Bank in London. He also coheads the bank's Global Economics Group.

childhood during the last 10 years, it may well turn into a troubled teen-ager, suffering from considerable stress and perhaps even from existential crises.

Euro's Happy Childhood

The economic literature has identified a number of characteristics that a currency needs to play an important role at the global level.[29] Prominent among those features are (1) the issuing country's share in world output and trade; (2) macroeconomic and price stability in the issuing country; (3) the size, state of development, depth, and regulatory framework of financial markets there; and (4) network externalities. The euro has ben-efited from all these factors. As table 3.14 shows, in 2007 the euro area was the largest economy in the world after the United States (when GDP is converted into common currency using purchasing power parities); it was the largest global trader (measured as share of exports in world exports) and had lower inflation and a lower government budget deficit than the United States (indicating a high degree of macroeconomic stability). As a result of this and the increasingly heavy use of the euro in neighboring countries, users of the European common currency seem to benefit from substantial positive network externalities (although the US dollar is still likely to offer even more of these externalities given its greater use in Asia and Latin America).

Reflecting the economic size of the euro area, deepening European fi-nancial integration, and the heavy use of the euro internationally, the sizes of euro-denominated money market instruments, securities, and cross-border bank liabilities all have increased significantly and even overtaken the respective sizes of US dollar instruments since the introduction of the common European currency (figures 3.18 to 3.20).

Moreover, the euro also gained in attractiveness as a store of value for official international reserve holders. However, as figures 3.21 and 3.22 show, despite the rise of the euro in the portfolios of both industrial- and developing-country central banks, the US dollar's dominant position as the preeminent international official reserve currency has so far remained unchallenged. Similarly, the US dollar has remained the most important international medium of exchange, as evidenced by its share in the cash foreign exchange market (figure 3.23) and in foreign exchange derivatives (figure 3.24).

At the same time, however, the euro has exerted a stronger influence on other currencies than the Deutsche mark did when it was the second

---

29. See, for instance, G. Galati and P. Woolridge, *The Euro as a Reserve Currency: A Challenge to the Pre-eminence of the US Dollar?* BIS Working Paper 218, October 2006. Basel: Bank for International Settlements.

Table 3.14 Key economic characteristics of the euro area, United States, and Japan, 2007 (percent of GDP unless otherwise indicated in parentheses)

Characteristic	Euro area	United States	Japan
Population (millions)	320	302	128
GDP (percent share of world GDP, PPP)	16.1	21.4	6.6
GDP per capita (thousands of euros, PPP)	27.9	39.3	28.8
Value added by economic activity			
Agriculture, fishing, and forestry	1.9	1.1	1.4
Industry (including construction)	26.8	22.4	29.1
Services	71.3	76.5	69.5
Unemployment rate (percent)	7.4	4.6	3.8
Inflation (percent)	2.1	2.9	0.1
Stock market capitalization	77.0	142.0	94.0
General government			
Surplus (+) or deficit (−)	−0.6	−3	−1.4
Gross debt	66.3	49.2	159.5
Revenue	45.6	30.4	33.0
Expenditure	46.2	33.5	34.4
External (excluding intra–euro area) transactions			
Exports of goods and services	22.4	11.9	18.4
Imports of goods and services	21.2	17.0	16.5
Exports (percent share of world exports)	17.5	9.9	6.1
Current account balance	0.3	−5.3	4.8

PPP = purchasing power parity

Sources: European Commission, Eurostat Database; International Monetary Fund; Organization for Economic Cooperation and Development; Reuters; European Central Bank; national authorities.

most important international currency. This can be see in figure 3.25, which gives the coefficients of regressions of the dollar exchange rate of a currency on the dollar-mark and dollar-euro exchange rates, respectively, before and after the introduction of the euro. A coefficient of one indicates that the respective currency moves entirely with the Deutsche mark or euro while a coefficient of zero suggests that the currency moves completely independently from the exchange rate of the Deutsche mark or the euro. The figure plots the coefficients of the regressions for the Deutsche mark on the horizontal axis and those of the regressions for the euro on the vertical axis. Points in the diagram that lie exactly on the 45 degree line imply that there was no change in the coefficients from the period before to that after the introduction of the euro. Most coefficients moved north of the 45 degree line, suggesting that regression coefficients—and hence the euro's influence on exchange rate movements of these currencies against the US dollar—increased with the introduction of the common European currency.

Figure 3.18   Euro-denominated money market instruments overtaking US dollar market, 1989–2007

percent of total amount outstanding

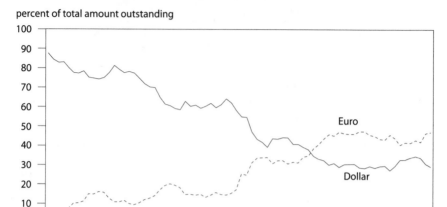

Note: Pre-1999 data are for Deutsche mark.

Figure 3.19   Euro debt securities markets overtaking US dollar market, 1993–2007

percent of total amount outstanding

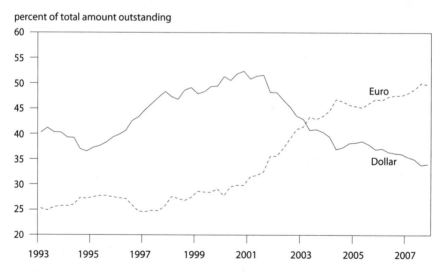

Note: Pre-1999 data are for Deutsche mark.

Source: Bank for International Settlements.

Figure 3.20   European euro area banks attract more international business, 1977–2007

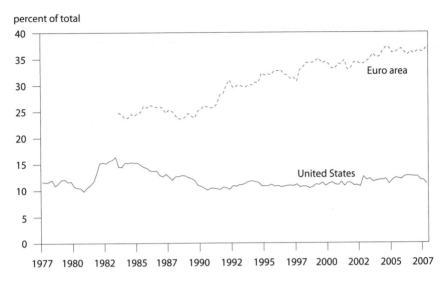

percent of total

Source: Bank for International Settlements.

Euro Weathers the Financial Crisis

Skeptics have argued that the lack of a strong political component in the EMU would prevent effective supervision and regulation of the euro area financial sector and make the sharing of the costs from financial crises difficult if not impossible. Hence, financial stability has been seen at severe risk in the euro area during financial crises. However, the events so far during the present financial crisis have proven the skeptics wrong.

At the national level, regulation and supervision of the financial sector in euro area countries were found to have been no worse than in other key countries, including the United States, and in some cases much better (e.g., Spain, where the central bank helped to prevent murky practices of putting business off-balance sheet and forced banks to build their reserves anticyclically). Moreover, governments have shown that they were able to handle failures of banks with large cross-border activities. Perhaps more importantly, euro area (and EU) governments quickly found a common approach to dealing with the banking crisis (giving guarantees for bank debt and providing funds for the recapitalization of banks), even though schemes were implemented on a national level. The ECB and the European Commission have played an important role in bringing governments together in a cooperative approach to resolve the crisis.

Given its role as the second most important international currency, the

Figure 3.21 Euro gaining moderately as official reserve currency, 1995–2008

percent share of total reserves

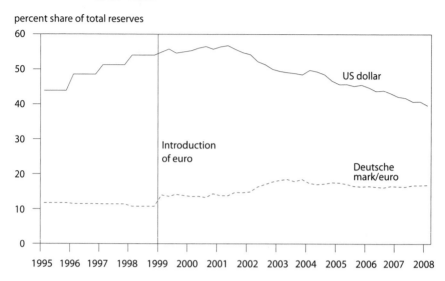

Source: International Monetary Fund, Currency Composition of Official Foreign Exchange Reserves (COFER) Database.

Figure 3.22 Euro gaining as official reserve currency in both industrial and developing countries, 1995–2008

percent share of total reserves

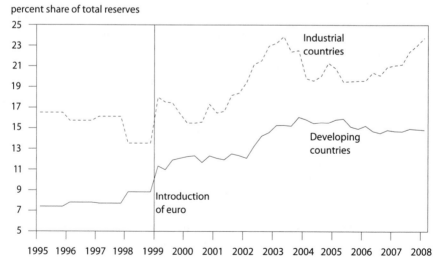

Source: International Monetary Fund, Currency Composition of Official Foreign Exchange Reserves (COFER) Database.

Figure 3.23   US dollar maintaining its lead in foreign exchange markets

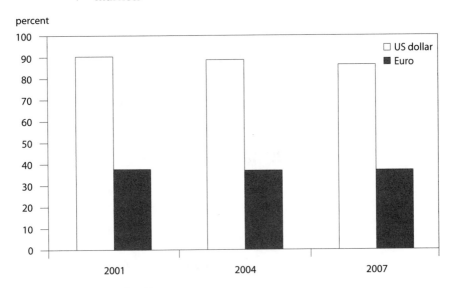

percent

Source: Bank for International Settlements.

Figure 3.24   US dollar maintaining its lead in foreign exchange derivatives markets

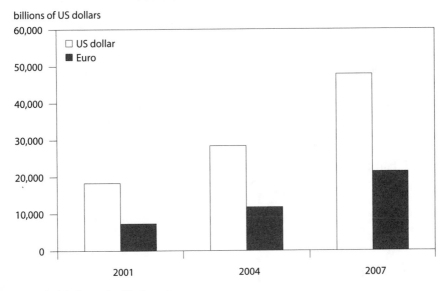

billions of US dollars

Source: Bank for International Settlements.

Figure 3.25 Euro exerting a stronger influence on exchange rates than Deutsche mark did

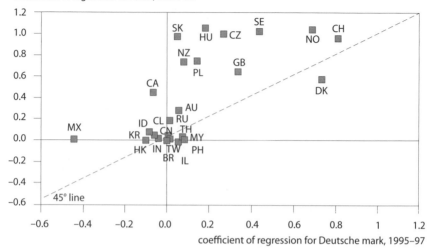

coefficient of regression for euro, 2002–08

coefficient of regression for Deutsche mark, 1995–97

AU = Australia; BR = Brazil; CA = Canada; CH = Switzerland; CL = Chile; CN = China; CZ = Czech Republic; DK =Denmark; GB = United Kingdom; HK = Hong Kong; HU = Hungary; ID = Indonesia; IN = India; IL = Israel; KR = South Korea; MX = Mexico; MY = Malaysia; NO = Norway; NZ = New Zealand; PH = Philippines; PL = Poland; RU = Russia; SE = Sweden; SK = Slovakia; TH = Thailand; TW = Taiwan

Note: Data points represent the coefficients of the regression of the dollar exchange rate of a currency on constant dollar-mark (euro) and dollar-yen exchange rates, estimated with daily data over the periods shown. Currencies above the 45 degree line respond more to the euro now than they did to the Deutsche mark in the past.

Source: Bloomberg.

euro turned into a shield especially for smaller EMU member countries against currency and capital-market turbulences triggered by the financial crisis. The relative tranquility in euro area financial markets contrasted sharply with the severe difficulties experienced by other smaller European countries, most spectacularly by Iceland, where the entire banking sector defaulted, but even by generally very stable countries, such as Denmark, which had to defend its currency through interest rate increases. Against the background of this experience, euro skeptics in several EU countries outside the EMU are having second thoughts about EMU entry, and a number of new EU member countries in Central Europe have intensified efforts to bring forward their eventual EMU membership.

Euro's Future as a Teenager

The euro's happy childhood between 1999 and 2009 is likely to be followed by a much more difficult period as a teenager. In fact, as in human

Figure 3.26 House prices in key EMU member countries (deviations of inflation-adjusted prices from their long-term trend), 1971–2007

percent deviation from trend

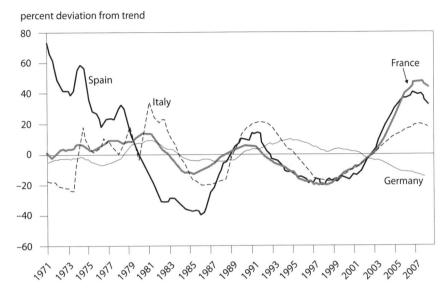

Source: Organization for Economic Cooperation and Development.

life, existential crises during this phase cannot be excluded. Key challenges for the euro include real economic adjustment within the euro area and the maintenance of fiscal and financial stability without a central fiscal authority.

In the first decade of its existence, the euro area benefited from low inflation and falling interest rates, first as a result of the convergence of national rates to the low level of Germany and then on the back of global rate reductions in the wake of the bursting of the dotcom bubble. The low level of interest rates stimulated demand financed by credit. As a result, real estate prices, construction investment, and private household consumption grew strongly, especially in those countries where interest rates reached lows never seen before. Divergence in house price developments played an important role in divergence in economic growth. As figure 3.26 shows, house prices in all major countries except Germany (and all smaller countries) rose substantially in real terms during the first 10 years of the EMU. Against this, prices stayed weak in Germany after the bursting of the unification house price bubble in the mid-1990s. The difference in house price developments exerted a significant influence on domestic demand growth. This is illustrated in figure 3.27, which plots real house price changes in a number of euro area countries between 1998 and 2006 against real consumption growth during this period.

Figure 3.27   Real house price and consumption growth across selected EMU countries, 1998–2006

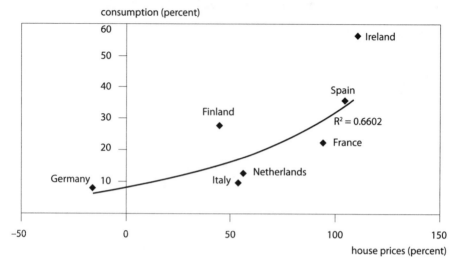

consumption (percent)

Source: Organization for Economic Cooperation and Development.

An unhealthy "division of labor" developed, where some EMU countries borrowed heavily to consume and invest while a few others, notably Germany, produced to satisfy the foreign demand. Thus, the international current account imbalances that developed during the last decade at the global level were mirrored by similar imbalances within the EMU. In 2007 Germany recorded a current account surplus of 7.6 percent of GDP, or 183 billion euros (figure 3.28). With the euro area running a surplus of 36 billion euros, this implies an aggregate deficit of other EMU member countries of 147 billion euros, or 2.3 percent of GDP. Within this group, some countries had very large and unsustainable deficits (notably Greece with 14.1 percent of GDP, Spain with 10.1 percent, Portugal with 9.8 percent, and Ireland with 5 percent).

Reflecting divergent developments of domestic demand through the first decade of the EMU, large differences in unit labor cost—and hence relative external competitiveness—developed. By the third quarter of 2008 unit labor costs in Germany and France stood at about 13 and 11 percent, respectively, below their levels at the beginning of the EMU. Against this, unit labor costs in Spain and Italy stood at 44 and 23 percent, respectively, above the starting levels (figure 3.29).

As risk aversion in financial markets increased in the course of the credit crisis, sovereign credit spreads of EMU deficit countries widened relative to Germany, making the funding of large current account positions ever more costly and difficult (figure 3.30). Clearly, deficit countries

Figure 3.28   Current account balances of key EMU countries, 1995–2008

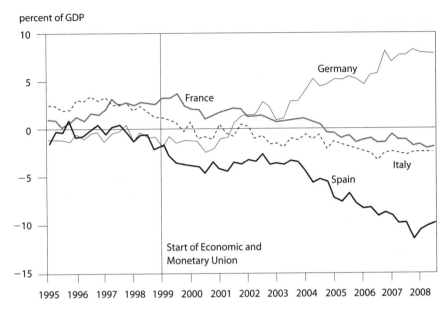

percent of GDP

Sources: European Commission, Eurostat Database; Deutsche Bank Global Markets Research.

Figure 3.29   Unit labor costs in key EMU countries, 1995–2008

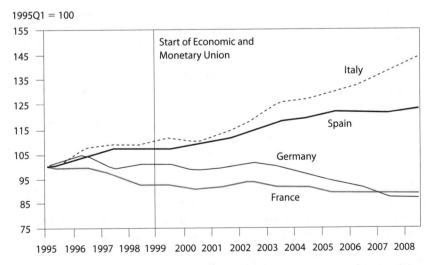

Sources: Organization for Economic Cooperation and Development; Deutsche Bank Global Markets Research.

**Figure 3.30   Interest rate spreads of 10-year government debt
over Germany, 2008**

percentage points

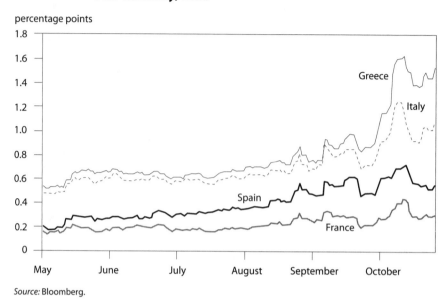

Source: Bloomberg.

need to bring their current account balances to more sustainable levels to avoid excessive risk premia on both public and private debt or even funding crises. This requires both reducing domestic expenditure and allocating resources from the nontraded to the traded goods sector.

The downturn in housing markets in Spain, Greece, Ireland, and several other EMU member countries with large current account deficits will certainly dampen domestic demand growth. However, in order to avoid an excessive increase in unemployment due to layoffs in the nontraded goods sector, competitiveness of the traded goods sector needs to increase. Without the ability to devalue the exchange rate, this has to be achieved by nominal cost reduction.

After having joined the EMU at a relatively high real exchange rate, Germany managed to do just this during the first decade of the currency union (see figure 3.29). But whether the countries presently suffering from a lack of competitiveness are able to follow the German example is an open question. Before the EMU, these countries normally recouped lost competitiveness through nominal exchange rate devaluations. It will require a profound institutional and cultural change to enable them to bring their relative costs down without the help of devaluations. Moreover, to allow them to adjust successfully, the surplus countries, and notably Germany, have to be prepared to let their costs and prices rise at a faster pace. The more sticky cost and price inflation in the deficit country is, the higher the cost and price inflation required in the surplus countries to make adjustment possible. But deflationary pressures in deficit countries and inflationary pressures in surplus countries may cause popular dissatisfaction with the workings of the EMU in both country groups. Although a break-up of the EMU remains very unlikely, given the huge political costs of such an event, political tensions among EMU member governments and between governments and the ECB are likely to rise as all parties involved struggle to find a feasible adjustment path to more sustainable internal current account balances.[30]

The other challenge for the euro in coming years is maintaining fiscal and financial stability without a central government authority. Before the EMU, many economists—including some who later held senior positions at the ECB—argued that a monetary union without a political union is a risky undertaking. How could fiscal policy discipline be maintained and financial stability ensured when there was no central government authority supporting the central bank's stability policy in a consistent way? The Stability and Growth Pact (SGP)—an agreement establishing constraints for government budget deficits and debt—was developed to give part of the answer. The other part relating to financial stability was given in the course of the financial crisis in the form of close and successful cooperation of national governments in crisis management. Yet, despite these efforts, questions on how to secure fiscal and financial stability on a lasting basis remain.

The present recession is testing governments' resolve to respect the (already mellowed) rules of the SGP. According to this pact, only countries with sufficient room for fiscal policy maneuver ought to take fiscal policy measures to support growth. However, pressure on the rules of the pact is mounting. Germany, a country with fairly sound government finances, a large current account surplus, and therefore some room for fiscal policy maneuver, has shown limited appetite for a fiscal stimulus to boost growth. In the view of German authorities, the additional debt incurred as a result of fiscal expansion will fall on future German taxpayers, while other EMU members, due to significant spillover effects of a fiscal expansion in Germany, would benefit from it. Without a major German fiscal impulse they could benefit from, other countries with much less solid public

---

30. Scenarios for a breakup of the EMU, which were popular in the first few years of the euro's existence, have made a comeback with the financial crisis. Suffice it to say that leaving the EMU is a bad option for a country seeking a weaker currency to boost growth in the short term. Its debt would be denominated in an appreciating foreign currency, and it would be entirely at the mercy of international capital markets, which would probably impose a hefty default premium on this debt. Things would be easier if a country wanting a stronger currency left the EMU: Its debt would be denominated in a falling foreign currency. However, the exchange rate appreciation would pose a serious threat to its competitiveness and growth. This and the political costs of leaving the EMU would most likely be more than enough to deter any EMU participant from seriously considering exit.

finances and hence little room for fiscal policy maneuver, such as Italy, are mulling significant fiscal policy measures to support growth.

At the same time, the financial crisis has revealed some defects in the arrangements for financial stability in the EMU. Initially, banking and financial-market supervision was left in national hands. Over time, and certainly with the onset of the financial crisis, cooperation among national supervisors and between them and the European System of Central Banks intensified. The crisis management has been praised widely and indeed with some justification. But an Achilles' heel remains in the arrangements due to the lack of a central fiscal authority. To appreciate this, consider the question of how the national authorities of a smaller euro area country could cope with bank failures that exceed the authorities' capacity to mobilize funds for a public rescue. According to its statutes, the ECB must not "bail out" any EMU member government. But what if such a government is overwhelmed by the costs of bank failures within its jurisdiction? Would the ECB accept the bonds issued by this country to support its banks as collateral when they are submitted for repurchase by the very same banks that urgently need the funds? Would other countries regard such an operation as monetization of government debt by the ECB and block the transaction, possibly causing the default of the distressed government?

A move toward joint issuance of government bonds by EMU member countries would make these questions irrelevant. Bonds issued this way would be backed by the financial standing of all EMU governments combined (and eventually, of course, also by the ECB, which is an agency of these governments), like traditional sovereign issues. Joint issuance of government debt would also establish a common sovereign euro area bond market, which many international investors in the euro would most likely find much more attractive than the present smaller national bond markets. But would countries with a high credit rating (e.g., Germany) be willing to dilute their rating by issuing debt jointly with governments with weaker ratings? This and the earlier questions reveal gaps in an EMU that is not backed by political union, gaps that may introduce a risk premium on the euro as an international reserve currency, which does not apply to the US dollar.

Conclusion

In its first decade of existence, the euro has been an impressive success. However, challenges are likely to arise during the next decade. First, the present financial crisis and economic recession are likely to mark a structural break for the development of finance and credit-driven growth not only at the global level but also for the euro area. But while adjustment to a world without credit-financed domestic demand growth and big international current account imbalances can be facilitated by exchange rate changes at the global level, this is not possible within the euro area. There, adjustment in the deficit countries needs to be engineered through expenditure reduction and relative cost deflation. This is likely to be very painful and may test the resolve of politicians to maintain the EMU as a hard currency area (or even the EMU itself).

Second, the recession and financial crisis are threatening fiscal and financial stability in a currency union without a central political authority. Fiscal discipline is likely to come under pressure as the recession deepens, and financial stability may be threatened when smaller or weaker euro area governments are overwhelmed by the cost of the financial crisis. As a result, markets are beginning to differentiate more clearly among government and financial debt of individual EMU countries. Differentiation will be reinforced in the future when more EU member countries join the euro—as seems now increasingly likely—and economic divergence among EMU countries will increase further. While a widening of bond yield spreads among EMU member countries may be welcomed by those who thought that the earlier narrowing would undermine fiscal policy discipline, it is also a step toward reducing the financial integration achieved during the last decade.

The implications for the international role of the euro are mixed. On the one hand, as the EMU expands, the euro's role as an anchor and international transaction currency will grow. On the other hand, the role of the euro as a store of wealth for global investors may be undermined by the lack of an integrated euro area financial system and market. Compared with the US dollar, the euro may come to look like a king without a country. Perhaps it was not entirely coincidental that the euro weakened against the dollar as the financial crisis deepened. It may well have reminded investors that history has not been too kind to kings without countries.

4

Is the Present Crisis the Moment for the Euro's Global Emergence?

A Panel Discussion with Antonio de Lecea, Leszek Balcerowicz, C. Fred Bergsten, Erkki Liikanen, and Lawrence H. Summers

ANTONIO DE LECEA

I am somewhat uncomfortable with the title or the main question of this panel. It has two implicit assumptions that I find questionable. The first one concerns the reference to global emergence, which needs some explanation. The euro has already acquired an international currency status and therefore, in my opinion, it is inappropriate to refer to a possible future global emergence of the euro when it is already the second largest currency in the world.

The second issue is the link between the current crisis and the future of the euro-dollar balance because the underlying assumption seems to be that there can be only one dominant international currency. This assumption is based partly on history and partly on the concept of

Antonio de Lecea Flores de Lemus has been director for international affairs in the European Commission's Directorate General for Economic and Financial Affairs since November 2004. Leszek Balcerowicz, former deputy prime minister and minister of finance of Poland and former president of the National Bank of Poland, is a professor of economics at the Warsaw School of Economics. C. Fred Bergsten has been director of the Peterson Institute for International Economics since its creation in 1981. Erkki Liikanen, former finance minister of Finland (1987–90), has been the governor and chairman of the Board of the Bank of Finland since July 12, 2004. Lawrence H. Summers, US secretary of the treasury from 1999 to 2000, is the director of the National Economic Council. He was the 27th president of Harvard University (2001–06) and the Nathaniel Ropes Professor of Political Economy there. Until January 2009, he was the Charles W. Eliot University Professor at Harvard University.

network externalities. Again, network externalities may play a role in some functions of international currency but not all of them. They may play a role for the currency as a unit of account and as a vehicle currency but not so much as a currency of investment (including foreign exchange reserves) because there are other considerations, as put forward by other speakers, particularly that of currency diversification.

If we look at one of the main determinants of the use of a currency as an international currency—size of capital markets—we find that capital markets in the European Union match the size of those in the United States. It is true that the composition differs. Equity capitalization is half that of the United States, but EU capital markets have been catching up in terms of efficiency, liquidity, and breadth. Therefore, rather than having a single dominant currency in the global monetary system, we can have two—I mean a bipolar system—and there may be room for more than two in the future.

This takes me back to the second issue: the relevance of the current crisis to bring about a bipolar monetary system. In a bipolar world, I do not think a single crisis will determine the shift or the tipping one way or another; change will probably be incremental. Crises are certainly destabilizing but are unlikely to shift from one currency to the other.

Having said that, what will be the impact of the current crisis on the role of the euro? Until now, the idea of crisis triggering a possible shift from one currency to another was based on a very different type of crisis, that resulting from disorderly unwinding of global current account imbalances. The argument went like this: The adjustment of current accounts would involve the depreciation of the dollar, which would expose the dilemma of countries holding a large amount of dollar-denominated reserves. By moving out of the dollar, they would stem their own evaluation losses. But eventually, they might lose confidence in the dollar and trigger its decline.

The current crisis started off as an adjustment to an imbalance but a different imbalance—reversal of the housing boom in the United States— and this is the only similarity. Since the crisis started, financial contagion, uncertainty about the allocation of the losses stemming from those bad assets, and the loss of trust have been the trigger.

And once contagion has spread, it does not matter whether the crisis originated on this side or the other side of the Atlantic. The original idea that the euro area financial sector might be immune to this crisis, unfortunately, did not prevail. Therefore, I would claim that the current crisis will not tilt the balance of power in one or the other direction. And even if the financial industry experiences profound transformations as a result of this crisis, the relative attractiveness of the financial markets in the United States and the euro will not dramatically change as a consequence of this crisis. The response of policymakers to this crisis and to other challenges will matter more.

Provided no massive policy mistakes are made on either side of the Atlantic, this crisis will not have a significant impact on the relative international status of the dollar or the euro.

LESZEK BALCEROWICZ

Before I address the relative role of the euro, let me comment on the present situation. I will skip the most difficult question of crisis resolution and mention what seems to be absent from today's discussion: the diagnosis and long-term lessons.

There is a tendency to discuss the reasons for the present crisis in terms of insufficient or wrong regulations and errors of specific institutions. These are very important reasons but probably only partial and approximate. The underlying reason is the excessive growth of credit in some countries, especially the United States. The faster credit grows, the more errors you accumulate, sooner or later leading to asset bubbles, which will eventually burst.

I belong to the group that thinks one should look at macroeconomic policies, especially monetary policy in the United States. This brings us a lesson for the future. To what extent should future monetary policy of the Federal Reserve—because, to some extent, the Fed dictates monetary policy to the world—consider asset price developments? This issue is highly disputed, but we cannot avoid its discussion. In fact, the discussion has already started.

The argument that you cannot fine-tune asset price developments is not sufficient to reject the general case that monetary policy should, at a minimum, not contribute to asset bubbles. So this is the first point.

On the second point, I have participated in many heated debates about global imbalances. And the question was how it was going to end, soft landing or hard landing? We are in a financial crisis that has no connection to the previous discussion about global policy imbalances. Perhaps we are witnessing an unhappy ending to the previous discussion on global imbalances. And perhaps we should bring some of those issues to the debates about the present financial crisis. Some very interesting issues have not been sufficiently discussed. What were the interconnections between the so-called global saving graph and excessive soft monetary policy? What were the dynamics of these two factors?

I agree with my predecessors that the most likely outcome of the present crisis, however it ends, would be neutral for the respective global roles of the euro and the dollar. One should not rush to the conclusion that the euro is going to benefit because the world is interconnected. Besides, the euro area's own economies are not as flexible as that of the United States. In the long run, certain factors prevent the euro from becoming a more important global currency, including faster rate of long-term growth and greater political cohesion in the United States than in the European Union.

C. FRED BERGSTEN

The dollar has been the world's dominant currency for about a century for a simple reason: It had no competition. No other economy was anywhere near the size of the American economy. No financial markets underlying any currency were anywhere near the size of the US financial markets. Through bad times and good for the US economy, the dollar was dominant.

This was true even in the late 1970s and early 1980s, when the United States ran three consecutive years of double-digit inflation; interest rates went to 20 percent plus; and we had the deepest recession since the 1930s. The dollar lost a little market share in that period but not much because there was no competition. The Deutsche mark was the closest competitor, and it never achieved a market share more than about one-quarter that of the dollar, mirroring the fact that the West German economy was about one-fourth the size of the US economy and, as Helmut Schmidt always reminded us, West Germany was "the size of Oregon, so don't expect us to play a global role."

All that changed with the advent of the euro because now we do have a currency based on an economy as large as or larger than the United States and financial markets that, while not equal in every respect even prior to the crisis, are certainly a competitor and are superior on some metrics. So the whole international competitive position for global currency status changed with the creation of the euro.

However, it is unlikely that the euro will seamlessly ascend to an equivalent role to the dollar for another simple reason that comes out of the study of the history of global currencies: inertia and incumbency advantages. We do not have very many observations to study this topic, but the history of the pound sterling suggests that incumbency advantages and inertia are very important. Sterling retained a major international role for more than 50 years beyond any conceivable notion that the United Kingdom was a major world economy, let alone the dominant world economy that it was when sterling first achieved its global dominance when it had no real competitor a century earlier.

So the crucial question is whether the inertia and incumbency advantages will be overcome by some significant event that would permit the newly eligible international currency, the euro, to move up alongside the dollar. In short, the United States has to make a mistake. The incumbent has to mess up badly when there is a competitor in place for the situation to change.

The United States did mess up considerably back in the late 1970s. Later, productivity growth was very slow. But there was no competitor.

Now there is a competitor, and so the immediate question, to link to the short term, is whether the current crisis originating in the United States is going to represent the mistake that would open the door for the competitor to ascend to a more or less equivalent position.

There are two responses to the question if one wants to conclude that this will not change it very much. One is that the United States could recoup rapidly. Yes, there is a crisis but the United States responds quickly and successfully. Recovering from the crisis in a sufficiently effective way not to lose global credibility, reputation, confidence, and the like has happened quickly, but we do not know yet if it has happened successfully.

The other possible savior from a dollar standpoint is that the Europeans do as badly as, or worse than, the United States in responding to the crisis. As Leszek Balcerowicz suggested, there would then be no net effect at all. I think the honest answer is we cannot know yet.

The interesting point is that the United States and Europe must cooperate to get the world out of the crisis. The issuers of the two key currencies have got to intensively cooperate to enable the world to come out of the problem. But at the same time, within that cooperation, there is inherently some competition because whichever one does better, whichever one resolves its own problems more successfully, whichever one comes out of the current difficulties more rapidly, will produce some important inferences about what the long-term market reaction is going to be to "euro versus dollar" and whether this situation will bring about the historic change required for a global currency relationship to change in the way it did in the past when the dollar replaced sterling, and now, when at least the potential exists for the euro not to replace the dollar but to move up alongside it into a true bipolar monetary system.

The other interesting question from the US standpoint is whether the ascendance of the euro to a more or less equivalent position would be a good or bad thing. Adam Posen earlier implied that it would be a bad thing. He noted that if Taiwan or Korea or some big dollar holder ever thought about moving off the dollar, the National Security Council guy would be out there to tell them to hold on. That might well be an accurate prediction, and we certainly saw it in the case of Saudi Arabia from time to time over the years. But the question is whether that is right and whether the United States should resist or welcome the advent of the euro as a more or less equivalent currency.

The United States must obviously do everything it can to restore the strength and stability for the dollar in terms of its own economy and in terms of the world economy as well. But the key currency role is more ambiguous from a US standpoint. In the short term, it is great to finance those big imbalances and live beyond your means as long as you can. But, as Leszek just said, that set of imbalances and persistent overvaluation of the dollar in trade terms clearly contributed to the big capital inflow that kept interest rates low and enabled the United States to live beyond its means, which at least in significant part is an underlying cause of the current crisis.

I believe it would be healthy for the United States to move to a bipolar monetary system where there is competition. We all believe in competition in goods markets, financial markets, indeed practically all markets, so why not on the international currency front as well? History shows that you can run bipolar monetary systems (and Barry Eichengreen's recent work has reaffirmed that). There is no reason why the United States and Europe could not cooperate effectively to manage a bipolar monetary system. The competition it would promote might be a healthy element as we reflect on the causes of the current crisis and how to avoid them in the future. It might be a healthy element in reducing the prospect that we have to go through this dreary cycle again, having more bubbles that are bound to burst, and trying to keep the United States as well as others from living too far beyond their means.

ERKKI LIIKANEN

The European Central Bank (ECB) decided on October 8, 2008 to participate in a coordinated rate cut and later the same day decided to implement a new monetary policy. We should have announced the two simultaneously, but the rate cut decision was a coordinated one and the implementation decision only our own. Euro area banks will, henceforth, be able to get liquidity to the full amount of their bids at our policy rate. This is a major change in liquidity policy.

On the international role of the euro, Fred said that he sees the possibility of a bipolar world here. I am quite agnostic on this issue. I think we, as European central bankers, should not promote the euro and that the euro's international role should rather reflect the economic development of the euro area.

Although we are in the middle of the storm in the United States, after it is over, I expect the dollar to remain the safe haven or the last resort. I do not know whether Adam Posen's point is correct that this is a national security issue for the United States, because I am not in that business. Actually, my country is more known for peace and reconciliation. Martti Ahtisaari has got the 2008 Nobel Peace Prize, and I use this opportunity to pay tribute to him.

What are the critical issues for the international role of the euro? I think they are the size and dynamism of the European economy, financial-market development, and supervision of our evolving financial markets.

First, regarding the European economy, the critical issue is how we can promote growth, implement structural reforms, and increase competition in product and labor markets. If these reforms, known as the Lisbon objectives, are implemented, there will be more growth, more productivity, and more dynamism. And there will be more interest in investing in European equity markets, this return chasing element, which was mentioned earlier. So that is the first and most critical issue.

Second is financial-market development. The European financial markets have advanced quite a bit but are still not ready. We need deeper, more integrated, and more liquid financial markets. The ECB has contributed to that development by trying to create a uniform infrastructure for securities settlement in Europe. It sounds very technical, but the key issue in securities markets is that across-the-border transactions in Europe are expensive, about four to seven times more expensive than similar US securities transactions. To unblock that bottleneck we need to have common infrastructures and more competition. So when European financial markets become deeper and more liquid, and the assets made available to investors are also developed, I am sure the role of the euro will also become stronger internationally.

The third challenge is how to efficiently supervise these financial markets. André Sapir spoke about it at this conference. I think that these past months have taught us well that liquidity and solvency are twins. If you have trouble in liquidity, you may later have a problem with solvency. For that reason, I am a proponent of the position that supervision should be close to central banking but independent. And countries where they are in the same infrastructure, even though independent, have acted rather quickly.

Of course, we have a particular challenge because the European Union has 27 countries and the euro area has 15. The solution must be such that the basis is national supervision, which operates within national borders. But home- and host-country supervisors must cooperate if the bank being looked at is systemically important in more than one country. And for those truly European players—we may have 10 or 15 of these—we need to go even further in the future. They should have one supervisory counterparty at the European level. We cannot, in the long term, imagine that one of your major banks will have to operate with 25 different administrative practices in as many countries. Some of these issues are actually under consideration in the European Union because the European Commission has made proposals on how to move forward. We just need to use this opportunity to get it right.

Finally, on financial crises, Kenneth Rogoff and others wrote a paper some time ago about the five big crises. That was the first time I heard that Finland, Sweden, and Norway are big countries because these three had crises in the late 1980s and early 1990s. All the current issues are well documented in our literature on the last crisis. In order to get out of the problem, we need solutions for bank recapitalization and equity, "bad banks" need more time to realize bad assets, and we need bank guarantees.

Some people ask why we are not dealing with the current problem at the European level. When I served at the European Commission with Sir

Leon Brittan, I was the commissioner for the budget. The ceiling for the EU budget is 1.275 percent of the total GDP of EU countries. It is small but still extremely controversial. Margaret Thatcher became famous when she wanted "her money back" from that small budget. So, there are no financial resources to solve this with the EU budget.

Second, if you need to put in taxpayers' money to save a bank, it is difficult to justify to the electorate across national borders. The taxpayers must know that it is targeted at the territory for which they are liable. For that reason, I do not expect that the EU budget is the solution for injecting equity or granting guarantees.

But the question of harmonizing practices remains. The best way to do this would be to define basic criteria for action beforehand and have all countries follow the same rules. It has not happened quite this way, but we are not terribly far. The EU scheme has three elements: guarantees, recapitalization, and takeover provisions. We have all more or less signed on to the so-called British plan. But in the European Union, member states must submit all these measures to the European Commission for scrutiny because we have strict rules on state aid. Sir Leon Brittan was running that area. State aid rules allow the Commission to prohibit any state aid that distorts competition within the EU market. So there is no precise ex ante harmonization of rescue operations but ex post.

To conclude, I cannot imagine meeting this crisis with independent currencies in Europe. I was in Brussels in the 1990s when huge tensions broke out between the European currencies. People could not accept that 15 to 20 percent changes in exchange rate could take place overnight. Regardless of what people think about the European project, there is wide agreement today that the Economic and Monetary Union, the euro, has been a major pillar of stability in our economy.

LAWRENCE H. SUMMERS

Old habits die hard, so let me begin by remarking that a strong dollar is in the interest of the United States. My view is that the United States is best served by not conceptualizing itself as in competition with the euro. If the United States runs its economy and manages its currency well, life will work out okay, and in general, I do not favor a US strategy of seeking to assert with great force the primacy of the dollar. So in that sense, I agree with Fred.

Where I have difficulty with his argument is the notion that the United States should actively encourage currency competition so as to discipline itself, which reminds me of a particularly exotic doctrine in automobile safety: If daggers were placed in steering wheels, people would find it in their interest to drive much slower and there would be fewer automobile accidents.

This notion has a certain logic to it but is not usually accepted. In the same way, to seek to create a situation where we will do damage to ourselves by doing the wrong thing and, therefore, we will do the right thing seems to me to expose us more to ill consequences than to potential gain. Currencies, like languages, involve extremely important elements of coordination. That is the reason for the incumbency advantage a number of people have talked about at this conference. To have two currencies trying to be in complete equipoise risks substantial instability, as things rush from one direction to the other. None of this is to say that the United States should seek to thwart the euro.

The world will tend to maintain the strength of the dollar, the primal role of the dollar, unless we mess up quite badly, and that is a fine outcome. If we make a mistake, that will be unfortunate. We should certainly support the Economic and Monetary Union, but the notion that we actively profit from a kind of knife's edge to deter us from bad conduct doesn't strike me as being a healthy one. We will know much more 18 months from now about a question that seems to be central to thinking about many monetary and financial questions, not least the view of the euro.

One can have two views with respect to the current crisis. The first, which I call the made-in-America view, is that America rammed large deficits that created substantial imbalances, elected an administration that did not believe in regulation, fomented in retrospect a crazy set of mortgage practices, built up a phenomenal bubble, and created for itself a tremendous financial crisis that, being the world's focal economy, inevitably had spillovers because others purchased its assets substantially. And so America is the epicenter of this financial crisis. The financial crisis has an unfortunate fallout. The lessons to be learned concern various dysfunctional features of American financial practices and financial regulation. The event is a substantial boon to those who favor the view that the American model of capitalism, or more generally the Anglo-Saxon model of capitalism, is somehow inferior to alternative, more corporatist, and dirigiste models. This is one view with respect to the financial crisis.

The second is that in a period of high global liquidity and globally lax supervision encouraged by the enormous complexity of financial instruments, a financial crisis developed with respect to imprudent practices of financial institutions everywhere and the first incarnation of the crisis happened to be American subprime lending. But that was largely coincidental; because America has more mark-to-market accounting, more institutions that operate on a hair-trigger because they are outside the system of large state-embraced banks, the crisis was felt first in America, was dimensioned first in America, was reflected first in America. But the magnitude of the financial system rot in Europe is not so much smaller as it is less discovered than the financial system rot in the United States. Europe is behind because of slightly different exigencies of the real estate cycle and because of slower revelation of financial pain. But the crisis is fundamentally global or at least transatlantic and should be interpreted in transatlantic terms.

I do not know which of these views is right. I was always educated by Ted Truman when we worked together that my habit of posing things as dichotomies was wrong because the truth always lay somewhere in between. Perhaps the right way to frame the question is less as which of these views is right and more as where along the spectrum between "made in America" and "first discovered in America" should one see this crisis.

If you live in Europe, you tend very much to the first view: that it was more made in America. Many in the United States, particularly those associated with institutions that would be thought of more as part of the shadow banking system than of the official banking system, would tend more to the second view, that it was first discovered in the United States.

I am genuinely not sure where the truth lies. But the question will be enormously important because the more the reality is in the first category, the more these events threaten the dollar and the model for which it stands and the more likely they are to portend a change in currency arrangements. But if the reality is more in the second category, the less likely these events would point to the euro gaining share relative to the dollar.

It is certainly not the case that European stock markets have vastly outperformed American stock markets over the last nine months. Depending on how you choose your dates, they may have outperformed American stock markets or underperformed a little bit. But the same is much closer. Suppose one had said a year ago, "America's going to have a huge financial crisis. Bear Stearns is going to go down. Lehman is going to go down. AIG is going down. Merrill Lynch is going to be sold, and five Latin American countries are going to be able to borrow money cheaper than Goldman Sachs," and then asked, "How will the US stock market do relative to the European stock market?" The answer would seem obvious. But the fact that it is not does make one wonder how much of this is an export situation and how much of this is a global situation. Certainly, the dramatic movements in the dollar vis-à-vis the euro recently also point in the same direction. I will leave the question on where the truth lies between the two views for others more knowledgeable than me to answer. The answer to that question will bear on the future of the dollar and the euro and also on how different economic systems are assessed.

QUESTION AND ANSWER SESSION

C. Fred Bergsten: I was delighted, Larry, to tee things up for you to come back at with some vigor, as you always do. But I cannot resist then coming back to you by simply noting that when you said that the United States should not seek to subject itself to currency competition, it did sound a bit like a former and perhaps future secretary of the Treasury speaking.

But I was basically pleased because, I think, we agreed. You said the United States should not seek primacy for the dollar and should not seek to thwart an increased international role for the euro. We should, indeed, support the euro project. That is what I was saying. And, in a sense, let the best currency win.

I certainly did not say that we should do damage to ourselves in order to promote a bigger role for the euro, nor did I advocate for a complete equipoise, in your elegant term. But rather to say that within this framework of necessary cooperation, which we had for many years, will have for the indefinite future, and certainly have had to come out of this crisis, there will be an element of competition. And you said, in posing your dichotomy, it is really going to be a judgment matter that the markets and world opinion as a whole will develop over the next several years, as to how Europe and the United States do coming out of this and therefore, in part, in understanding how we got into it.

So, I think fundamentally we agree on it. We are both agnostic as to how it is going to come out. I guess the difference would be that I have greater equanimity about the prospect that, on this particular criterion of international currency roles, a bigger role for the euro might actually be a healthy thing, especially for future secretaries of the Treasury.

Erkki Liikanen: Just two comments. On the exchange rate, I feel uncomfortable when people explain everything with short-term changes in exchange rates. There have been changes recently, but let us look at them in the long term.

On the financial markets, Larry said that we have a problem in Europe that we know exists but has not yet been revealed. Europe is not isolated. But let us not take extremely strong positions before we know for certain. Of course, the banks that depend on wholesale funding have had a very tough time because markets are tight, the risk premia are high, and so forth.

George Soros: The current crisis has revealed a fundamental flaw in the design of the euro. In such a crisis, the central bank can do certain things, and the treasury has to do certain things. In the case of the euro, you have a common central bank but no common treasury. This issue has come to the forefront now when there is a need to effectively underwrite or rescue banks. France and Germany prefer to do it on a national basis. Smaller countries that are weaker would like to do it on a European basis. How this issue is going to be resolved will have a major influence on whether the euro is qualified to be an international reserve currency.

This factor has played into the fluctuation in the value of the euro because it is very hard to know exactly why currencies move the way they do. Certainly, the more pressing issue is the shortage of dollars. The euro, in fact, was overbought in the early stages of the recession, which started in the United States. In fact, the economic slowdown was transmitted to

Europe via the declining dollar. And now that the financial crisis has become more severe, there is a pressing shortage of dollars among European banks. They have to pay tremendous premiums for it. That is the other factor that has accounted for the move to the euro.

Leon Brittan: On George Soros' point that the European side of the crisis cannot be dealt with exclusively by the European Central Bank but has to be dealt with by treasuries, this may not be an acceptable pragmatic British approach, but as far as I see it, it does not matter whether it is done by European institutions, so long as it is done by Europe. By this I mean that if, for historical institutional reasons, it is impossible for Europe to agree on a big plan to be implemented, it does not matter so long as the European finance ministers agree on the principles that should be applied by individual countries, which have a degree of flexibility as to how they apply them but at the same time are dealing with the same problems with the same broad objectives.

Not everyone on this panel entirely shares the theme about the euro replacing the dollar or not. But the framework of discussion implies that it is a good thing. Your side wins, as it were.

Larry said he was in favor of a strong dollar, in a slightly mantra-like fashion at the beginning of his remarks. I was going to agree with Fred, but then he said in his concluding remarks, "Let the best currency win," implying that this is a contest and that winning is a good thing. Erkki, with whom I agree, said that it is not a European objective to make the European currency, the euro, an international reserve currency.

I want to bring to bear a little bit of the experience of the United Kingdom. I remember the time when Britain was struggling to retain the international role for sterling. It became very clear to the younger among us that having this international role as a reserve currency was not only not a big prize but also a major handicap to dealing with the British economy.

One thing is clear, if the cap fits, wear it. If you are a major country where economic fundamentals are pushing your currency away from its central role in the world, there is nothing more disastrous than to try and follow policies that are designed to cling on to that role because those policies are going to be seriously disadvantageous.

Erkki Liikanen: On the role of subsidiaries, there is a difference between a subsidiary of a bank and a branch of a bank. The subsidiary is legally independent. So in these crisis resolutions that we have had, countries were able to take action in the case of subsidiaries because the national supervisor of the subsidiary supervised the bank. They knew the situation and had the ability to act nationally. A branch, however, is outside the full national supervision of the host country. So if it is a question of a branch, it will be more difficult. In the subsidiary case, it has worked.

To George Soros, one comment on the European treasury issue. The last two or three years have been rather positive in that area even though we do not have a big European budget. But certain good, sound, basic principles have been applied due to the Stability and Growth Pact, which aims at cutting excessive deficits and which has been working. The pact has been respected in Germany and also in France; we have given a greater role to automatic stabilizers. Everybody has to accept that excessive deficits are harmful to economic development.

C. Fred Bergsten: Just to clarify Sir Leon Brittan's last point. When I said let the best currency win, I meant in a market sense. Let the market determine whose policies are better, whose performance is better. That will, as Larry and I both said, probably determine which currencies will play which relative roles in the future.

I distinguish market choice from national interest or certainly any driven by national policy to promote either currency as the dominant one. I thought I was clear in my remarks that I had a preference, which Larry did not care for. But my preference for that kind of competitive international currency role is based in part on its disciplinary grounds. And I hope I will, therefore, retain your support for my view in this debate.

Leszek Balcerowicz: On banking supervision in Europe, whatever arrangement that emerges should be country-specific because countries differ. For example, some small European banks are of systemic importance in some new EU members. And second, it would not be advisable to have complete harmonization of supervision. And I give you one example from my own experience as a former central bank governor: The rate of growth of housing credit denominated in Swiss francs has been excessive, specifically in Poland and some other new EU members. We introduced special regulations that have slowed this growth. One can call it a reverse of subprime because it makes it more expensive and more difficult for poor people to get housing credit. I think it was working in the sense that it slowed the rate of previously excessive growth of credit. Such solutions cannot be European; they have to be country-specific.

Lawrence Summers: The issue of European crisis governance is profoundly important. We will know better how well the system works a year from now than we do today. I'm inclined to agree with Leon Brittan, that whatever defenses can be offered for it are more in the pragmatic domain than in the theoretical domain. We will know just how pragmatically effective and successful it is.

At a WP3 meeting 10 years ago, I had inquired, "Could you just help me understand, suppose the third largest bank in Spain is about to fail, who are the players and who is responsible for what. What is up to the Spanish Treasury? What is up to the Spanish central bank, which no longer has a currency? What is up to the ECB? What is up to Brussels? Just tell me what the protocol is."

And again, this was 10 years ago. At that point, half a dozen European hands were raised. It was like any group of economists: Half a dozen answers were offered to the question by half a dozen Europeans. I assume that matters have been rationalized since then, but I do think it is an important issue, particularly when you have to move rapidly.

Erkki Liikanen: Larry asked 10 years ago about a Spanish bank. But I would like to take a more complicated question, that of Fortis, a Belgian bank that got into trouble. Its balance sheet is 225 percent of the Belgian GDP. How was the crisis handled?

As far as emergency lending is concerned, the rules are clear. The central bank has the responsibility after authorization of the ECB Governing Council.

As far as equity is concerned, Fortis has headquarters in Belgium and subsidiaries in two other countries. The treasuries got together on that particular Sunday and decided how they would inject equity. All the decisions were announced at the same time, 10 o'clock on Sunday. The Spanish case is simpler because there are fewer participants in the discussion.

Alexander Swoboda: In the mid-1960s there were already discussions in the United States on whether it was worth keeping the link to gold and the international role of the dollar and so on. And there was the case of Britain, which Sir Leon Brittan mentioned. It is not a question of actively promoting the international role of one's currency for the sake of actively promoting the role of the currency and winning a competition on international markets. It is a matter of the costs and benefits of having a currency that is an international currency.

A number of small countries—Germany was mentioned and Switzerland, my own country—actively discouraged the international use of their currencies because it had many disadvantages. So, I think, you decide you want a strong currency or you want a good, deep, resilient market for assets denominated in your currency, which encourages use of your currency in markets. And that contributes quite naturally to your currency being more used as an international currency. But it is not a political decision: "I want my currency to be the dominant one." If Britain was trying to retain its currency's dominance, it was partly because it was afraid of what would happen to the British economy if the Commonwealth dumped British reserves. It was not because it wanted to maintain the empire.

Edwin (Ted) Truman: I have a slightly broader question that goes beyond the European discussion, and it was raised in part by the discussion about bank subsidiaries in Eastern Europe. I'm not quite sure it makes a difference whether an entity is a subsidiary or branch. I mean it makes a legal difference, but as we have learned from this crisis, there are reputational risks. And once your reputation is at risk, it does not matter why.

My broader issue is: A country has a national supervisor, and the national treasury is responsible for solvency support. But some countries have financial institutions that are large relative to the country's GDP, for example, Iceland, Malta, Belgium, and Switzerland. It is a tragedy for Iceland, but if the country were the size of Germany and had comparable institutions as a multiple of GDP, it would be a problem for everybody. So if we are going to insist on principally national supervision and principally national treasuries to do the solvency operation, or if they cannot do it, then there are implications for everybody else. You have a question for the global system and whether others in the system will say, "Your bank cannot get that large." That would be one answer. I am not sure what the right answer is, but this crisis has raised this question.

Peter B. Kenen: What is important to a country is not that its currency is the reserve currency. What is important to a country—and this implies that two or three currencies can play international roles at the same time and not compete for dominance—is that its nationals, for example, enjoy the advantages of its currency being used widely abroad (invoicing of trade, private-sector uses, and so on) and not the fact that the Chinese, for example, may be holding X billion US dollars in their reserves.

Too much attention is being given to the role of the currency in the official sector or in the monetary system narrowly defined. We should be looking at the role of currencies in the international business sector. And there it is obvious that more than one country or entity, such as the monetary union, can promote the international use of its currency or assist its nationals in doing so without necessarily competing with some other government.

Of course, exchange rate movements are of some proposition. You do want a modicum of exchange rate stability. But that speaks to the kind of monetary policies you follow, not policies designed to encourage reserve accumulation by foreigners but rather policies to assure domestic financials and price stability. This debate is cast too narrowly in terms of competition between currencies as reserve currencies and insufficiently in terms of a role for your currency that is commensurate with your role in the world economy and that promotes or assists this role rather than trying to displace another currency in the system.

Lawrence Summers: I will comment on a couple of issues. First, how good is it in terms of lowering borrowing costs to have your currency be a favored reserve currency? Second, how good is it to be a transaction currency, which is Peter's issue. And there is a third issue, which is awkward to talk about but I suspect may be quantitatively more important: How attractive is your paper money as an asset for hoarders outside the law to hold? And what does that mean for seigniorage? I suspect the numbers from extra seigniorage loom fairly large relative to some of the other numbers you calculate in this area. It is obviously not the most consequential issue in the world, but we in the Treasury in the 1990s were of the view that it was a modestly internationally uncivil act for the Europeans to introduce the €500 note when we had made a very conscious decision to resist issuing the $500 note so as to make our currency less attractive for drug dealers and black marketers. If you calculate the seigniorage gain that results from the European act—it is essentially an interest-free loan forever of that amount of money—$50 billion to $100 billion can plausibly be attributed to it. Let me leave it at that.

Erkki Liikanen: I just want to comment on Ted Truman's two critical questions. He asked about the size of the country and size of the balance sheet of the bank. I think it is a serious issue. We have been very closely following Iceland. Icelandic banks have branches and subsidiaries in Finland also.

The balance sheet of Icelandic banks was 10 times bigger than the GDP of that country. So we should always remember—and everybody is learning it—that the central bank should be strong enough with its balance sheet so that it is able to do its job as the lender of last resort. That is the first point. The second is that the treasury of each country must be able to assess its capacity to act in case of a problem with solvency. And that is where the Fortis case is interesting because it was relatively big. Belgium was able to act, together with the Netherlands and Luxembourg.

The difference between a subsidiary and a branch is not only theoretical. I am in the middle of a problem at home (Finland) because three Icelandic banks are now in receivership. Two of them have subsidiaries and one has a branch in my country. I have been following Norway and Sweden. They have considered it possible to give liquidity assistance—emergency lending—to a subsidiary because that is independently supervised by the host country. But to give emergency lending to a branch is a different case. So there are concrete differences between those two structures in a crisis.

C. Fred Bergsten: Let me close with two empirical and hopefully not very provocative points. Peter rightly noted the distinction between the private or vehicle use of a currency and its reserve currency use. Historically, there has been a pretty high correlation between those two uses. I do not think there is a strong theoretical reason for that, although some logic links the two. But they have always been parallel. So whereas I think you are conceptually right, I do not think it leads to a big difference in terms of one's judgment on the impact of the international role of your currency—if you get one, you get the other, and you have to look at them as a package.

The other is on Larry's point about the gains from seigniorage. If you are right, Larry, that the gains are as much as $50 billion to $100 billion for the European Union by issuing those mafia-friendly notes, it still does not necessarily swamp the other effects of the international role of your currency. It depends on the answer to the question Leszek and I posed earlier, the extent to which the international role of your currency has an important measurable impact on your domestic economic outcomes.

And again, that comes back to the provocative point. If the international role of the dollar was an important factor in promoting the imbalances, promoting the huge capital inflow, promoting the low interest rates, excessively easy monetary policy, and promoting the mispricing of risk, then the quantitative implications could swamp any seigniorage gain or loss. Now that is an if, because we have a lot of controversy over that analytical linkage. But those kinds of comparisons would have to be made because there is no definitive answer. It would have to be part of the equation as to whether you thought it was a good thing or not such a good thing for your currency to play a big global role.

Adam S. Posen: Five years ago, we held a conference at the Institute and I edited the volume on the euro at five, then also with the support of the European Commission. Euro skepticism in the United States remained a significant factor at the time, and we had to sell the idea that the euro was succeeding. Five years later, that is no longer the issue.

Our conference today considered whether and how the euro could play a more global role. A number of empirically grounded reasons were presented for skepticism that such a much-expanded role, let alone displacement of the dollar, would be soon achieved. Yet, all participants viewed both the continued domestic success and continually increasing global usage of the euro as nearly inevitable, as well as in the world's common interest. The euro at 10 is regional, stable, and a legitimate source of pride in European achievement.

About the Contributors

Joaquín Almunia is the European commissioner for economic and monetary affairs. He has been a member of the European Commission since April 2004. He was an economist at the Council Bureau of the Spanish Chambers of Commerce in Brussels and in 1976 became the chief economist of the Spanish trade union UGT.

From 1979 to 2004, he served as a member of the Spanish parliament, becoming minister of employment and social security in 1982 and minister of public administration in 1986. He served as leader of the Parliamentary Party from 1994 to 1997, preceding his appointment as leader of the Spanish Socialist Party from 1997 to 2000. In 2000 he stood as Socialist candidate for prime minister.

He is the author of several books and numerous academic articles and press columns. He graduated in law and economics from the University of Deusto (Bilbao) and completed postgraduate studies at L'École Practique des Hautes Études de Paris.

Maria Celina Arraes is the deputy governor for international affairs at the Central Bank of Brazil. In this capacity, she is a member of the Executive Board of the Central Bank and of the Monetary Policy Committee. She is responsible for regulation of the foreign exchange market and for the relationship of the Central Bank of Brazil with international organizations and with other central banks, mainly in Latin America, under the aegis of Mercosur and other financial and monetary integration arrangements. She is also the central bank deputy in the Group of Twenty.

Arraes has been a public official since 1973. Before being appointed to her current post at the Central Bank of Brazil, she held several positions there in the international area and in the central bank governor's office. She was also senior adviser to the executive director for Brazil in the International Monetary Fund. Before returning to the central bank in 2008, she spent nine years at the United Nations Development Program.

She holds an MA in economics from the University of Brasilia (1977) and degrees in economics and public administration. She has published articles on the national financial system and central banks and financial and monetary integration in different publications, including in International Economic Development and Law Series (United Kingdom), Institute for the Integration of Latin America and the Caribbean Series of the Inter-American Development Bank, and the Center for Latin-American Monetary Studies (CEMLA).

Leszek Balcerowicz, former deputy prime minister and minister of finance of Poland and former president of the National Bank of Poland, is a professor of economics at the Warsaw School of Economics (WSE). He is the architect of Poland's economic reforms initiated in 1989 and has been at the center of Poland's economic and political life since the fall of communism in Poland in 1989. In 2005 he was awarded with Poland's highest decoration, Order of the White Eagle, for his contribution to Poland's economic transformation.

In September 1989 Balcerowicz became deputy prime minister and minister of finance in the first noncommunist government in Poland after World War II. He was also president of the Economic Committee of the Council of Ministers. During this vital period in Poland's transition he designed and executed the radical stabilization and transformation of Polish economy. He retained his positions in the government until December 1991. From April 1995 to December 2000 he was the president of the Freedom Union, a free market–oriented party. From 1997 to June 2000 he again became deputy prime minister and minister of finance. In January 2001, he was appointed president of the National Bank of Poland.

Since October 1992, Balcerowicz has been a professor of economics at WSE and since 1993 a director of the chair of international comparative studies at WSE. In 1992–2000 he was chairman of the Council of the Center for Social and Economic Research (CASE) in Warsaw. He is on the board of directors of the Peterson Institute for International Economics.

He graduated in 1970 with distinction from the foreign trade faculty of the Central School of Planning and Statistics (CSPS) in Warsaw, now the Warsaw School of Economics. In 1974 he received an MBA from St. John's University in New York; in 1975 he received his PhD in economics from CSPS.

C. Fred Bergsten has been director of the Peterson Institute for International Economics since its creation in 1981. He has been the most widely quoted think tank economist in the world over the eight-year period 1997–2005. He testifies frequently before Congress and appears often on television. He was ranked 37 in the top 50 "Who Really Moves the Markets?" (Fidelity Investment's *Worth*) and as "one of the ten people who can change your life" in *USA Today*.

He was assistant secretary for international affairs of the US Treasury (1977–81); undersecretary for monetary affairs (1980–81), representing the United States on the G-5 Deputies and in preparing G-7 summits; assistant for international economic affairs to Dr. Henry Kissinger at the National Security Council (1969–71); and senior fellow at the Brookings Institution (1972–76), the Carnegie Endowment for International Peace (1981), and the Council on Foreign Relations (1967–68). He is co-chairman of the Private Sector Advisory Group to the United States–India Trade Policy Forum. He was chairman of the Competitiveness Policy Council, which was created by Congress, throughout its existence from 1991 to 1995; and chairman of the APEC Eminent Persons Group throughout its existence from 1993 to 1995.

He has authored, coauthored, or edited 40 books on international economic issues including *The Long-Term International Economic Position of the United States* (2009), *China's Rise: Challenges and Opportunities* (2008), *China: The Balance Sheet—What the World Needs to Know Now about the Emerging Superpower* (2006), *The United States and the World Economy: Foreign Economic Policy for the Next Decade* (2005), *Dollar Adjustment: How Far? Against What?* (2004), *Dollar Overvaluation and the World Economy* (2003), *No More Bashing: Building a New Japan-United States Economic Relationship* (2001), and *The Dilemmas of the Dollar* (2d ed., 1996).

He has received the Meritorious Honor Award of the Department of State (1965), the Exceptional Service Award of the Treasury Department (1981), and the Legion d'Honneur from the Government of France (1985). He has been named an honorary fellow of the Chinese Academy of Social Sciences (1997). He received MA, MALD, and PhD degrees from the Fletcher School of Law and Diplomacy and a BA magna cum laude and honorary Doctor of Humane Letters from Central Methodist University.

Lorenzo Bini Smaghi has been a member of the Executive Board of the European Central Bank since June 2005. He was director general for international financial relations at the Italian Ministry of the Economy and Finance from 1998 to 2005, deputy director general for research at the European Central Bank in 1998, and head of the Policy Division at the European Monetary Institute in Frankfurt from 1994 to 1998. He was head of the Exchange Rate and International Trade Division at the Research Department of Banca d'Italia from 1988 to1994 and economist in the International Section of the Research Department of Banca d'Italia from 1983 to 1988.

He was vice president of the Economic and Financial Committee of the EU (2003–May 2005); chairman of the Committee on Financial Markets of the OECD (2003–June 2005); president of SACE S.p.A. (Italian Export Credit Agency) (2001–May 2005); member of the boards of the EIB, Finmeccanica S.p.A, and MTS S.p.A (2001–May 2005); and chairman of Working Party No. 3 of the OECD (2005–April 2008).

He is the author of several books on international and European monetary and financial issues, including *Il paradosso dell'euro* (2008), *L'Euro* (2001), *Open Issues in European Central Banking* (2000), and *Chi Ci Salva dalla Prossima Crisi Finanziaria?* (2000).

He graduated from the Université Catholique de Louvain (Belgium) and holds an MA degree in economics from the University of Southern California and a PhD in economics from the University of Chicago.

Kristin Forbes is a nonresident visiting fellow at the Peterson Institute for International Economics and associate professor at the Massachusetts Institute of Technology's Sloan School of Management. Over the last few years she has rotated between academia and economic policy positions in the US government. From 2003 to 2005 she served as a member of the White House's Council of Economic Advisers (where she was the youngest person to ever hold this position). During 2001–02 she worked in the US Treasury Department as the deputy assistant secretary of quantitative policy analysis, Latin American and Caribbean nations. She has also been honored as a Young Global Leader as part of the World Economic Forum at Davos since 2005.

Forbes is a research associate at the National Bureau of Economic Research, a member of the Trilateral Commission, and a term member of the Council on Foreign Relations. She has written extensively on international capital flows, capital controls, currency depreciations, financial crises, financial market contagion (including a coedited book *International Financial Contagion*, 2001) and the relationship between income inequality and economic growth. She was awarded the Milken Award for Distinguished Economic Research in 2000. She has been honored with several teaching awards, including the Sloan School of Management's Jamieson Award for a history of excellence in teaching, Teacher of the Year Award, and Excellence in Teaching Award.

She has been a visiting scholar at a number of institutions, including the US Federal Reserve Board, Indian Council of Research on International Economic Relations, and International Monetary Fund. Prior to joining MIT, Forbes worked in the investment banking division at Morgan Stanley and in the policy research department at the World Bank.

Forbes received her PhD in economics from MIT in 1998, where she won the Solow Prize for excellence in teaching and research. She obtained her BA, summa cum laude with highest honors, from Williams College in 1992.

Linda S. Goldberg is a vice president of international research at the Federal Reserve Bank of New York and visiting officer at the Board of Governors of the Federal Reserve System. She is also a research associate of the National Bureau of Economic Research. She was a visiting professor at Princeton University, Department of Economics, Bendheim Finance Program (January to July 2005, January to July 2007). Prior to joining the Federal Reserve in 1995, she was a professor of economics at New York University and a visiting professor at the University of Pennsylvania.

She has worked or consulted for numerous international agencies, including the International Monetary Fund, the World Bank, and the Organization for Economic Cooperation and Development. She has served as an associate editor of the *Economic Policy Review*, a journal of the Federal Reserve Bank of New York, and is the book review editor of the *Journal of International Economics*.

Goldberg has a PhD in economics from Princeton University (awarded 1988), and a BA in mathematics and economics from Queens College, City University of New York with honors, where she graduated with the honors of Phi Beta Kappa and summa cum laude.

C. Randall Henning, visiting fellow, has been associated with the Peterson Institute since 1986. He serves on the faculty of the School of International Service, American University. He specializes in the politics and institutions of international economic relations, international and comparative political economy, and regional integration. His research focuses on international monetary policy, exchange rate and macroeconomic policy coordination, the G-7, G-8, and G-20 forums, East Asian financial cooperation, and European monetary union.

He is the author of *Accountability and Oversight of US Exchange Rate Policy* (2008), *East Asian Financial Cooperation* (2002), *The Exchange Stabilization Fund: Slush Money or War Chest?* (1999), *Cooperating with Europe's Monetary Union* (1997), and *Currencies and Politics in the United States, Germany, and Japan* (1994); coauthor of *Transatlantic Perspectives on the Euro* (2000), *Global Economic Leadership and the Group of Seven* (1996) with C. Fred Bergsten, *Can Nations Agree? Issues in International Economic Cooperation* (1989) and *Dollar Politics: Exchange Rate Policymaking in the United States* (1989); and coeditor of *Governing the World's Money* (2002) and *Reviving the European Union* (1994). He is also the author of recent journal articles on the exchange rate policy of the euro area.

Mohsin S. Khan has been a senior fellow at the Peterson Institute for International Economics since March 2009. Before joining the Institute, he was the director of the Middle East and Central Asia department at the International Monetary Fund (IMF) from 2004 to 2008. He first joined the IMF in 1972 as an economist in the Financial Studies Division of the Research Department, where he held senior positions including adviser, assistant director, and senior adviser. He also served as deputy director of the Research Department and became director of the IMF Institute in 1996. Other affiliations include visiting lecturer and research fellow at the London School of Economics (1975–76), adviser to the Central Bank of Venezuela (1976), and chief of the Macroeconomics Division of the Development Research Department at the World Bank (1985–86).

He has published widely on macroeconomic and monetary policies in developing countries, economic growth, international trade and finance, Islamic banking, and IMF programs. He is the editor or coeditor of *Economic Development in South Asia* (2005), *Macroeconomic Management: Programs and Policies* (2002), *External Debt and Capital Flight in Sub-Saharan Africa* (2000), *Trade Reforms and Regional Integration in Africa* (1998), *Macroeconomic Models for Adjustment in Developing Countries* (1991), *Theoretical Studies in Islamic Banking and Finance* (1987), and *Growth-Oriented Adjustment Programs* (1987). He has also published numerous articles in major economics journals. In 2003 he was awarded, jointly with A. Mirakhor, the Islamic Development Bank Prize in Islamic Economics for outstanding contributions to the field.

He received his PhD from the London School of Economics and holds an MA from Columbia University, a BSc in economics from the London School of Economics, and a BA from Punjab University.

Antonio de Lecea Flores de Lemus has been director for international affairs in the European Commission's Directorate General for Economic and Financial Affairs since November 2004. He is in charge of the international issues relevant for the Economic and Monetary Union and of shaping and implementing the economic dimension of EU external policies. This involves both bilateral economic relations with non-EU countries as well as participation in the preparatory work of key multilateral and regional economic institutions and fora (International Monetary Fund, World Bank, G-7/G-8, Organization for Economic Cooperation and Development, and multilateral development banks) where he acts as the European Commission's financial sous-sherpa.

He was economic adviser in the Private Office of Romano Prodi, former European Commission president, from 1999 until 2004. He has worked for the European Commission since 1986, holding management positions in the EU budget and control areas, as well as in economics and finance. Before joining the European Commission he was a member of the Private Office of the Spanish Secretary of State for Finance in Madrid and held other academic positions.

He obtained his PhD in 1983 from the Catholic University of Louvain's European Doctoral Programme for Quantitative Economics jointly run by university with the London School of Economics and Bonn University. He received a first degree in economics from the Barcelona Autonomous University (UAB). He has been an associate professor of applied economics since 1986 at Basque Country University in Bilbao, Spain, a position that he now holds on secondment.

Erkki Liikanen, former finance minister of Finland (1987–90), has been the governor and chairman of the Board of the Bank of Finland since July 12, 2004. He has also been a member of the Governing Council of the European Central Bank and governor of the International Monetary Fund for Finland since 2004. In June 2008 he was appointed president of the Finnish Red Cross.

He was a member of parliament (1972–90), secretary general of the Social Democratic Party (1981–87), ambassador extraordinary and plenipotentiary and head of the Finnish Mission to the European Union (1990–94), member of the European Commission for Budget, Personnel and Administration (1995–99), and member of the European Commission for Enterprise and Information Society (1999–2004).

He obtained a masters degree in political science (economics) from the University of Helsinki in 1975. He has also been awarded an honorary doctorate, DSc (Tech) (h.c.), from the Helsinki University of Technology.

Philippe Martin is professor at Sciences Po (Paris) and research fellow at the Centre for Economic Policy Research (CEPR), London. He is co-managing editor of *Economic Policy*, member of Institut Universitaire de France, and codirector of the macroeconomics program at CEPREMAP, Paris. He was assistant professor at the Graduate Institute of International Studies in Geneva and economist at the Federal Reserve Bank of New York. His fields of research are international macroeconomics, international trade, and economic geography.

His research has been published in the *American Economic Review*, *Review of Economic Studies*, *Journal of International Economics*, *Journal of Public Economics*, and other academic journals. He is coauthor of Economic Geography and Public Policy (2005, Princeton University Press). He was an academic adviser to the World Bank's *2009 World Development Report on Economic Geography*.

Thomas Mayer is a managing director and chief European economist at Deutsche Bank in London. He also coheads the bank's Global Economics Group. He and his team provide economic and interest rate forecasts for European countries and the global economy to Deutsche Bank's clients as well as to the trade and sales desks of the bank.

Before joining Deutsche Bank in 2002, he worked for Goldman Sachs in Frankfurt and London (1991–2002), and for Salomon Brothers in London (1990–91). Before moving to the private sector, he held positions at the International Monetary Fund in Washington (1983–90) and at Institut für Weltwirtschaft in Kiel (1974–78).

Mayer has published numerous articles on international and European economic issues in professional journals and commented on these issues in the media. He received a PhD in economics from the University of Kiel (1978) and has been a CFA Charterholder since 2002.

Jean Pisani-Ferry is director of Bruegel, the Brussels-based think tank, and professor at Université Paris-Dauphine. He was executive president of the French prime minister's Council of Economic Analysis; senior adviser to the French minister of finance; director of CEPII, the French institute for international economics; and economic adviser with the European Commission.

Pisani-Ferry's research is mainly devoted to European and global economic policy topics. Recent books he coauthored or coedited include *Coming of Age: Report on the euro area* (2008), *An Agenda for a Growing Europe* (2004), and *Exchange Rate Policies in Emerging Asian Countries* (1999).

He is also a member of the European Commission's Group of Economic Policy Analysis and of the French prime minister's Council of Economic Analysis. He has held teaching positions with various universities including the Ecole polytechnique in Paris and the Université libre de Bruxelles.

Adam S. Posen is deputy director of the Peterson Institute for International Economics, where he has been a senior fellow since 1997. A widely cited expert on monetary policy, he has been a visiting scholar at central banks worldwide, including on multiple occasions at the Federal Reserve Board, the European Central Bank, and the Deutsche Bundesbank. In 2006 he was on sabbatical leave from the Peterson Institute as a Houblon-Norman Senior Fellow at the Bank of England. He has also been a consultant to several US government agencies (including the Departments of State and Treasury and the Council of Economic Advisers), the European Commission, the Japanese Ministry of Economy, Trade, and Industry, and the International Monetary Fund on a variety of economic and foreign policy issues. He is a member of the Panel of Economic Advisers to the Congressional Budget Office for 2007–09.

He is the author of *Restoring Japan's Economic Growth* (1998; Japanese translation, 1999); coauthor with Ben Bernanke et al. of *Inflation Targeting: Lessons from the International Experience* (1999); and editor and part-author of three collected volumes: *The Euro at Five: Ready for a Global Role?* (2005), *The Future of Monetary Policy* (2008), and *The Japanese Financial Crisis and its Parallels with U.S. Experience* (2000; Japanese translation, 2001). He has also published more than 30 papers on monetary and fiscal policy in leading economics journals and academic and central bank conference volumes. He cofounded and chairs the editorial board of the refereed journal *International Finance*. He is a frequent contributor to the opinion page of the *Financial Times* and has also published in Foreign Affairs, New

York Times, *Wall Street Journal*, *Washington Post*, *Die Zeit*, and Nihon Keizai Shimbun, among many other leading newspapers.

From 1994 to 1997, he was an economist at the Federal Reserve Bank of New York, where he advised senior management on monetary strategies, the G-7 economic outlook, and European monetary unification. In 1993–94, he was Okun Memorial Fellow in Economic Studies at the Brookings Institution and won the Amex Bank Review Awards Silver Medal for his dissertation research on central bank independence. In 1992–93, he was resident in Germany as a Bosch Foundation Fellow. Posen is a member of the Council on Foreign Relations. He is a research associate of the Center for the Japanese Economy and Business of Columbia University, a fellow of the CESifo Research Network, and has been a Public Policy Fellow at the American Academy in Berlin (2001). He received his PhD and AB (Phi Beta Kappa) from Harvard University, where he was a National Science Foundation Graduate Fellow.

André Sapir is senior fellow at Bruegel and professor of economics at Université Libre de Bruxelles (ULB), where he holds a chair in international economics and European integration. He was economic adviser to the president of the European Commission. In 2004 he published *An Agenda for a Growing Europe*, a report to the president of the Commission by a group of independent experts, known as the Sapir report.

His publications include *EMU and Economic Policy in Europe: The Challenge of the Early Years* (2002), *Market Integration, Regionalism and the Global Economy* (1999), *Trade and Jobs in Europe: Much Ado about Nothing?* (1999), *Economic Policy in EMU* (1998), *Flexible Integration: Towards a More Effective and Democratic Europe* (1995), and *European Policies on Competition, Trade and Industry—Conflict and Complementarities* (1995).

He is also a research fellow of the Centre for Economic Policy Research and a member of European Commission President Jose Manuel Barroso's Economic Policy Analysis Group. He is a founding Editorial Board Member of the World Trade Review, published by Cambridge University Press and the World Trade Organization. He holds a PhD in economics from the Johns Hopkins University (1977).

Dominique Strauss-Kahn is the managing director of the International Monetary Fund (IMF). Before taking up his position at the IMF, he was a member of the French National Assembly and professor of economics at the Institut d'Etudes Politiques de Paris. From 2001 to 2007, he was reelected three times to the National Assembly, and in 2006, he ran for the Socialist Party's nomination for the French presidential election. In 2000 and 2001, he taught economics at the Institut d'Etudes Politiques de Paris and was named visiting professor at Stanford University. He was also a personal adviser to the secretary general of the OECD.

He served as minister of economy, finance, and industry of France from June 1997 to November 1999. In this capacity, he managed the launch of the Euro. He also represented France on the Board of Governors of a number of international financial institutions, including the IMF. Between 1993 and 1997, he was in the private sector as a corporate lawyer. From 1991 to 1993, he served as minister of industry and international trade, during which time he participated in the Uruguay Round of trade negotiations.

He began his career as assistant professor, then professor of economics at the University of Paris, where he was tenured in 1978. He was then appointed deputy commissioner of the Economic Planning Agency (1981–86). He was elected deputy (member of Parliament) to the National Assembly (1986), where he chaired the Finance Commission from 1988 to 1991. He holds a PhD in economics from the University of Paris.

Lawrence H. Summers, US secretary of the treasury from 1999 to 2000, is the director of the National Economic Council. He was the 27th president of Harvard University (2001–06), the Nathaniel Ropes Professor of Political Economy at Harvard, and until January 2009 the Charles W. Eliot University Professor there. He received his PhD in economics from Harvard in 1982, by which time he had taught for three years as an economics faculty member at MIT, where he was named assistant professor in 1979 and associate professor in 1982. He then went to Washington as a domestic policy economist for the President's Council of Economic Advisers. In 1983, he returned to Harvard as a professor of economics.

In 1987 he became the first social scientist ever to receive the annual Alan T. Waterman Award of the National Science Foundation. In 1993 he was awarded the John Bates Clark Medal. In 1993 he was named US undersecretary of the treasury for international affairs, and on July 2, 1999, he was confirmed by the Senate as secretary of the treasury. After leaving the treasury in January 2001, he served as the Arthur Okun Distinguished Fellow in Economics, Globalization, and Governance at the Brookings Institution.

He is a member of the National Academy of Sciences and has written extensively on economic analysis and policy publishing over 150 articles in professional economic journals. His many publications include *Understanding Unemployment* (1990) and *Reform in Eastern Europe* (1991).

György Szapáry is a visiting professor in economics at the Central European University in Budapest and member of the board of directors of Hungary's OTP Bank. From 1993 to 2007, with a short break as adviser to the governor, he served as deputy governor of the National Bank of Hungary and a member of its Monetary Council. As deputy governor, he was also a member of the Economic and Financial Committee of the European Commission and of the European Central Bank's International

Relations Committee during 2004–07. From 1997 to 2001, he was a member of the Board of the Budapest Commodity Exchange.

During 1965–66, he worked at the European Commission in Brussels. From 1966 to1990, he worked at the International Monetary Fund in Washington. His last position there was assistant director in the Asian department. During 1990–93, he was senior resident representative of the IMF in Hungary.

Szapáry is a member of several foundations in Hungary and the recipient of the Hungarian Sándor Popovics Award for outstanding contribution in the field of banking and monetary policy. He has published numerous articles in professional journals. He graduated from the Louvain Catholic University (Belgium) in 1961 and gained a PhD in economics there in 1966.

About the Organizations

Peter G. Peterson Institute for International Economics

The Peter G. Peterson Institute for International Economics is a private, nonprofit, nonpartisan research institution devoted to the study of international economic policy. Since 1981 the Institute has provided timely and objective analysis of, and concrete solutions to, a wide range of international economic problems. It is one of the very few economics think tanks that are widely regarded as "nonpartisan" by the press and "neutral" by the US Congress, it is cited by the quality media more than any other such institution, and it was recently selected as Top Think Tank in the World in the first comprehensive survey of over 5,000 such institutions.

The Institute, which has been directed by C. Fred Bergsten throughout its existence, attempts to anticipate emerging issues and to be ready with practical ideas, presented in user-friendly formats, to inform and shape public debate. Its audience includes government officials and legislators, business and labor leaders, management and staff at international organizations, university-based scholars and their students, other research institutions and nongovernmental organizations, the media, and the public at large. It addresses these groups both in the United States and around the world.

The Institute's staff of about 50 includes more than two dozen experts, who are conducting about 30 studies at any given time and are widely viewed as one of the top group of economists at any research center. Its agenda emphasizes global macroeconomic topics, international money and finance, trade and related social issues, energy and the environment, investment, and domestic adjustment measures. Current priority is attached to the worldwide financial and economic crisis, globalization (including its financial aspects) and the backlash against it, global trade imbalances and currency relationships, the creation of an international regime to address global warming and especially its international trade dimension, the competitiveness of the United States and other major countries, reform of the international economic and financial architecture and particularly sovereign wealth funds, and trade negotiations at the multilateral, regional, and bilateral levels. Institute staff and research cover all key regions—especially Asia, Europe, Latin America, and the Middle East, as well as the United States itself and with special reference to China, India, and Russia.

Institute studies have helped provide the intellectual foundation for many of the major international financial initiatives of the past two decades: reform of the International Monetary Fund (IMF), adoption of international banking standards, exchange rate systems in the G-7 and emerging-market economies, policies toward the dollar, the euro, and other important currencies, and responses to debt and currency crises. The Institute has made important contributions to key trade policy decisions including the Doha Round, the restoration and then the extension of both trade promotion authority and trade adjustment assistance in the United States, the Uruguay Round and the development of the World Trade Organization, the North American Free Trade Agreement (NAFTA) and other US trade pacts (notably including Korea), the Asia Pacific Economic Cooperation (APEC) forum and East Asian regionalism, initiation of the Strategic Economic Dialogue between the United States and China and the related "G-2" concept, a series of United States–Japan negotiations, reform of sanctions policy, liberalization of US export controls and export credits, and specific measures such as permanent normal trade relations (PNTR) for China in 2000 and import protection for steel.

Other influential analyses have addressed economic reform in Europe, Japan, the former communist countries, and Latin America (including the Washington Consensus), the economic and social impact of globalization and policy responses to it, outsourcing, electronic commerce, corruption, foreign direct investment both into and out of the United States, global warming and international environmental policy, and key sectors such as agriculture, financial services, steel, telecommunications, and textiles.

The Institute celebrated its 25th anniversary in 2006 and adopted its new name at that time, having previously been the Institute for International Economics. It moved into its award-winning new building in 2001.

Bruegel

Bruegel is a European think tank dealing with international economics. It was created in Brussels in early 2005 with the intention of bringing a new voice to Europe's economic policy debate.

Bruegel's governance and funding model make it unique, as it is the only think tank partly funded by European Union member states. It is supported by 18 European governments, as well as a number of leading private corporations.

Bruegel does not represent any particular policy doctrine. It aims to contribute to economic policymaking in Europe through open, facts-based, and policy-relevant research, analysis, and discussion.

Bruegel has five key features:

- **Outward-looking stance**. The European Union is a major world player. But it needs to broaden and deepen its policy debate, which suffers too often from an inward-looking bias, and to foster genuine policy discussion with other international economic players. Bruegel aims to contribute to a better understanding of the economic challenges and responsibilities facing Europe in the context of globalization and, latterly, the crisis.

- **Evidence-based policy recommendations**. Bruegel does not represent any particular policy doctrine. Its research, which is conducted both in-house and through partnerships with other research organizations, draws on state-of-the-art analysis to assess economic change, discuss policy options and make recommendations—while always keeping an eye on their do-ability.

- **Demand-driven questions, independent answers**. Bruegel's annual research program is set by its Board, which represents the diversity of Bruegel's stakeholders, after consultation with members. Once research areas are chosen, research work is carried out, and decisions to publish are taken, fully independently. All publications are released under the name of individual authors. Bruegel itself does not adopt positions on policy.

- **Linking government, research, business, and civil society**. Bruegel provides a forum for informed debate between individuals from diverse backgrounds. It builds on the diversity of experience of its researchers and stakeholders to develop interaction between communities. Bruegel also cooperates with leading European and international research institutions on specific research projects.

- **European reach**. From the outset, Bruegel adopted a pan-European approach. It addresses topics for which policy responsibility rests with individual states, the European Union or international organizations. It is developing a presence in national debates across Europe, as well as in Brussels and in international discussion forums.

See www.bruegel.org for more information.

Index

Eastern Europe)
response to global financial crisis (*See*
crisis management)
weaknesses of, 6
euro banknote trade figures, 134
eurobonds. *See* bond markets
Eurofirst 300, 49
Eurogroup, 2
crisis management, 10, 19, 77–78
on entry criteria, 74–75
role of, 81–82, 82*n*
euroization, 91
promotion of, 13
unilateral, 7, 7*n*
European Bank for Reconstruction and
Development, 13
European Central Bank (ECB), 2, 23, 28
crisis management, 10, 18–19, 29, 36, 75,
186
on entry criteria, 74–75
liquidity policy, 186
neutral stance on global role, 7–8, 26, 121
price stability definition, 165
Review of the International Role of the Euro,
61, 104, 121
European Commission
crisis management, 19, 77
on entry criteria, 74–75
European Economic Recovery Plan, 80
macroeconomic stability report, 73
European Economic Recovery Plan, 80
European Investment Bank, 20
European Payments Union, 162
European Recovery Programme, 80
European System of Central Banks, 178
European Union (EU)
entry criteria (*See* entry criteria)
neutral stance on global role, 7–8, 26, 121
role in international coordination, 21, 185
weaknesses in, 4
European Union Treaty, Article 99, 73
euro peg
African countries, 90–91
determinants of, 88–89
economic case for, 91
hard power and, 7
Latin America, 161–62, 162*f*
neighbor countries, 91
neighboring countries, 122, 123*f*
network externalities and, 5
Exchange Rate Mechanism. *See* ERM
exchange rate misalignments, 36, 73–74, 74*f*
exchange rate pass-through, trade invoicing
and, 66

exchange rate regimes. *See also* currency
pegs
Africa, 90–91
Asia, 108–10, 109*t*
choice of, implications of, 124–26, 161–62
currency internationalization and, 26
Europe, 91 (*See also* ERM)
GCC, 92, 147–51
geostrategic relationships and, 87–93
Latin America, 161–62, 162*f*
MENA, 142*f*, 142–43
neighboring countries, 122–26, 123*f*, 125*f*
trade invoicing and, 64
exchange rate stability criterion, 94–95
Exogenous Shocks Facility, 38
exports. *See* trade
external representation, 12, 75, 76*t*, 93

fair value, 34, 38
"fair weather" governance, 10, 70–75
FDI. *See* foreign investment
financial assets
Asia, 110, 112*f*
trade in, 53–59
financial conditions, currency internationalization and, 26–28
financial crisis. *See* global financial crisis
financial gravity equation, 55
financial integration, 78–80
effects of single currency on, 55
gains from, 53–54
lack of, 6, 11, 29
financial liberalization
currency internationalization and,
29–30
euro effect, 56, 58
preferential, 56, 58
welfare implications of, 58
financial markets. *See also* bond markets
competition between, 54
crisis management, 33–34
effect of euro on, 57–58
global currency status and, 41–50, 186
US dollar versus euro markets, 27
Financial Sector Assessment Programs
(FSAPs), 38
financial-sector reforms, 20, 38–39
financial services, Single Market in, 78–80
Financial Stability Forum (FSF), 20, 38, 76*t*
financing instruments, currencies used
as, 27
Finland, 57, 187, 196
fiscal policy
governance structure and, 74–75

regulatory failure, 38
reserve accumulation, geopolitical ties and, 87–93
return on investment
    currency internationalization and, 27–28, 48–49
    US liabilities, 44f, 44–45, 97, 97n
risk aversion, 18
risk diversification, 48–49, 54, 55, 58
risk management, failure in, 38
Romania
    bank loans, 129
    entry criteria and, 94, 95n, 134
    exchange rate depreciation, 130
    exchange rate regime, 91, 123f, 124
    external debt, 127, 129t
    foreign exchange reserves, 127, 128t
ruble zone, breakup of, 91–92
Russia, 9, 121
    economic ties with euro area, 122
    exchange rate depreciation, 130
    exchange rate regime, 123f, 124, 136
    geopolitical ties, 97

Sarbanes-Oxley Act, 47
Sarkozy, Nicolas, 78
Saudi Arabia, 92, 144n, 150, 151f, 185
saving rate (US), 117
scale economies, 27
Scandinavian countries. See also specific country
    asset trade, 57, 58
SDR (special drawing rights), 9, 143, 149, 149n, 150n, 153
securities trading
    cross-border, 6, 6n
    euro versus US dollar, 166, 168f
    in global currency, 8, 187
security relationships. See geopolitical ties; hard power
seigniorage, 24, 196, 197
Serbia, 91, 123f
SGP. See Stability and Growth Pact
Singapore, 108
Single Market in financial services, 78–80
Slovakia, 122, 123f, 126, 127, 128t, 134
Slovenia, 81, 122, 123f, 127, 129t, 130, 130f
Snow, John, 43
social safety net programs, 38
soft power, 29
Soros, George, 191–92
Southeastern Europe. See Eastern Europe; specific country

South Korea, 62, 63t, 92–93, 108, 185
sovereign risk spreads, 9, 11, 27, 174, 176, 176f
sovereign wealth funds (SWFs), 108, 142, 142n, 146–47, 147n
Soviet Union, collapse of, 91–92
S&P 500, 49
Spain
    bond spreads, 81
    crisis management, 169
    deficit, 174, 175f
    fiscal policy, 72
    house prices in, 173, 173f
    recession, 73–74
    unit labor costs, 174, 175f
special drawing rights (SDR), 9, 143, 149, 149n, 150n, 153
Stability and Growth Pact (SGP), 2
    Eastern Europe and, 94
    effectiveness of, 28, 72
    effect of global financial crisis on, 20–21
    purpose of, 177, 193
    reform of, 13n
stateless currency, 100
"stormy weather" governance, 10, 70–71, 75–82, 178, 193–94
Strauss-Kahn, Dominique, 33
subprime mortgage market (US), 116, 182, 189, 193
Summers, Lawrence H., 3, 8n, 103–104, 188–90, 193–94, 195–96
supervisory failure, 38
swap lines
    Asia, 114
    extension of, 8, 12–13
Sweden, 55, 57, 91, 165, 187, 196
SWFs (sovereign wealth funds), 108, 142, 142n, 146–47, 147n
Syria, 143

Taiwan, 92–93, 185
Thailand, 62, 63t, 108
Thaksin Shinawatra, 115
Thatcher, Margaret, 188
"tipping point" in currency usage, 106, 116–17
trade
    euro area's share of, 27
    in financial assets, 53–59
    in goods, 55
trade flows
    Asia, 111, 114f
    effect of euro on, 53, 57–58

Other Publications from the Peterson Institute for International Economics

WORKING PAPERS

* = out of print

POLICY ANALYSES IN
INTERNATIONAL ECONOMICS Series

Measuring the Costs of Visible Protection
in Korea*　　　　　　　　　　Namdoo Kim
November 1996　　　　　ISBN 0-88132-236-9
The World Trading System: Challenges Ahead
Jeffrey J. Schott
December 1996　　　　　ISBN 0-88132-235-0
Has Globalization Gone Too Far?　Dani Rodrik
March 1997　　　ISBN paper 0-88132-241-5
Korea-United States Economic Relationship*
C. Fred Bergsten and Il SaKong, editors
March 1997　　　　　　ISBN 0-88132-240-7
Summitry in the Americas: A Progress Report
Richard E. Feinberg
April 1997　　　　　　ISBN 0-88132-242-3
Corruption and the Global Economy
Kimberly Ann Elliott
June 1997　　　　　　ISBN 0-88132-233-4
Regional Trading Blocs in the World
Economic System　　　　Jeffrey A. Frankel
October 1997　　　　　ISBN 0-88132-202-4
Sustaining the Asia Pacific Miracle:
Environmental Protection and Economic
Integration　　Andre Dua and Daniel C. Esty
October 1997　　　　　ISBN 0-88132-250-4
Trade and Income Distribution
William R. Cline
November 1997　　　　ISBN 0-88132-216-4
Global Competition Policy
Edward M. Graham and J. David Richardson
December 1997　　　　ISBN 0-88132-166-4
Unfinished Business: Telecommunications
after the Uruguay Round
Gary Clyde Hufbauer and Erika Wada
December 1997　　　　ISBN 0-88132-257-1
Financial Services Liberalization in the WTO
Wendy Dobson and Pierre Jacquet
June 1998　　　　　　ISBN 0-88132-254-7
Restoring Japan's Economic Growth
Adam S. Posen
September 1998　　　　ISBN 0-88132-262-8
Measuring the Costs of Protection in China
Zhang Shuguang, Zhang Yansheng,
and Wan Zhongxin
November 1998　　　　ISBN 0-88132-247-4
Foreign Direct Investment and Development:
The New Policy Agenda for Developing
Countries and Economies in Transition
Theodore H. Moran
December 1998　　　　ISBN 0-88132-258-X
Behind the Open Door: Foreign Enterprises
in the Chinese Marketplace　Daniel H. Rosen
January 1999　　　　　ISBN 0-88132-263-6
Toward A New International Financial
Architecture: A Practical Post-Asia Agenda
Barry Eichengreen
February 1999　　　　ISBN 0-88132-270-9
Is the U.S. Trade Deficit Sustainable?
Catherine L. Mann
September 1999　　　　ISBN 0-88132-265-2

Safeguarding Prosperity in a Global Financial
System: The Future International Financial
Architecture, Independent Task Force Report
Sponsored by the Council on Foreign Relations
Morris Goldstein, Project Director
October 1999　　　　　ISBN 0-88132-287-3
Avoiding the Apocalypse: The Future
of the Two Koreas　　　　Marcus Noland
June 2000　　　　　　ISBN 0-88132-278-4
Assessing Financial Vulnerability:
An Early Warning System for Emerging
Markets　　　　　　　Morris Goldstein,
Graciela Kaminsky, and Carmen Reinhart
June 2000　　　　　　ISBN 0-88132-237-7
Global Electronic Commerce: A Policy Primer
Catherine L. Mann, Sue E. Eckert, and Sarah
Cleeland Knight
July 2000　　　　　　ISBN 0-88132-274-1
The WTO after Seattle　Jeffrey J. Schott, ed.
July 2000　　　　　　ISBN 0-88132-290-3
Intellectual Property Rights in the Global
Economy　　　　　　　Keith E. Maskus
August 2000　　　　　ISBN 0-88132-282-2
The Political Economy of the Asian Financial
Crisis　　　　　　　Stephan Haggard
August 2000　　　　　ISBN 0-88132-283-0
Transforming Foreign Aid: United States
Assistance in the 21st Century　Carol Lancaster
August 2000　　　　　ISBN 0-88132-291-1
Fighting the Wrong Enemy: Antiglobal
Activists and Multinational Enterprises
Edward M. Graham
September 2000　　　　ISBN 0-88132-272-5
Globalization and the Perceptions of American
Workers　Kenneth Scheve/Matthew J. Slaughter
March 2001　　　　　　ISBN 0-88132-295-4
World Capital Markets: Challenge to the G-10
Wendy Dobson and Gary Clyde Hufbauer,
assisted by Hyun Koo Cho
May 2001　　　　　　ISBN 0-88132-301-2
Prospects for Free Trade in the Americas
Jeffrey J. Schott
August 2001　　　　　ISBN 0-88132-275-X
Toward a North American Community:
Lessons from the Old World for the New
Robert A. Pastor
August 2001　　　　　ISBN 0-88132-328-4
Measuring the Costs of Protection in Europe:
European Commercial Policy in the 2000s
Patrick A. Messerlin
September 2001　　　　ISBN 0-88132-273-3
Job Loss from Imports: Measuring the Costs
Lori G. Kletzer
September 2001　　　　ISBN 0-88132-296-2
No More Bashing: Building a New
Japan–United States Economic Relationship
C. Fred Bergsten, Takatoshi Ito, and
Marcus Noland
October 2001　　　　　ISBN 0-88132-286-5
Why Global Commitment Really Matters!
Howard Lewis III and J. David Richardson
October 2001　　　　　ISBN 0-88132-298-9

Leadership Selection in the Major Multilaterals
Miles Kahler
November 2001   ISBN 0-88132-335-7
**The International Financial Architecture:
What's New? What's Missing?**   Peter Kenen
November 2001   ISBN 0-88132-297-0
**Delivering on Debt Relief: From IMF Gold
to a New Aid Architecture**
John Williamson and Nancy Birdsall,
with Brian Deese
April 2002   ISBN 0-88132-331-4
**Imagine There's No Country: Poverty,
Inequality, and Growth in the Era
of Globalization**   Surjit S. Bhalla
September 2002   ISBN 0-88132-348-9
Reforming Korea's Industrial Conglomerates
Edward M. Graham
January 2003   ISBN 0-88132-337-3
**Industrial Policy in an Era of Globalization:
Lessons from Asia**   Marcus Noland
and Howard Pack
March 2003   ISBN 0-88132-350-0
Reintegrating India with the World Economy
T. N. Srinivasan and Suresh D. Tendulkar
March 2003   ISBN 0-88132-280-6
**After the Washington Consensus:
Restarting Growth and Reform
in Latin America**   Pedro-Pablo Kuczynski
and John Williamson, editors
March 2003   ISBN 0-88132-347-0
**The Decline of US Labor Unions and the Role
of Trade**   Robert E. Baldwin
June 2003   ISBN 0-88132-341-1
**Can Labor Standards Improve under
Globalization?**   Kimberly A. Elliott
and Richard B. Freeman
June 2003   ISBN 0-88132-332-2
**Crimes and Punishments? Retaliation
under the WTO**   Robert Z. Lawrence
October 2003   ISBN 0-88132-359-4
Inflation Targeting in the World Economy
Edwin M. Truman
October 2003   ISBN 0-88132-345-4
**Foreign Direct Investment and Tax
Competition**   John H. Mutti
November 2003   ISBN 0-88132-352-7
**Has Globalization Gone Far Enough?
The Costs of Fragmented Markets**
Scott Bradford and Robert Z. Lawrence
February 2004   ISBN 0-88132-349-7
**Food Regulation and Trade:
Toward a Safe and Open Global System**
Tim Josling, Donna Roberts, and David Orden
March 2004   ISBN 0-88132-346-2
**Controlling Currency Mismatches
in Emerging Markets**
Morris Goldstein and Philip Turner
April 2004   ISBN 0-88132-360-8
**Free Trade Agreements: US Strategies
and Priorities**   Jeffrey J. Schott, editor
April 2004   ISBN 0-88132-361-6

Trade Policy and Global Poverty
William R. Cline
June 2004   ISBN 0-88132-365-9
**Bailouts or Bail-ins? Responding to Financial
Crises in Emerging Economies**
Nouriel Roubini and Brad Setser
August 2004   ISBN 0-88132-371-3
Transforming the European Economy
Martin Neil Baily and Jacob Kirkegaard
September 2004   ISBN 0-88132-343-8
**Chasing Dirty Money: The Fight Against
Money Laundering**
Peter Reuter and Edwin M. Truman
November 2004   ISBN 0-88132-370-5
**The United States and the World Economy:
Foreign Economic Policy for the Next Decade**
C. Fred Bergsten
January 2005   ISBN 0-88132-380-2
**Does Foreign Direct Investment Promote
Development?**   Theodore Moran,
Edward M. Graham, and Magnus Blomström,
editors
April 2005   ISBN 0-88132-381-0
American Trade Politics, 4th ed.   I. M. Destler
June 2005   ISBN 0-88132-382-9
**Why Does Immigration Divide America?
Public Finance and Political Opposition
to Open Borders**   Gordon Hanson
August 2005   ISBN 0-88132-400-0
Reforming the US Corporate Tax
Gary Clyde Hufbauer and Paul L. E. Grieco
September 2005   ISBN 0-88132-384-5
The United States as a Debtor Nation
William R. Cline
September 2005   ISBN 0-88132-399-3
**NAFTA Revisited: Achievements
and Challenges**   Gary Clyde Hufbauer
and Jeffrey J. Schott, assisted by Paul L. E. Grieco
and Yee Wong
October 2005   ISBN 0-88132-334-9
**US National Security and Foreign Direct
Investment**
Edward M. Graham and David M. Marchick
May 2006   ISBN 978-0-88132-391-7
**Accelerating the Globalization of America:
The Role for Information Technology**
Catherine L. Mann, assisted by Jacob Kirkegaard
June 2006   ISBN 978-0-88132-390-0
Delivering on Doha: Farm Trade and the Poor
Kimberly Ann Elliott
July 2006   ISBN 978-0-88132-392-4
**Case Studies in US Trade Negotiation,
Vol. 1: Making the Rules**   Charan Devereaux,
Robert Z. Lawrence, and Michael Watkins
September 2006   ISBN 978-0-88132-362-7
**Case Studies in US Trade Negotiation,
Vol. 2: Resolving Disputes**   Charan Devereaux,
Robert Z. Lawrence, and Michael Watkins
September 2006   ISBN 978-0-88132-363-2

DISTRIBUTORS OUTSIDE THE UNITED STATES

**Australia, New Zealand,
and Papua New Guinea**
D. A. Information Services
648 Whitehorse Road
Mitcham, Victoria 3132, Australia
Tel: 61-3-9210-7777
Fax: 61-3-9210-7788
Email: service@dadirect.com.au
www.dadirect.com.au

India, Bangladesh, Nepal, and Sri Lanka
Viva Books Private Limited
Mr. Vinod Vasishtha
4737/23 Ansari Road
Daryaganj, New Delhi 110002
India
Tel: 91-11-4224-2200
Fax: 91-11-4224-2240
Email: viva@vivagroupindia.net
www.vivagroupindia.com

**Mexico, Central America, South America,
and Puerto Rico**
US PubRep, Inc.
311 Dean Drive
Rockville, MD 20851
Tel: 301-838-9276
Fax: 301-838-9278
Email: c.falk@ieee.org

Asia (*Brunei, Burma, Cambodia, China,
Hong Kong, Indonesia, Korea, Laos, Malaysia,
Philippines, Singapore, Taiwan, Thailand,
and Vietnam*)
East-West Export Books (EWEB)
University of Hawaii Press
2840 Kolowalu Street
Honolulu, Hawaii 96822-1888
Tel: 808-956-8830
Fax: 808-988-6052
Email: eweb@hawaii.edu

Canada
Renouf Bookstore
5369 Canotek Road, Unit 1
Ottawa, Ontario KlJ 9J3, Canada
Tel: 613-745-2665
Fax: 613-745-7660
www.renoufbooks.com

Japan
United Publishers Services Ltd.
1-32-5, Higashi-shinagawa
Shinagawa-ku, Tokyo 140-0002
Japan
Tel: 81-3-5479-7251
Fax: 81-3-5479-7307
Email: purchasing@ups.co.jp
*For trade accounts only. Individuals will find
Institute books in leading Tokyo bookstores.*

Middle East
MERIC
2 Bahgat Ali Street, El Masry Towers
Tower D, Apt. 24
Zamalek, Cairo
Egypt
Tel. 20-2-7633824
Fax: 20-2-7369355
Email: mahmoud_fouda@mericonline.com
www.mericonline.com

United Kingdom, Europe
(*including Russia and Turkey*)**, Africa,
and Israel**
The Eurospan Group
c/o Turpin Distribution
Pegasus Drive
Stratton Business Park
Biggleswade, Bedfordshire
SG18 8TQ
United Kingdom
Tel: 44 (0) 1767-604972
Fax: 44 (0) 1767-601640
Email: eurospan@turpin-distribution.com
www.eurospangroup.com/bookstore

**Visit our website at:
www.piie.com
E-mail orders to:
petersonmail@presswarehouse.com**

ML   ½